LET'S TAKE THE KIDS!

LET'S TAKE THE *K*IDS!

Great Places to Go with Children in New York's Hudson Valley
(including the Catskills, the Adirondacks to Lake George, the Berkshires, and Cooperstown)

MARY BARILE AND JOANNE MICHAELS

ST. MARTIN'S PRESS

NEW YORK

Design by Robert Bull Design

Library of Congress Cataloging-in-Publication Data

Michaels, Joanne.
    Let's take the kids! / Joanne Michaels & Mary Barile.
      p.   cm.
    ISBN 0-312-04050-4
    1. Hudson River Valley (N.Y. and N.J)—Description and travel-
-Guide-books. 2. Children—Travel—Hudson River Valley (N.Y. and
N.J.)—Guide-books. I. Barile, Mary. II. Title.
F127.H8M54   1990
917.47'30443—dc20   89-77918

First Edition

10 9 8 7 6 5 4 3 2 1

To Erik, our favorite young adventurer,
and to the eternal kids, Ralph and Stuart.

CONTENTS

ACKNOWLEDGMENTS

We know that it is impossible to thank everyone who helps in creating a travel book; for every department head who answers a question, there are scores of office and administrative people who provide additional assistance, source material, and suggestions. So, a heartfelt thanks to everyone we spoke to throughout the region in our travels, and an extra-special thanks to the following people for their enthusiasm during our research and writing: Sheryl Woods, New York State Department of Tourism; Joanne DeVoe, Schenectady County Chamber of Commerce; Carol Sensenig and Mollie Maloney, Albany County Convention and Visitors Bureau; Linda Toohey, Saratoga Springs Chamber of Commerce; Doris Herwig, Warren County Department of Tourism; Laurie Arnheiter Konis, Sagamore Resort, Bolton Landing; Faire Hart, Mohonk Mountain House, New Paltz; Pamela Jones and Sue Bain, Greene County Promotion Department; Doris Holdorf, Otsego County Tourism; Delaware County Historical Association; Delaware County Chamber of Commerce; New York State Department of Parks and Recreation; and Judy Salsbury, Salsbury/Ziglar, Lenox, Mass.

This book would have taken a lot longer to produce and would have been a lot less fun to write without the suggestions and patience of Barbara Anderson, our editor. On many a cold winter afternoon, Margaret and Joe Barile's hot gourmet meals gave us the impetus to continue writing and traveling. Ralph Barile's sacrifice of computer time and office space was irreplaceable. Stuart Ober's gift of time, support, and baby-sitting went beyond the call of duty. Stacy Jarit and Jacqueline Sobel were enthusiastic researchers, and particularly helpful with the Lake George section of the book. Alan McKnight did a fine job on the maps.

And, of course, Erik Michaels-Ober was always willing to drop his toys and travel with us all over the region, acting as the final arbiter of taste for this project!

INTRODUCTION

This book provides many answers to the Big Question: What can we do with the kids on a weekend outside of the metropolitan area? When faced with this question for our own and friends' young ones, we discovered that there is no central source of information for the upstate region. Very often we had to call each county and track down the tourism bureau if we wanted specific information—no easy task, because some tourism bureaus are not listed as such in the phone book but are part of a town's planning board. Even when we could locate them, we discovered that few tourism bureaus were equipped with listings of local activities and sites for children anyway. So, we set ourselves the task of finding the best places to take children, ages two to twelve, in upstate New York and the Berkshires.

Children will be enchanted by the variety of experiences awaiting them in this region. Rich with culture, history, and even some magic, upstate New York and the Berkshires have captured the imagination of writers, artists, and visitors for more than three centuries. This is the land where Rip Van Winkle slept (you can still search for his treasure in Greene County); and what child wouldn't want to explore the bridge in Tarrytown where Ichabod Crane outran the headless horseman? Wild animals still roam the land at the Catskill Game Farm, and revolutionary war battles continue to be fought at the Old Stone Fort in Schoharie. Rare gems can still be dug out of the earth by young prospectors in the Adirondacks, and canoes can be paddled down the Delaware River. The parks come alive each summer with puppet shows, dancing, storytelling, and music, and the region boasts some of the best hands-on museums in the country. You don't have to travel far to find one of the best areas in the United States for vacationing with children.

We've organized our book by county to provide travelers with a tourism "loop" around the region. The counties

follow the Hudson River northward, then west through the
Catskills and Leatherstocking regions, and then north again to
the capital district and, finally, the lower Adirondacks. The
Berkshires, because they are a little further afield, have been
given their own chapter. It would take at least a week to ten
days to follow the loop in its physical entirety; however, most
of the seasonal events would be missed in so short a trip. We
hope you will find the book useful in planning day trips and
weekends as well as longer vacations.

There are certain annual events, celebrations, and festivals
that are particularly child oriented; these you will find listed by
county and by month at the back of the book. We discovered
that there is no such thing as an exact date for any given festival.
The dates change yearly, so in order to make it easier for you to
find out when a particular event is scheduled, we have provided
phone numbers for each monthly event and suggest that you call
ahead before taking off for a county fair or a lumberjack festival.
We have included hundreds of established events, but many
new festivals and celebrations are offered every year. The best
information sources for these events are local newspapers and
free tourist guides, which can be obtained at news shops, delis,
and chambers of commerce.

Traveling with children is an art: no matter how many
trips you have taken on your own, once you put a kid in the
car, a whole new world must be taken into account. Food,
travel time, boredom, rest stops—all of these should be considered, especially when planning an overnight trip to un-
familiar territory. The following ideas evolved out of our own
experiences with children during trips throughout upstate New
York and the Berkshires. These tips may not solve all of your
travel concerns, but we think you'll be glad you thought about
some of these issues beforehand.

• **Map out your route ahead of time.** We traveled thousands of
miles during our research excursions and found that this part
of New York State contains a great number of vast rural areas.

While the scenery really is lovely, you will find that places to stop for rest rooms or snacks are few and far between, especially in the off-season. Finding a rest room in a tiny hamlet on a Sunday evening can be impossible and very uncomfortable for everyone in the car. Make certain that your itinerary includes at least a few larger villages and towns, which generally have a fast-food restaurant or a diner with rest rooms open to the public. If you don't mind the extra driving time, take some of the older side roads instead of just thruways. This kind of route allows you to stop if the kids see something of interest (like cows and sheep) and often has clean, quiet picnic stops along the way.

• **Take along a good supply of snacks.** Unless you and the kids are thrilled with eating at fast-food restaurants, it is advisable to bring your own snacks. This will accomplish three things: cut down on expenses; reduce travel time (especially during summer lunch hours); and provide more nutritious items for the kids. We suggest a small ice chest filled with juice boxes, cheese, fresh fruit, nuts, crackers, and other easy-to-carry, easy-to-open snacks. And a damp washcloth, towelettes, and tissues in the car will make clean-up much easier.

• **Keep a collection of small toys and coloring books in the car.** This will keep even the youngest traveler happy for some of the time on a long drive, especially when there is not much to look at out the windows. We found that kids enjoy drawing pictures of what it is they are going to see, whether it is cows, houses, trains, or boats. This type of activity helps make the journey part of the excitement. Older children may want to have their own maps, so they can follow the journey's progress.

• **Dress the kids in layers of clothing.** Parts of upstate New York are mountainous, which means that huge temperature fluctuations between day and night can be expected year-round. Summer temperatures can go from the nineties during the day to the forties at night; spring and fall temperatures may drop from the seventies to the twenties; and winter can mean below-zero temperatures. Dressing in layers allows the most flexibility and ensures that you won't be stuck in the car when you really want to be outdoors. In winter or threatening weather, don't forget hats and boots (sneakers are fine for dry, warm days but not for mud and ice). If you are planning to spend time at a farm where you pick your own fruits and vegetables, bring hats, long-sleeved shirts, comfortable shoes, and sunscreen. River trips are always very windy, so bring along sweaters and scarves or hats, even on a balmy spring day.

• **Make sure a site is appropriate for your child's age.** Because many of the sites in this book are considered historic, you should consider your child's age before going to them, especially if your child is very young. Some of these sites are geared for all ages, and they allow kids to explore and participate in special hands-on areas; others are for observation only, and while kids are welcome, they are not allowed to touch anything. We have tried to make this distinction clear in each of the entries, but if you are unsure about a site's appropriateness for your child, call before you go or ask before you pay. At one site, we had trouble getting a refund when we discovered that it was not suitable for a four year old, although no one in the ticket office had warned us when we bought the tickets.

• **Find out about a tour before plunging ahead.** While one five year old may enjoy a thirty-minute tour, another may tire in the first ten minutes. You know your child best. Most sites will allow adults who are not taking a tour to wait outside with children, charging either no admission or a reduced admission; if this fee is not displayed at the ticket office, ask about it. Even if your child is well behaved on tours, you may want to schedule a stop afterward at an amusement park or a nature center, where children can participate fully in the activities or just run around freely. This not only prevents kids from associating history with boredom but also lets parents see some adult-oriented sites on outings with their children.

• **If you are taking a group of children, bring along enough adults to keep the group carefully supervised.** Many smaller sites are understaffed, and besides, it is more pleasant for all visitors when groups of children are well behaved and stay together with adult guides. If you are bringing more than ten

children to a site, you are well advised to call ahead; some sites limit the number of visitors they can accommodate and may require special group reservations and fees.
• **In the winter months, always call before you go.** Outside of ski areas, many sites close down between November and March or are open for very limited hours. Calling ahead will prevent disappointment and a ruined outing. The flip side is that with enough notice, many smaller sites will make special arrangements for groups in the off-season. Parks and recreation areas are notorious for neglecting to post winter hours in their publicity literature; if you like to spend time outdoors in the winter, call the park first and inquire about its hours.
• **Protect yourself and your family against Lyme disease.** This tick-borne infection has spread throughout the upstate New York and Berkshire regions, so if you are planning to hike or camp in wooded areas, check with your doctor or local health department for information. They can provide handy booklets that tell you everything you need to know about this disease.

Let's Take the Kids was written from a car traveler's point of view, but you can get around certain areas quite easily by bus and train. If you want to plan a trip by train call Amtrak (1-800-USA-RAIL) for information; for bus trips call Pine Hill Trailways ([914]331-0744) and Adirondack Trailways (1-800-342-4101). All offer special children's fares.

We grew up in the area covered in this book, and we remember many wonderful years exploring the region with our families. While some of the older attractions, such as Howe Caverns, have remained unchanged for decades, others, such as Storytown in Lake George, have metamorphosed into giant amusement parks like Great Escape. We hope that a new generation of travelers will enjoy discovering the wonder and magic of this diverse region as much as we enjoyed rediscovering it.

Mary Barile
Joanne Michaels
Woodstock, New York

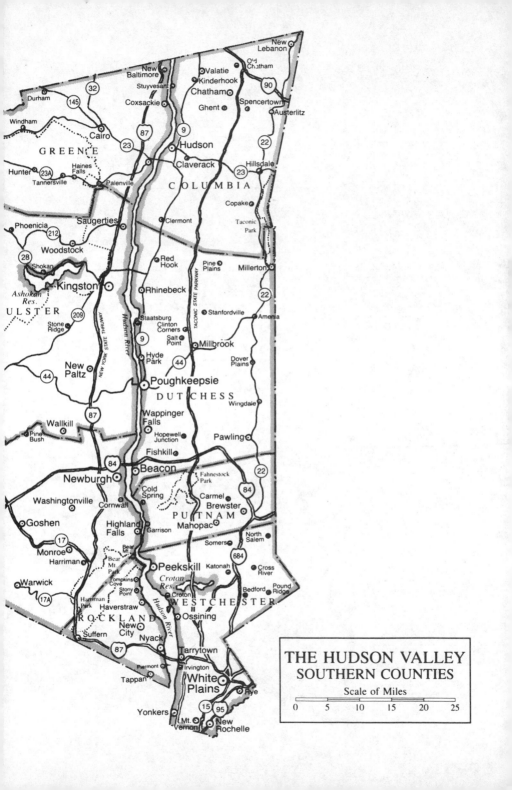

THE HUDSON VALLEY
SOUTHERN COUNTIES

Scale of Miles

0   5   10   15   20   25

NEW YORK

AREA SHOWN

THE HUDSON VALLEY
NORTHERN COUNTIES
Scale of Miles

0   5   10   15   20   25

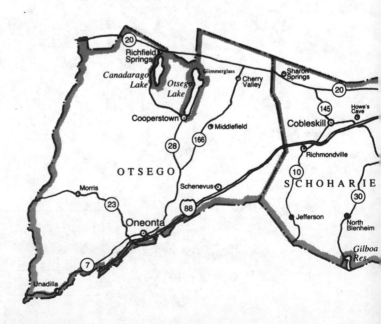

THE HUDSON VALLEY
BERKSHIRE COUNTY
MASSACHUSETTS
Scale of Miles
0   5   10

NEW YORK

AREA SHOWN

Williamstown

North Adams

②

②

Adams

New Ashford

⑦

⑧

Cheshire

Windsor

Dalton

Hancock Shaker Village

⑳

Pittsfield

B E R K S H I R E

Lenox

⑧

Becket

⑨⓪

⑳

Lee

Stockbridge

⑦

⑨⓪

Great Barrington

Otis

㉓

South Egremont

⑦

⑧

● Mt. Washington

Sheffield

Andrus Space Transit Planetarium at the Hudson River Museum. 511 Warburton Avenue, Yonkers, N.Y. 10701. (Take Sawmill River Parkway to the Executive Boulevard exit in Yonkers. Follow to the end and make a left onto North Broadway, then a right onto Odell Avenue. Go to the end of Odell Avenue and turn left onto Warburton Avenue. Follow the signs 1.3 miles to the museum.) (914) 963–4550. Open year-round for public showings: Wednesday and Friday, 4 pm; Thursday, 4 and 7 pm; and Saturday and Sunday, 1, 2:30, and 4 pm. Admission. Group rates are available for group shows Tuesday through Friday at 10 am, 11:15 am, noon, and 1 pm.

The Andrus Space Transit Planetarium, one of eleven of its kind in the world, is home to a state-of-the-art Zeiss M1015 Star Machine, a powerful scientific tool that can project thousands of stars and planets onto the planetarium's forty-foot domed ceiling. A quadriphonic sound system makes the planetarium the perfect setting for their multimedia programs, which include viewing stars, comets, constellations, and galaxies up close. The shows are accompanied by explanatory narratives that fit the season of the year and the age of the audience, from kindergarten to college. Past shows, which are changed at least five times a year, have included "Mars, the Red Planet," "The Sky's the Limit," and "Jewels of the Night Sky." The planetarium also sponsors a series of free night observations in the summer, in conjunction with local astronomy clubs, a "Night Under the Stars" camping experience for kids, and even planetarium birthday parties, where the guest of honor's name appears in a star! Other exhibits about science are offered in the nearby **Troster Science Hall,** a good place to visit while you wait for the planetarium show.

Facilities: Rest rooms; gift shop. Wheelchair accessible; stroller accessible.

* * *

If you plan to spend several hours in Yonkers, then go early and stop in at the **Hudson River Museum,** which adjoins the Andrus Planetarium. (Open Wednesday, Friday, and Saturday from 10 am to 5 pm; Thursday, 10 am to 9 pm; and Sunday, noon to 5 pm. Admission. Wheelchair accessible.) Housed in an old mansion, the museum contains exhibits of art and science through the ages. Some of the museum's tours are for smaller children, covering such topics as color, shapes, art, and animals; call ahead for tour schedules. Teachers should note that special tours and workshops are available, but reservations are required. There is also the unique **Red Grooms Bookstore,** a colorful shop where art, magic, and books come together for people of all ages.

Bicycle Sundays. From County Center Road in White Plains to Scarsdale Road in Yonkers, N.Y., via the Bronx River Parkway. (914) 285–2643. May through mid-October, every Sunday except holiday weekends, 10 am to 2 pm. Free.

If you enjoy bicycling and would like to spend a Sunday afternoon teaching the kids to ride safely, try this comfortable and convenient bike path. The ride, which is fourteen miles round-trip, is held on the Bronx River Parkway, a relatively flat, well-paved road that is closed to traffic during this weekly event. The parkway, one of the oldest in the region, is lined with flowering shrubs and trees in the spring and summer; in autumn the rides are a great way to see the foliage as well as to get some exercise as a family. Hundreds of people take advantage of the program, and all ages participate. You must bring your own equipment for this ride.

Facilities: None.

Bill of Rights Museum. 897 South Columbus Ave., Mt. Vernon, N.Y. 10550. (914) 667–4116. Open year-round, Saturday, noon to 4 pm, with tours at 12:30, 1:30, and 2:30 pm; also open Tuesday through Friday, 9 am to 5 pm, by appointment only.

Group tours are available by reservation for grades four and up. Free.

This young museum was founded only a few years ago to commemorate the Bill of Rights and the libel trial of printer and journalist John Peter Zenger, which was held nearby. This is actually a museum complex, with walking tours that take in the graveyard, the village green, the museum, and St. Paul's Church, which was built in 1763. We recommend this excursion especially for older children who are studying American history, since it is one of the more accessible prerevolutionary sites in the region. The tour's focus is on freedom of the press and free speech. A replica of an eighteenth-century printing press is used during each tour, in which kids are invited to participate in a mock-operation of the press (no ink is used). The church was once used as a courthouse, and Aaron Burr argued cases there. Inside the church are highbacked pews that were constructed to protect churchgoers from drafts in the winter and from animals that wandered through in the summer. There is even a resident ghost: Reverend Thomas Standard, who is said to turn on and off the lights and the heat. Special events at the site include an Independence Day celebration with bands and speakers and, on Tuesday afternoons in August, Listen and Lunch concerts featuring classical music on the village green.

Facilities: Rest rooms; gift shop, with old-fashioned toys. Wheelchair accessible, except for the church, which has limited access.

Blue Mountain Reservation. Welcher Avenue, Peekskill, N.Y. 10566. (914) 737–2194. Open year-round, from 9 am until dusk. Free.

This lovely county park in northeastern Westchester offers a full range of year-round outdoor activities for youngsters. Summer brings lots of action on the sandy beach, which fronts a unique chlorinated lake. Groups that want to stay overnight may make arrangements to camp in the rustic lodge (available for rental year-round). There are hiking trails, extensive picnic areas, horseback riding trails (bring your own horse), and fishing ponds. In the winter there is excellent cross-country skiing and some fine sledding hills for bobsledders and tobogganers.

Facilities: Rest rooms (wheelchair accessible); picnic areas with tables. Parents will have a difficult time maneuvering strollers off the paved paths.

Emelin Theatre for the Performing Arts. Library Lane, Mamaroneck, N.Y. 10543. (Take I-95 to Exit 18A [Mamaroneck Avenue] and go east to Prospect Avenue. Turn right onto Prospect; the first left is Library Lane.) (914) 698–3045. Open year-round, but performance times and dates vary, so call ahead for a schedule. Admission. You can buy tickets individually or for the winter or the spring performance series, which are usually held over seven weekends; the price is extremely reasonable for shows of such high quality. Group rates are available for individual performances.

This performing arts center was an unusual gift to Westchester County: the money for the Emelin Theatre's construction was donated to the Mamaroneck Library. The Emelin offers a broad spectrum of theater, music, dance, and children's programming. Past performances have included the Paper Bag Players (who use many costumes and props made out of paper bags and cardboard); the Hello Show, with its dozens of large puppets; the Emmy Award–winning Rags, Bags, and Dragons Puppet Theater; and folk singers, magicians, and mimes. The classics also have been represented, with shows about Cinderella, Beauty and the Beast, and the Wizard of Oz. The children's series is called Super Stuff for Kids, and it runs all year, with most shows offered on weekends.

Facilities: Rest rooms; snack bar. Wheelchairs are accommodated, but strollers don't really belong there; call ahead if that is a problem.

Greenburgh Nature Center. Dromore Road, Scarsdale, N.Y. 10583. (914) 723–3470. (Located off Central Avenue; watch for signs.) The grounds are open year-round, every day from 10 am until dusk. *Nature Museum:* Open from 10 am to 4 pm every day except Friday. Free. Groups are welcome.

The Greenburgh Nature Center, a thirty-two-and-a-half-acre oasis in the center of bustling Westchester's greenbelt, offers a unique opportunity for families to discover nature together. Younger visitors will enjoy the Nature Museum, housed in a former mansion, which contains more than 145 exotic and local animals some of which can be handled by the children, along with displays concerned with the natural world of the surrounding area. Greenburgh's short, marked nature trails; pond; brooks; rock outcroppings and glacial boulders; apple orchard; and various trees and ferns make it a good place to introduce very young children to ecology. More than forty types of flowering plants may be found in the woods, and because the property is located near bird migration routes, you may see any of several dozen types of songbirds. There are chocolate egg hunts in the woods, mushroom walks, grape-picking parties, maple sugaring in March, Halloween night walks for four to ten year olds (those who survive the walk may buy spider cider), and twilight lawn concerts. The center also sponsors child-oriented special events on weekends, year-round. Those who attend the "Spring Holiday Camp" are kept busy with nature-related games, walks, and crafts. There are also classes and workshops, some of which last one session, others of which are scheduled over several afternoons or weekend mornings. Teachers may want to ask about the center's special nature programs. Although this is a nature center, art exhibits are held in the manor house; some of these (such as a basket exhibit we saw) will appeal to older children.

Facilities: Rest rooms; gift shop. Strollers will be difficult to maneuver outside of the paved areas.

Indian Point Energy Education Center. Broadway and Bleakley Avenue, Buchanan, N.Y. 10511. (Take the Welcher Avenue exit off U.S. 9 and follow the signs.) (914) 737–8174. Open year-round, Monday through Friday, 10 am to 5 pm. Free. Group tours are available by advance reservation.

This educational center is located at one of the first nuclear power plants built in the United States. Opened in 1962, the original unit was shut down in 1974. Today the plant serves as a support for the two remaining units—which supply 25 percent of New York City's and Westchester County's electricity—and power research center. (Adults should be aware that this is a working nuclear site.) Visitors will find many fascinating exhibits about the history and uses of electricity and solar energy. On display are some of Thomas Edison's early inventions and a hands-on computer that lets kids find out about energy use at home. During the tour you will watch nuclear reactor operators train on a computerized control-room simulator, while a self-guided display allows kids to measure the natural radiation of everyday objects. A working system—the center is heated in part with solar energy—with its display of wind, solar, and water energy resources, should intrigue older children. Teachers should note that special discussions and films may be arranged for all school ages, from first grade to college; tours are offered as well.

Facilities: Rest rooms. Some wheelchair and stroller accessible areas.

Mountain Lakes Park. Hawley Road, North Salem, N.Y. 10560. (From New York City head north on I-684 to Exit 6, then take New York 35 east to New York 121, proceed to Grant's Corner Road, and turn right onto Hawley Road.) (914) 669–5793. Open year-round, 9 am until dusk. Free, but there is a charge for camping.

This one-thousand-acre camping park is a little more rugged than others in the region, so it is one park that offers older children a chance to "rough it" with an experienced adult. There are both cabin sites and tent sites for rent here throughout the year (some sites are limited to groups of six or more). Most do not have running water or toilet facilities. If you enjoy this type of challenge, you can explore some beautiful country—and still be only an hour from New York City. Other parts of the park, including its swimming pools, beaches, boat rental area, and fishing ponds, are open to day trippers. Winter in the park offers areas for snowshoeing, cross-country skiing, ice-skating (Hemlock Lake), and ice fishing (only on weekends). Notices about skiing and ice-skating conditions are posted at the entrance to the park.

Facilities: Rest rooms (wheelchair accessible); picnic area with tables.

Muscoot Farm Park. New York 100, Somers, N.Y. 10689. (From I-684 take the Cross River Road–Katonah exit, then follow New York 35 west to the intersection with New York 100, turn left, and drive one mile to the park entrance.) (914) 232–7118. Open May through October, Wednesday through Sunday, 10 am to 4 pm. Admission. Group rates and tours are available.

Now run by Westchester County, Muscoot Farm Park is a seven-hundred-acre farm built in 1885. This is a unique chance to visit a model farm of the late–nineteenth century, built at a time when technical advances such as electricity and indoor plumbing were just being introduced into the area. Younger children will be especially impressed with the multitude of farm life to be seen (and pet), including horses, cows, chickens, pigs, and ducks. The farm is complete with outbuildings: corn cribs, an outhouse hidden by a grape arbor, a wagon shed with a fine collection of antique wagons and sleighs, and a huge dairy barn. Throughout this still-working farm are interpretive exhibits, ranging from farm tools and houseware to hardware that was created in the farm's own blacksmith shop. In the summer, the herb garden blooms with plants used in cooking and medications. Corn and other crops are grown and harvested here too; what you see will depend on the season. The emphasis at Muscoot Farm is on *working*, so that visitors will see farm life in action: special programs may show the skills needed to be a blacksmith or a beekeeper on a farm, for example; often there are hayrides to be enjoyed. In addition to the farm, there are many acres of park to explore along marked trails that are home to beaver, raccoon, birds, and many wildflowers. Teachers and parents should note that a Young Farmers Program is held every summer for children three to six years old; the sessions last one week and are offered several times during the season.

Facilities: Rest rooms (wheelchair accessible); gift shop, picnic area. Strollers can be maneuvered on the paths, but be advised that working farms can be muddy and slippery.

If you are in Somers at Muscoot Farm on a Friday, you may want to stop at the **Historic Elephant Hotel,** now a county office building. (Located at the junction of New York 100 and U.S. 202 in Somers. [914] 227–4977. Open only on Fridays, from 2 to 4 pm. Free. No wheelchair accessibility.) The hotel was built by showman Hachaliah Bailey, who imported the first elephant to America in 1796. Today the third floor of the building houses a delightful circus exhibit arranged in five rooms. Visitors are treated to displays of circus memorabilia, posters, and three miniature big tops. This stop is wonderful for anyone who is interested in the history of circuses in America—which is just about everyone under the age of ninety.

Museum of Cartoon Art. Comly Avenue, Rye Brook, N.Y. 10573. (914) 939–0234. Open year-round, Tuesday through Friday, 10 am to 4 pm; and Sunday, 1 to 4 pm. Admission (children under 5 are admitted free). Group rates and tours are available by reservation.

This museum, which is housed in a five-story concrete castle, the only one of its type in the world, celebrates the color, history, and exuberance of cartoon art. Every cartoon character you or your children have ever loved is here, either on the walls, in one of the original comic strips on display, or under your feet in the unique rug. There is even cartoon graffiti in the bathrooms! Exhibits focus on the history of cartoon art, from political satire to early color comics and through magazines like *Mad*. Past exhibits have included "The Golden Age of Children's Illustration," "The Art of Walt Disney," and "A Tribute to Batman and Superman." A television set plays a con-

stant schedule of animated cartoons and movies that will entertain viewers for as long as they want to watch. Visitors can
request some of the classic cartoon tapes, including Betty Boop
and Superman (from the 1930s). Adults should also enjoy the
building itself, which resembles a fine Charles Addams castle
and was the largest concrete structure of its time. An annual
cartoon contest for children is held annually; the deadline for
entries is May 31. Contact the museum for specifics.

Facilities: Rest rooms; gift shop. There is no access for
wheelchairs, but strollers can be maneuvered easily.

Phillipsburg Manor. U.S. 9, North Tarrytown, N.Y. 10591.
(914) 631–8200. Open year-round, but hours vary: January and
February, weekends only, 10 am to 4 pm; March, November,
and December, every day except Tuesday, 10 am to 4 pm; and
April through October, every day except Tuesday, 10 am to 5
pm. Closed Thanksgiving, Christmas, and New Year's Day. Admission (children under six are admitted free). Group rates and
tours are available by reservation. Also, discount tickets are
available for this site in conjunction with tours of Sunnyside
and the Van Cortlandt Manor (see entries for those sites).

Created between the years 1662 and 1693, the Phillipsburg
Manor was once the center of a ninety-thousand-acre estate
owned by Frederick Phillipse. An orientation movie puts visitors back in the seventeenth century, then costumed guides
lead them across the Pocantico River to the main site. The old
grist mill has been restored and is in working order, and the
flours it produces are sold in the gift shop. The miller lets in
the water from the millrace to run the great grinding stones;
children are often invited to help him with his work. A
crowded, creaky place, full of noise and motion, the mill should
entertain all but the smallest visitors. Inside the manor house,
children will probably be surprised to discover how small the
living quarters were back then, and how many of the rooms
served several functions (one might sleep in one's office, and
one had to go through everyone else's bedroom to reach one's
own). Outside the house are some farm animals, a sheep pen,

and ducks on the mill pond. Special events throughout the year take advantage of the manor's site: in June, for example, the wheat harvest is celebrated with a frolic—an old-fashioned fiddle-and-dance party held after the winter wheat is brought in from the fields. For those Royalists among you, King George II's birthday is commemorated in November with fanfare, dancing, and refreshments. Candlelight tours are offered in early December.

Facilities: Rest rooms; gift shop, with lots of flours and meals that were ground in the old grist mill; picnic area with tables.

Pick-Your-Own Farms. Westchester County was once a farming region, but today there are only a few farms left that welcome visitors to pick their own produce. You pay by the pound—the produce is weighed after you pick it—and the savings are substantial when compared to market prices. Summer days in the fields call for hats, sunscreen, and long-sleeved shirts for comfort. At **Outhouse Orchards** (Hardscrabble Road, Croton Falls, N.Y. [Take I-684 to Exit 8 and go one and a quarter miles east to the orchards.] [914] 277–3188. Open weekends only for pick-your-own) there are apples for the picking in September and October, plus a farm tour. Call ahead for the tour schedule. At **Wilkens Fruit and Fir Farm** (1313 White Hill Road, Yorktown Heights, N.Y. [Take the Taconic Parkway to the U.S. 202 exit. Go one-quarter mile to Mohansic Avenue, then head south one mile to White Hill Road] [914] 245–5111. Open August through April, weekends only, for pick-your-own) enjoy a haywagon ride to the orchards to pick apples in September and October. This is the only farm in the county where you can cut your own Christmas tree in December.

Playland. Playland Parkway, Rye, N.Y. 10580. (Take Exit 19 off I-95 and watch for signs.) (914) 921–0373. Open mid-May through Labor Day, Tuesday through Thursday, noon to 11 pm; Friday and Saturday, noon to midnight; and Sunday, noon to 11 pm. Admission (there is no charge to enter the park, but you have to buy tickets for the rides). Group rates are available. *Ice Casino Skating Rink:* Open October through March, but the hours are varied, so it is recommended that you call ahead ([914] 967–2040). Admission.

Built in 1928, this was the first amusement park with family fun as its focus. The park is still popular, with dozens of rides, carousel music, art deco architecture, and an ocean view along its fabulous boardwalk. Children are dazzled by the rides, old and new, including the carousel, which is complete with painted horses and other brightly clad animals; the eighty-two-foot-high Dragon Coaster; the Thriller, which spins around; the newly refurbished Ye Olde Mill boat ride; and the Wildcat Coaster. Smaller, quieter rides enchant toddlers in the special Kiddy Land section. After the rides you may want to spend some time at the swimming pool or at the beach on Long Island Sound (both are open from Memorial Day through Labor Day), which charge separate admission. Playland is actually located in the **Edith G. Read Natural Park and Wildlife Sanctuary,** so while you are there you can take advantage of the hiking trails, fishing sites, and special programs that are organized by the Westchester County Parks Department. Playland closes for the winter, but the **Ice Casino** is open for indoor ice-skating from October through March. You can skate there to old-fashioned organ music or newer rock tunes, or take a lesson with the kids.

Facilities: *Playland:* Rest rooms (wheelchair accessible); souvenir shops; picnic areas; snack stands. Some areas in the park are wheelchair accessible; parents with strollers will have no trouble. *Read Park:* Rest rooms (they are not wheelchair accessible); picnic areas; fishing (with a license only). *Ice Casino:* Rest rooms; snack bar; skate rentals.

Sunnyside. U.S. 9, Tarrytown, N.Y. 10591. (Located one mile south of the Tappan Zee Bridge.) (914) 631–8200. Open year-round, but hours vary: January and February, weekends only, 10 am to 4 pm; March, November, and December, every day except Tuesday, 10 am to 4 pm; and April through October, every day except Tuesday, 10 am to 5 pm. Closed Thanksgiving, Christmas, and New Year's Day. Admission (children under six are admitted free). Group tours and rates are available by advance reservation.

Sunnyside was the home of author Washington Irving, who described his charming house as "full of angles and corners as an old cocked hat." The creator of Ichabod Crane began living and working at Sunnyside in the 1840s, and it is a fine place to introduce children to American literature. The house remains much as it was in Irving's time, with a graceful carriage drive and wisteria draped over the front door. Inside, costumed guides take visitors through the cottage, which still contains many of Irving's personal belongings, including his writing desk and piano. Although Irving had no children of his own, he did have many nieces and nephews living with him, and many of the bedrooms with nineteenth-century toys and clothing reflect the children who lived at Sunnyside. Younger visitors who are familiar with the "Legend of Sleepy Hollow" and "Rip Van Winkle" will be fascinated to learn that Ichabod Crane did indeed live in the neighborhood (Irving based the character on a neighbor) and that the ghostly hoofbeats still can be heard on windy nights along the local roads. Outside the cottage, many walking paths offer lovely views of the Hudson River. There are several outbuildings to visit as well: the woodshed; the root cellar and milk room; the outhouses; and the icehouse. Next to a graceful swan pond, which Irving dubbed the "Little Mediterranean," are picnic tables—a perfect rest spot for lunch in the summer. For kids who love trains, Amtrak trains can be seen (and heard) shooting by several times a day on the railroad tracks alongside the Hudson (the same route taken by Irving on his trips to New York). Special events are held throughout the year, many of them especially for children. Past events have included a Strawberry Fest, an Independence Day celebration, an ice-cream-making workshop, a celebration of nineteenth-century baseball, an apple festival, a nineteenth-century Thanksgiving dinner, and Christmas candlelight tours. Teachers should note that there are many workshops for school classes. Call ahead for details.

Facilities: Rest rooms; gift shop, with many lovely children's items; picnic area with tables. Not recommended for wheelchairs. If wheelchair accessibility is needed, call ahead. Strollers are fine on the grounds, but there are some steep stairs inside the house.

After touring Sunnyside there are a few other places to see in the area. Make a stop at the **village park** (on U.S. 9 in the center of Tarrytown). The park has markers showing where Major John André (the British soldier who was Benedict Arnold's contact) was captured during the American Revolution and a bridge over the stream where, legend has it, Ichabod Crane was chased away by the headless horseman. The kids will also enjoy stopping at the **Old Dutch Church,** built in the late seventeenth century and still used for services. (The Church is on U.S. 9 north of Tarrytown near Phillipsburg Manor; watch for the parking area signs. Call [914] 631–1123 for church hours and for times for guided tours of the cemetery.) The Old Dutch Church cemetery contains many fascinating old tombstones, many of them in Dutch, dating back to the seventeenth century. Washington Irving's grave is there, and it is now a national historic landmark. An old belief holds that the ghost of a headless Hessian soldier haunts the site. You may want to call ahead ([914] 285–2652) for a tour of the **Tarrytown Lighthouse** (follow the signs from the center of town to Kingsland Point Park on the Hudson River), which offers displays of logbooks, photos, and furnishings that illustrate what life was like in a lighthouse over the past one hundred years. Even if you decide not to take the tour, the lighthouse and the Hudson River traffic are wonderful attractions for kids. The lighthouse is also the focus of several school- and group-centered tours and workshops; call for schedules and reservations.

Van Cortlandt Manor. Croton-on-Hudson, N.Y. 10520. (Nine miles north of the Tappan Zee Bridge on U.S. 9, exit onto Croton Point Avenue, go one block northeast to South Riverside Avenue, turn right and proceed one-quarter mile to the entrance.) (914) 631–8200. Open year-round, but hours vary:

January and February, weekends only, 10 am to 4 pm; March, November, and December, every day except Tuesday, 10 am to 4 pm; and April through October, every day except Tuesday, 10 am to 5 pm. Closed Thanksgiving, Christmas, and New Year's Day. Admission (children under six are admitted free). Group tours and rates are available by reservation.

This three-hundred-year-old manor has been restored to reflect life in a wealthy seventeenth-century Dutch-American home. The original estate consisted of eighty-six thousand acres. Although the site is small today, it still contains much of the manor's outbuildings and gardens. Inside the manor house there is a blend of family furniture and furnishings from the seventeenth, eighteenth, and nineteenth centuries (the Van Cortlandt family lived there until 1945, when the house was purchased by the Rockefellers). Children will delight at the huge fowling piece, which was used to bring down entire flocks of wild birds with one shot. If you are lucky, one of the costumed guides will be cooking at the brick hearth and will offer you a taste of gingerbread or other treats. There is some child-sized furniture in the house, as well as many interesting kitchen tools and implements. Outside there is the "Long Walk," a brick path that used to lead to a nearby inn. The walk is surrounded by lovely gardens and orchards.

Although this site is really for older children who enjoy history, there are many special events throughout the year that will please those of all ages. Every weekend in late September and October the manor takes on an eighteenth-century atmosphere with its Autumn Marketplace. Apple cider, pumpkins, apples, and crafts are all for sale, and there is entertainment. October also hosts Crafts and Tasks Day, when preparations for winter are done the same way they were a century ago. Summer offers demonstrations of cooking, baking, and herbal medicine preparation, and in the winter special candlelight tours make the manor house glow as it did three centuries ago.

Facilities: Rest rooms; gift shop; picnic area. People in wheelchairs may have difficulty; if accessibility is a problem, call ahead. Strollers can be maneuvered on the brick walk, but there are steep stairs in the house.

Ward Pound Ridge Reservation. Box 461, Cross River, N.Y. 10518. (From I-684 take the Cross River Road–Katonah exit and go east on New York 35 for four miles to New York 121; turn right and proceed to the entrance.) (914) 763–3993. Open year-round, daily, 7 am until dusk. *Trailside Nature Museum:* Open Wednesday through Sunday, 9 am to 5 pm. There is a small parking fee. Group rates are available; school visits to the museum are by appointment only. Camping is by advanced reservation only (two night minimum stay required) and is allowed only in the park's rustic shelters—no tents or trailers are permitted.

A forty-seven-hundred-acre park, Ward Pound Ridge Reservation is both a wildlife sanctuary and an educational center. A variety of outdoor activities may be enjoyed there, including hiking, fishing in the Waccabuc River, camping, cross-country skiing on marked trails, and sledding in the meadow area. In addition, there is the excellent fieldstone sided **Trailside Nature Museum,** which contains wildlife (the molar of a mastodon), nature, and Delaware Indian exhibits. A honeybee hive vibrates with activity behind a glass case; a black rat snake moves through an aquarium. Lining the walls are a few dozen taxidermic mounts from a coyote and bobcat to a kingfisher and raccoon. Even the youngest children will enjoy participating in the special workshops and events that are held continually at the park and at the museum. From late-February to mid-March there are maple syrup–making programs, in which participants learn the mysteries of sap boiling; bird walks, to see hawks and other wild birds; fiddling festivals; and winter carnivals. Just outside the museum is a half-acre wildflower garden with more than one hundred kinds of wildflowers, all labeled. (Note that children must be accompanied by an adult in this area.) There is also a replica of an Algonquin wigwam.

Facilities: Rest rooms; campsites, picnic areas with tables and grills. If wheelchair accessibility is needed, call ahead. Parents with strollers will be able to manage the paths and the museum.

Westmoreland Sanctuary. Chestnut Ridge Road, Mount Kisco, N.Y. 10549. (914) 666–8448. Open year-round, daily, dawn to dusk. Museum: Open Monday through Saturday, 9 am to 5 pm; and Sunday, 10:30 am to 5 pm. Free.

The special programs at the museum are the biggest attractions here for the younger visitor. A variety of classes, hikes, and workshops are offered throughout the year and in the past have included a timberdoodle watch (these birds' antics are well worth a hike into the woods), a birdfeeder-making workshop for preschoolers, nature craft classes for children, maple syrup–making classes, and sounds-around gatherings (where you sit in the woods and listen to the sounds with a naturalist who explains what it is you are hearing). A Halloween night hike and party enlivens the fall, as does the Fall Festival, complete with sheep shearing, blacksmithing, and spinning demonstrations, a petting zoo, and crafts demonstrations. Inside the museum you will find displays of local animals and plants and descriptive exhibits about the area's history. As it is one of the county's busiest nature centers, we recommend that you call ahead to find out what is scheduled.

Facilities: Rest rooms; picnic area. If wheelchair accessibility is needed, please call ahead. Not recommended for people with strollers.

Yorktown Museum. 1974 Commerce Street, Yorktown Heights, N.Y. 10598. (914) 962–2970. Open year-round, Tuesday through Friday, 9:30 am to 4:30 pm; and Sunday, 1:30 to 4:30 pm. Admission is free for individuals, but there is a minimal charge for groups.

A small, cozy museum contained in five rooms, the Yorktown Museum offers children a chance to look at daily life at the turn of the century, through either guided or self-guided tours. The Railroad Room contains a model of Yorktown's old railroad station, complete with a fully operational scale model of the Old Put Line as well as photos and artifacts of old-time railroading. One of the best-known rooms is the Small World, where dollhouse and miniatures enchant the viewer. The pick of the crop here is the Marjorie Johnson Victorian dollhouse, which is filled with tiny furniture and furnishings and has eight thousand hand-cut clapboards, a stonework base, and a resident ghost! In the Woodlands Room you may sit in a replica of a Mohegan village longhouse, grind some corn, and see what life was like for the native Americans of the area. Other rooms contain artifacts, farm tools, and furniture from homes and settlements of northern Westchester's past. A variety of changing exhibits throughout the year focus on topics such as nineteenth-century medicine and bridal gowns through the nineteenth century.

Facilities: Rest rooms; gift shop, which specializes in miniatures and dollhouse and craft kits, plus lots of small toys. Access for wheelchairs is by special arrangement; stroller accessible.

Bear Mountain State Park. U.S. 9W off the Palisades Interstate Parkway, Bear Mountain, N.Y. 10911. (914) 786–2701. Open year-round; 10 am to 4 pm. Call ahead for skiing and swimming schedules. Free. Group tours are accommodated by special reservation.

This huge park contains enough activities to fill up a week's vacation. Nature lovers will enjoy the hiking trails and spectacular views, bike trails (which vary in length so are suitable for all ages), swimming pool and lakes, and paddleboats, which may be rented during the summer. Even the youngest children will love the zoo, the beaver lodge, and the reptile house. Colorful birds and fuzzy mammals—snakes, bears, fox, coyotes, raccoons—cavort in their zoo homes while outside, the beaver busily chip away at trees and gambol in the waters near their winter lodge. In the reptile house face-to-face encounters with snakes and lizards will thrill all ages of adventurers. Note, however, that a lot of walking is involved and that it may take up to an hour to see the whole zoo complex, so it will be a good idea to bring a stroller for a very young child. At the Trailside Museum special exhibits explain the natural and human-constructed history of the park and the surrounding areas. Even during the winter the park is busy. Ski-jumping competitions take place in January and February, and ice-skating is offered from late October to late March (skates may be rented at the **Bear Mountain Inn**). In December don't forget to stop by for the Holiday Festival, which offers Santa Claus, a talking bear, carolers, and gingerbread house contests.

Facilities: Rest rooms; diaper-changing area; gift shop; picnic area with tables. Wheelchair accessible. Strollers can be used on the paved paths throughout the zoo and museum area. Pets are allowed if leashed. The *Bear Mountain Inn* offers breakfast, lunch, and dinner as well as overnight accommodations.

Paul Peabody Puppets. 10 Van Houten Avenue, Upper Nyack, N.Y. 10960. (914) 358–1463.

A craftsman with the soul of an artist, Paul Peabody is a master puppeteer who creates his own puppets and costumes by hand. The marionettes are patterned after characters in folk and fairy tales from around the world, and it can take him up to two months to complete one puppet. His puppet plays are offered at libraries and historic sites throughout the county. The motion and color of the entertainment intrigues people of all ages. And Peabody likes to spend time with his audience, explaining how the puppets are constructed and moved. While he doesn't have his own theater, you can always find him at local shows and festivals (see the calendar on page 191) or call him for information on upcoming performances. At the Holiday Marionette Show in Nyack each December, Peabody appears with elaborately costumed puppets for an old-world Christmas. The Rockland Historical Society and the Clearwater Great River Revival both sponsor his puppet demonstrations.

Pick-Your-Own Farm. Orchards of Conklin South Mountain Road, Pomona, N.Y. 10970. (Take the Palisades Interstate Parkway, Exit 12, and go half a mile north on New York 45.) (914) 354–0369. Open year-round, but pick-your-own is on weekends only, from 10 am to 5 pm.

This is the only orchard in Rockland County that offers tours during the harvest season. Many kids never get the chance to see where food comes from, and an orchard is a marvelous place to start exploring the food chain. You can pick what you like for as long as you like and then have the produce weighed; you are charged by the pound and sometimes have to pay for the container. In addition to picking your own apples, children and adults will enjoy gathering in the squash, spinach, peppers, raspberries, pears, peaches, and other fruits. It can get very hot out in the fields during the summer, so include a hat and a sunscreen when you pack. Also note that during berry season there are lots of bees around. Younger children may be disturbed by this. An October visit will yield a self-picked pumpkin, an especially satisfying way to start celebrating Halloween. The roadside market there stocks lots of local foods, including an array of vegetables as well as maple syrup, honey, and cider.

Rockland Lake State Park. U.S. 9W, Congers, N.Y. 10920. (914) 268–3020 or 268–7598. Open year-round, although the nature center is closed from October to May. Admission.

A park packed with activities and open spaces, this is a great place to stop no matter what time of year it is. In the spring and summer, fishing, boating, swimming, and picnics are popular. In the fall and winter pull on your hiking boots or grab your sled and head for the trails and hills. The nature center offers live animal exhibits and special nature-oriented events during the warmer seasons. Guided tours begin at the nature center (call ahead for topics and hours). It should be noted that a trail for the visually handicapped is offered along with the other marked nature trails. Many of the nature trails are easy to walk, even for the youngest in your party.

Facilities: Rest rooms; picnic areas with tables; snack stand; boat rental.

Stony Point Battlefield. U.S. 9W, Stony Point, N.Y. 10980. (914) 786–2521. Open from mid-April to October, Wednesday through Sunday, 8:30 am to 5 pm. Free. Group tours are available with park rangers, but call ahead.

Mad Anthony Wayne led his troops on a midnight raid here in 1779, and their victory over the British forces became one of the turning points of the American Revolution. At the orientation center a slide show describes the history of the site. A walking tour of this beautiful but wild park allows visitors to see the remnants of the battlefield and its fortifications. Even without a guided tour, there are many trail and battlefield markers that explain the movements of the troops during that fateful night. Popular with children is **Stony Point Lighthouse,** once used to aid ships on the Hudson River. We recommend this site for older children who are interested in the American Revolution, although younger children might enjoy the military displays and musters that are offered on holidays throughout the summer and fall.

Facilities: Rest rooms; picnic area with tables. Don't even think of bringing a stroller on the battlefield walk, which also may be a little long for children under age four. Pets are not allowed.

Swimming. The Palisades Park System, which includes Harriman State Park, Bear Mountain, Tallman Mountain, Rockland Lake, and Nyack Beach, all in Rockland County, offers some excellent spots to swim. There is no fee for swimming (only a small parking charge) at **Lake Tiorati, Lake Sebago,** and **Lake Welch,** which are all in Harriman State Park. Swimming is also available in the pools at Bear Mountain, High Tor State Park, Tallman Mountain, and Rockland Lake. **Rockland Lake** has two pools as well as a wading pool and there is a small charge for swimming there. All swimming facilities are fully operational by June 20th, and are open daily 10 am to 6 pm; on weekends and holidays 9 am to 7 pm. It is suggested that you call before going, since some schedules are subject to variation. (914) 786–2701.

Boscobel. U.S. 9, Garrison-on-Hudson, N.Y. 10524. (914) 265–3638. Open March through December, every day except Tuesday. Also closed Thanksgiving and Christmas. Hours: April through October, 9:30 am to 5 pm (last tour at 4:30 pm); November, December, and March, 9:30 am to 4 pm (last tour at 3:30 pm). Admission. Group rates and school tours are available by reservation.

This magnificent mansion, sited on a bluff high above the Hudson River, was once sold for thirty-five dollars to a scrap dealer. But local interest saved the house and restored it to its earlier magnificence, complete with antiques, decorations, and breathtaking flower gardens. Many older children enjoy seeing the sweeping staircases and elegant interior, although we don't recommend the house tour for the younger set. Outside, however, everyone will want to walk among the rose and tulip plantings, watch the boats on the Hudson, and visit the orangery (a greenhouse) and the gate house, a smaller, less pretentious nineteenth-century servant's home. There are outdoor concerts throughout the summer on the lawn, a Rose Day celebration in June, and holiday candlelight tours.

Facilities: Rest rooms; gift shop; picnic areas.

After Boscobel you may want to stop in the nearby village of **Garrison Landing** and walk down to the bandstand on the Hudson River, where children's events are held throughout the summer (the bandstand was once used as part of the set for the movie *Hello Dolly!*). Children like seeing the river up close. Another stop is **Constitution Marsh** (Indian Brook Road, Garrison), a favorite bird-watching area with self-guided walking tours along a boardwalk. There are even canoe tours of the marsh sponsored by the National Audubon Society (call [914] 265–3119), which will take individuals or school groups by reservation only. It is preferable that no one in the tour is under six years of age. Canoes are provided.

Mahopac Farm Museum. U.S. 6, Baldwin Place, N.Y. 10505. (914) 628–9298. Open April through November, daily, 10 am to 5 pm. Admission to museum; country store is free.

This small museum is not a museum in the strictest sense, but a collection of collections: antique and collector's cars, costumes of the late–nineteenth century, old bicycles (better known as "boneshakers"), and old farm wagons and carriages. Once you have finished enjoying the exhibits, stop next door at the country store and ice-cream parlor and try an old-fashioned sundae or malted.

Facilities: Rest rooms; gift shop; picnic area. Parents with strollers can move about freely, but wheelchair accessibility is limited.

Manitoga Nature Preserve. Old Manitou Road and New York 9D, Garrison-on-Hudson, N.Y. 10524. (914) 424–3812. Open year-round, spring and fall, 10:30 am to dusk; summer, 10:30 am to 6 pm; and November through March, 10:30 am to 4 pm. Admission for nonmembers.

Older children (eight and up) especially will enjoy this park, which was designed in the 1950s by Russell Wright to demonstrate how humans could live in harmony with nature. There are five miles of hiking trails, leading through evergreen forests or into wildflower and fern gardens. The trails are all organized around a theme having to do with people experiencing the natural world—for example, the Morning Trail faces the sunrise, and the Blue Trail contains brooks and wild laurel forests. The highlight for children is the wigwam, which is hidden in an oak forest. This life-size replica of a Woodland Indian dwelling was actually made with Stone Age tools. It now serves as a learning center for both professional scientists and schoolchildren. There are special workshops in natural basket making, foraging for food in the wild, and even winter track identification, which is taught by tracking an animal and then telling its story. If your kids enjoy seeing houses, call ahead and request a tour of **Dragon Rock,** a house that was built atop a quarry and faces waterfalls and evergreen forests. And serious hikers should note: Manitoga is the only site in this region of the Hudson where the Appalachian Trail is directly accessible.

Facilities: Rest rooms; picnic area; guide house (where maps are available). Parking is also available for the Appalachian Trail.

Pick-Your-Own Farms. Putnam County is lovely in the summer, and a fine way for kids to enjoy the outdoors is to spend some time picking their own fruit for dessert. After gathering the produce it is weighed. You are charged by the pound, at prices that are well below those at most supermarkets. **Salinger's Orchards** (Guinea Road, Brewster, N.Y. 10509). [914] 279–3521. Open August through June 1, daily, 9 am to 6 pm) has apples every autumn. Kids also will enjoy seeing the cider mill, which produces fresh cider that is for sale. **Ryder Farm** (Starr Ridge Road, Brewster, N.Y. 10509. [914] 279–3984. Open July through October, afternoons) is a two-hundred-year-old family farm of 125 acres, where pickers will find organically grown raspberries. Wear a hat and bring a sunscreen and your own baskets, if you can (otherwise you can purchase containers).

Skiing: Big Birch. New York 22, Patterson, N.Y. 12563. (914) 878–3181. Open December through March, Monday through Friday, 10 am to 10 pm; Saturday, 9 am to 10 pm; and Sunday, 9 am to 6 pm. Admission is charged for the lifts; there are reduced rates for children under twelve. Group rates are available.

This one hundred-acre ski center is especially fun for beginners and families with young children. There are full snowmaking facilities, lessons and rentals are available. This is the perfect place for your preschooler to learn the basics for downhill skiing—especially in the Sunshine Classes, for children age seven and under, and the Junior Racing Program, for more advanced youngsters. Night skiing is fun for older children, and because Big Birch is not as far north as many other ski centers, the temperatures there are often several degrees higher than at those farther upstate. Big Birch is close enough to New York City for residents to make it a day trip.

Facilities: Rest rooms; picnic areas; restaurant; ski equipment rental; ski school.

Southeast Museum. Main Street, P.O. Box 88, Brewster, N.Y. 10509. (914) 279–7500. Open March through December, Tuesday through Thursday, 2 to 4 pm; and Saturday and Sunday, noon to 4 pm. Free. Groups are accommodated by appointment.

This is a small museum but one with local interest and some off-beat exhibits. You will find a Borden Dairy Condensory (the inventor of condensed milk, Gail Borden, lived in the area), an exhibit that traces the history of the Croton Reservoir and water supply system, and local photos and memorabilia. Young rock hounds will enjoy the Trainor Collection of minerals, the most varied collection of minerals to be found in one American mine (the Tilly Foster Mine, which was located in the town of Southeast). This is a nice area in which to spend an hour or so. Right next door is the last unaltered **one-room schoolhouse** in the county—a national historic landmark that offers children a look at education experiences of the past. Located in the same historic district is the **Old Southeast Church** (New York 22. Open on Sunday only, from 2 to 5 pm), built in 1794, which offers costumed tour guides.

Facilities: Rest rooms; limited access to wheelchairs.

Taconic Outdoor Education Center in Clarence Fahnestock Memorial State Park. 12 Dennytown Road, Cold Spring, N.Y. 10516. (914) 265–3773. Open year-round, 9 am to dusk. Free, but there is a charge for camping and for cabin facilities. Call in advance for reservations. Groups are gladly accommodated.

One of the best outdoor educational sites in the region, this center offers year-round programs for all ages of children and adults. The center itself is located in the Hudson Highlands on a lake, with nearby hemlock ravines, wildflower meadows, swamps, and streams. Wildlife abounds, and program participants may see deer, owls, ruffed grouse, fox, and even wild turkey. Past youth program topics have included geology (how to interpret past geological history), aquatic ecology, maps and compasses, and survival (keeping safe in the woods). There are even night programs, with astronomy classes, night hikes in the woods, and a nature carnival. A family weekend takes place every October and includes many special events, such as workshops, apple-pressing demonstrations, and campfire singalongs. And for people who want to take their kids on an outdoor adventure but hate sleeping on the ground, in addition to the more rustic woodland sites the center offers deluxe cabin facilities at very reasonable rates (private rooms, bathrooms, a lounge, and a kitchenette).

Facilities: Rest rooms; picnic areas; lodge/dining hall with fireplace; wheelchair accessible. Facilities are available for other activities, including fishing, boating, ski touring, hiking, ice-skating, swimming, and horseback riding.

Museum of the Hudson Highlands. The Boulevard, Cornwall-on-Hudson, N.Y. 12520. (Take U.S. 9W to 107, follow it to 218 east, turn right on Payson Road, and look for signs.) (914) 534–7781. Open July and August, Monday through Thursday, 11 am to 5 pm; Saturday, noon to 5 pm; and Sunday, 1:30 to 5 pm. Open September through June, Monday through Thursday, 2 to 5 pm; Saturday noon to 5 pm; and Sunday, 1:30 to 5 pm. Suggested donation.

This museum is an excellent place to visit with children who love wildlife and want to learn more about the lives and habitats of various animals. Adults will appreciate the changing cultural exhibits in the smaller exhibit halls. Upon entering the natural history wing you will find a sort of indoor mini-zoo, which houses small animals and plants that are native to the Hudson River region. Lots of amphibians, reptiles, small mammals, and birds crawl, creep, and sing, to the education and delight of the younger children. The hall also contains a reproduction of an Algonkian wigwam, which demonstrates part of the history of native Americans in the area. Outside, you can take year-round nature walks over the seventy-acre preserve, where small ponds, evergreen forests, and even a prairie offer information about the natural world. An annual spring celebration called Children's Day is held, with live animal demonstrations, crafts, and special nature walks. There is also a Halloween get-together with apple bobbing and pumpkin carving. The museum is known for its summer workshops on the environment and for its arts and crafts classes (preregistration is necessary). Teachers will appreciate the natural history classes that are offered to groups ranging in age from preschool to high school.

Facilities: Rest rooms; gift shop with lots of handmade items and many nature guides; picnic area with tables. Strollers and wheelchairs can be navigated in the museum but will be difficult on the nature trails.

*   *   *

If you are in the area and your child enjoys gardens, take a tour of the **Bee and Thistle Herb Farm.** (51 Angola Road, P.O. Box N, Cornwall, N.Y. 12518. [914] 534–7436. Open Tuesday through Sunday, 1 to 5 pm. Call for tour hours.) The summer gardens are lovely, and the tour guides explain the use and history of each herb and flower.

Museum Village in Orange County. Museum Village Road, Monroe, N.Y. 10950. (Take Exit 129 off New York 17 west and watch for signs.) (914) 782–8247. Open May through the first week in December, Wednesday through Sunday, and all legal holidays; hours vary, although in general they are 10 am to 5 pm in the summer and 10 am to 2 pm in the spring and late fall. Admission. Special rates are available for groups of twenty or more; advance reservations are required.

America was once a rural nation, without electricity and dependent on horse- and people-power. At Museum Village, children are able to visit a re-creation of a typical crossroads village of the mid–nineteenth century. Many of the buildings were rescued from other parts of Orange County and moved to the village, where they now serve as working shops and houses. Children will enjoy visiting the wagon maker, the blacksmith (with a working forge), the schoolhouse, a log cabin homestead, and the barber shop. The Natural History Museum houses a mastodon skeleton, and you can buy penny candy at the General Store. There are craftspeople at work throughout the site, and children are welcome to watch the costumed weaver, printer, and broom maker go about their business. Kids will be entranced by the taste of open-hearth cooking and freshly pressed cider. Special children's events—a kite fly, craft workshops, dinner on the green with costumed villagers—highlight almost every month. This is a wonderful place to spend a day with kids. Teachers should note that there are extensive school programs.

Facilities: Rest rooms; gift shop; picnic tables; snack stand.

The site is fine for strollers, but wheelchairs will find it difficult once they leave the paths.

New Windsor Cantonment. Box 207, Vails Gate, N.Y. 12584. (From I-87, Exit 17, or I-84, Exit 7S, take Rte, 300 one and one-half miles to Temple Hill Road, turn left, and proceed one and one-half miles.) (914) 561–1765. Open from Mid-April to October 31, Wednesday through Saturday, 10 am to 5 pm; and Sunday, 1 to 5 pm. Open Memorial Day, Independence Day, and Labor Day. Free. Groups are accommodated by advance reservation only.

This is an unusual site: one of the few military village restorations in the country that depicts the everyday life of a soldier in George Washington's troops. The last days of the Revolution were waited out in the cantonment, where log cabins and more permanent buildings had been built to house the motley array of soldiers, officers, craftsmen, and camp followers that went into making up an army. Your tour should begin in the Visitors Center, where a slide show and exhibits discuss the life of an eighteenth-century soldier (there is also a fascinating exhibit, for adults, of the history of the Purple Heart, which Washington established). Then it's down a wooden walkway to the cantonment, where buildings have been reconstructed from old military prints. In fact, one small building is the only known surviving example of a structure built by revolutionary soldiers. On any given day, costumed site interpreters may be drilling on the green, cooking food over an open fire, forging army equipment in the blacksmith shop, or tootling on a fife. Special events, including concerts and the annual encampment of the Brigade of the American Revolution, are also held throughout the season.

Facilities: Rest rooms; picnic area with tables. Parents with strollers will not have too much difficulty, although some of the paths are graveled; wheelchairs may find limited accessibility outside of the museum or off the paths.

New York Renaissance Festival. Sterling Forest, Tuxedo, N.Y. 10987. (From New York City take New York 17 north to

New York 17A and follow the signs.) (914) 351–5171 (July through mid-September only). The festival runs from late July through mid-September, weekends only, 11 am to 6 pm. Admission (children under six are free). Reduced rates are available for groups of twenty-five or more (call [914] 351–5171). Off-season inquiries should be sent to Creative Faires, Ltd., 134 Fifth Avenue, New York, N.Y. 10011. Or call (516) 288–2004.

Step back into history and watch knights joust, ladies swoon in peril, and magicians spin their spells. Kids will absolutely adore spending a day with a knight at this enormous Renaissance festival. There are Shakespearean plays, opera, a petting zoo, and garden walks. Children may run into Maid Marion and Robin Hood or the queen herself. Popular attractions for youngsters are the mud fights, the Punch and Judy puppet shows, and the craft demonstrations, which run all day. The events are colorful and noisy, and there is plenty of room for kids to run around. The highlight of the day is the late afternoon joust, so don't leave early if you want to catch sight of the gaily dressed knights and horses. You can just sit in one place and watch the Renaissance world go by, or you can walk through the site, which is lovely with its gardens and ponds. One caveat: this is a rather pricey excursion, especially if you have a large family. The tickets run at least twelve dollars a day for adults, and many of the foods and snacks are on the expensive side. But the entertainment is marvelous—educational as well as fun—and an experience all ages will enjoy.

Facilities: Rest rooms; picnic areas; food of every description sold at booths; craft shows. The site is stroller and wheelchair friendly. Shuttle buses run from the parking areas to the main site.

Pick-Your-Own Farms. Orange County's Pine Island is known for its black-earth farming region, which produces fine crops of vegetables and fruits (as well as mastodon bones!). For pick-your-own, children will enjoy at least three farms in this area. All produce is weighed at the end of your stay, and you are charged by the pound. Prices are exceedingly reasonable. **Dat-**

tolico Organic Farm (Mission Land Road, Pine Island, N.Y. [located two miles west of Orange County Route 1.] [914] 258–4762. Open from late-May through mid-October) grows all of its produce without the addition of excess chemicals. A dazzling array of vegetables includes beans, carrots, corn, eggplant, peas, squash, and cucumbers. In the fall, a stop here will provide an industrious child with a pumpkin of his or her choice. At **Ayres Family Farm** (New York 302, Bullville, N.Y. [located three-quarters of a mile south of town.] [914] 361–4239. Open from June 1 to October 1) you can pick your own strawberries, asparagus, beans, tomatoes, cucumbers, and pumpkins (in season). **Linda O'Brien** (206 Hill Avenue, Pine Bush N.Y. [the farm is off New York 52, one-half mile east of town.] [914] 744–5495. Open from May through November) has fruits and vegetables in abundance, with pears, raspberries, strawberries, beans, potatoes, eggplant, beets, and corn—all yours for the picking. Just be sure to dress the kids in work clothes and hats and take along plenty of sunscreen.

Stewart International Airport and Airbase. 1035 First St., Newburgh, N.Y. 12550. (Take I–87 to Exit 17. Make a right onto New York 17 K west. At first traffic light, make a left and follow signs to the main entrance.) (914) 564–2100. Open from late spring to fall. Tours are for school groups only; call for an appointment. Free.

Kids who are studying aviation and transportation may want to ask their teachers to schedule a tour of this airport. During part of the school year, teachers and classes may take a tour of the firehouse (for planes) and the flight line, where you will see the various planes that are on site. Although the tour is short, it is interesting for children who have never seen a plane up close. We recommend this visit for younsters from five to ten years of age.

Facilities: Rest rooms; snack stand.

Storm King. Old Pleasant Hill Road. Mountainville, N.Y. 10953. (The site is just off New York 32 north; watch for signs.)

(914) 534–3115. Open from April 1 to November 30, every day except Tuesday, noon to 5:30 pm. Suggested donation. Group tours are available.

Situated in a 350-acre park, Storm King holds an enormous outdoor sculpture park. Between the small indoor museum and the outdoor area, more than ninety artists are represented, including Alexander Calder, Louise Nevelson, and Isamu Noguchi. There are more than 125 outdoor sculptures, amongst the landscaped gardens and walks. Although older children might appreciate viewing modern art up close, younger children will be more enthralled with hiding and climbing around the sculptures and in the park. There are very few places where huge sculptures can be displayed in a natural environment. Unlike some of the more conventional museums, where children are told to be quiet and not to touch, Storm King provides a good introduction to modern art for children of all ages. Plan to bring a lunch and spend a couple of hours. The views are magnificent and kids are allowed to play around the grounds.

Facilities: Rest rooms; picnic area with tables. This is a comfortable place for parents with strollers or wheelchairs.

Sugar Loaf Village. Sugar Loaf, N.Y. 10981. (The village is reached from New York 17 west, Exit 127; follow the signs.) (914) 469–4963. Open year-round. Most shops are open Tuesday through Sunday, 10 am to 5 pm; all are open Saturday and Sunday, 10 am to 5 pm. Free.

More than twenty years ago, Sugar Loaf established itself as a leading craft village, and today it offers lots of shops and demonstrations by working craftspeople. This is really a site for parents who want to shop but also want their kids to stay amused. One of the best offerings of Sugar Loaf is its selection of unique toy shops: Sugar Loaf Rag Dolls and Created with Love are only two of the stores where you may find something special for your children. Through the year, special events entertain visitors of all ages—these include concerts, a fall festival, and a Christmas caroling and candlelighting service (the

Saturday before Christmas), when Santa visits and the village glows with an old-fashioned, small-town atmosphere—a good holiday stop!

Facilities: Rest rooms in some of the restaurants. Coffee shops and restaurants. For those who tote strollers, remember that this is a town with narrow sidewalks and that you will have to carry the stroller in and out of many shops. Wheelchairs will have trouble with steps in and out of some shops.

Swimming. The following lakes and pools offer kids the best water fun in Orange County. **Arrow Park Lake** (Orange Turnpike, Monroe, N.Y. 10950, open 8 am to 5 pm daily, [914] 783–2044) is open to the public and charges a fee for swimming. **Maple Hill Pool** (at the corner of California and Maple streets, Middletown, N.Y. 10940. [914] 343–2768) is open from the end of June to the end of August every day from 1 to 5 pm and 6 to 8 pm (free on Tuesday and Thursdays from 9 to 11 am). There is a small use fee. **Fancher-Davidge Park** (at the corner of Lake and Oliver Streets, Middletown, N.Y. 10940. [914] 342–0621) is open from the end of June to the end of August, daily 1 to 5 pm and 6 to 8 pm. Tues. and Thursday 9 to 11 am. Free. **Wallkill Town Park** (Creamery Rd. off Route 302, Circleville, N.Y. [914] 692–5811) offers lake swimming from Memorial Day through Labor Day from 8 am to dusk.

Trotting Horse Museum and Historic Track. 240 Main Street, Goshen, N.Y. 10924. (914) 294–6330. Open Monday through Saturday, 10 am to 5 pm; and Sunday and holidays, noon to 5 pm. Admission. Group tours are available by special reservation.

Trotters and pacers (trotters move their right front and left rear legs at the same time, while pacers move both legs on one side at the same time) have long been part of American history. At this museum, the history of the sport can be traced through dioramas, prints, exhibits, and statues. Young children in particular will enjoy the Hall of the Immortals, with its dozens of lifelike statues, restored stalls, and full-size replicas of horses and their equipment. Children will have fun ringing the sleigh bells in the sleigh or sitting in the sulky behind the harness maker's horse in the sulky loft. A film that will appeal to older children explains the history of the track and trotting in America. Next door, the Historic Track (a national historic landmark) has lots of harness horses working out. The blacksmith is usually at work there, too. Matinee racing programs (free) are held on Saturdays during June. Every year on May 5th, a children's play is presented to celebrate Hambletonian's birthday.

Facilities: Rest rooms; Weathervane Gift Shop, which is especially worthwhile for those who love horse memorabilia and souvenirs; picnic facilities (at the track). The museum is not suitable for children in strollers because there is a long staircase to climb and narrow passageways on the first floor. Limited access for wheelchairs.

Horse Farms. Orange County is standardbred country in New York State and is home to several horse farms that welcome visitors, who can see firsthand the work that goes into horse breeding. It is best to call in advance for an appointment. **Blue Chip Farm** (Bates Lane, Wallkill, N.Y. [914] 895–3930. Open daily from 10 am to 4 pm) and **Castleton Farm** (Sarah Wells Trail, Goshen, N.Y. [914] 294–6717) both specialize in horse breeding. Also worth a visit are **Alnoff Farms** (Searsville Road, Walden, N.Y. [914] 778–5421. Open 9 am to 4 pm); **Excelsior Horse Farm** (Bullville, N.Y. [914] 361–2112); and **Lana Lobell Farm** (Route 416, Montgomery, N.Y. [914] 457–5572).

West Point (United States Military Academy). U.S. Military Academy, Information Center, West Point, N.Y. 10996. (Take U.S. 9W to Highland Falls and follow the signs.) (914) 938–2638. Open year-round except Thanksgiving, Christmas, and New Year's Day. The Visitors Center is open, March to December, daily, 8:30 am to 4:30 pm; and January to mid-March, Wednesday through Sunday, 8:30 am to 4:30 pm. Free, but there is a ticket charge for football games and special group tours. Tours—both group and individual—are arranged by West Point Tours, (914) 446–4724.

While everyone knows a little of West Point's history, a tour of this historic military site is unlike any other you will take the kids on. Overlooking the Hudson River, West Point offers dozens of places to visit that are on post: chapels, museums, drilling fields, stadiums, statues, and cemeteries. If you only have a day you will have to narrow down the number of stops on your itinerary; a few are especially popular among children. First, the Battle Monument, which commemorates the Union Army's Civil War dead. The monument overlooks the Hudson River and is ringed by large cannons that younger children love to play around on. Also in the area is a sample of the chain that was stretched across the Hudson in order to stop the British from bringing their warships up to West Point. A second stop on your tour should be the West Point Museum, which is broken down by wars (American Revolution, Civil War, and so on) and offers thousands of items that appeal to young viewers. Of particular interest are the colorful uniforms, guns, cannons, and tanks. There is even a mock-up of an atomic bomb. America's military history is part of our heritage, and it is all here in the museum for children to learn about part of their heritage. The last must-see for kids is Fort Putnam, which overlooks West Point. The fort has been partially restored to reflect the conditions of battle during the Revolution—before Benedict Arnold's plot to turn West Point over to the British. On Saturday in the fall you may want to see the cadet parades that are a prelude to each home football game. Hundreds of cadets are togged out in their dress uniforms and bands play. Kids will love the military panoply. If you have older children, you may want to try to get tickets to the home football games, held at Michie Stadium. These games are exciting and there are lots of colorful uniforms as well as the army's mascot mule. The setting makes this series one of the best in the Northeast.

Facilities: Rest rooms; gift shop; picnic areas; a restaurant (in the Hotel Thayer on the grounds). Strollers are fine for use on the site, but you may have to deal with graveled walks around the football stadium and grassy areas around the parade ground. Limited wheelchair accessibility in some outdoor areas.

Washington's Headquarters. 84 Liberty Street, Newburgh, N.Y. 12550. (914) 562–1195. Open April to December, Wednesday through Saturday, 10 am to 5 pm; and Sunday 1 to 5 pm. Limited winter hours—call in the off-season. Free. Group tours are available.

This, the first national historic site established in this country, is interesting for children as well as adult lovers of American history. Inside the Visitors Center are exhibits that offer a view of eighteenth-century military life: uniforms, equipment, tools used by soldiers of George Washington's troops, and some of Washington's personal items. The Hasbrouck House, used by the general during the last days of the Revolution, has been restored to reflect the furnishings and decorations that would have been there with George and Martha Washington. Although this site will be of particular interest to older children (ten and up), the special events that take place are first rate and will appeal to younger as well as older children. George Washington's birthday is celebrated with a punch-and-birthday-cake reception, folk singing, and other entertainment, as is the lesser-known birthday party for Martha. Kite flying is a popular offering, as are military demonstrations on Independence Day and school programs, which include workshops on kitchen crafts and other domestic skills.

Facilities: Rest rooms; picnic area. Strollers can be used around the grounds but they have to be carried upstairs in the museum and may be difficult to use in the Hasbrouck House. Very limited wheelchair accessibility.

If you are in Newburgh to visit Washington's Headquarters there are two other places of interest to children that you may want to visit. The **Delano-Hitch Recreation Center** (375 Washington Avenue. [914] 565–3260. Free) is open during ice-skating season until 11 pm. There is a warming hut on the premises, skate rental. The **Speed Skating Hall of Fame** at the

Recreation Center open Monday through Friday, 8:30 am to 4:30 pm) is a small museum that offers a look at American speed skaters from the early days through the most recent Olympics. And before you leave Newburgh, don't forget to stop at **Commodore Chocolatier** (482 Broadway. [914] 561–3960), where homemade ice cream and gourmet chocolate candies (hand-dipped) are there to tempt hungry travelers of any age.

Apple Pond Farming Center. Box 65, Hahn Road, Callicoon Center, N.Y. 12724. (Take I-87 to Exit 16, then take New York 17 west to Exit 100 at Liberty. Take New York 52 west eight miles to Youngsville, turn right at Shandalee Road and go one and a half miles. Then turn left onto Stump Pond Road, go two miles, and turn left again onto Hahn Road. The center is six-tenths of a mile up the road; watch for signs.) (914) 482–4764. Open year-round, daily, 10 am to 5 pm, but reservations are required for tours. Admission. Groups from 10 to 150 can be accommodated.

This is a very special working farm and educational center: all of the wagons and farm equipment are pulled by horses, and all crops are organically grown. Once you arrive (and park) in the farmyard, you take a walking tour that begins with an explanation of the how the farm works and introduces children to the animals and barns. You may get a chance to milk a goat or a cow and watch the Belgian workhorses (all eighteen hundred pounds of them) being harnessed. Then it's off to the fields in horse-drawn wagons that bump and lurch over the meadows. The farm's border collies, controlled only by voice commands, may demonstrate the art of sheepherding, guiding the flocks up and down the mountainside. Along the way, children learn about the history of horse-powered farming and about pioneer days. In the summer, hayrides are offered, and at other times of the year you may see maple syrup making, haying, beekeeping, and wool spinning. Overnight and week-long excursions in covered wagons can be arranged between July and October. Special group tours are also available: hayride parties, winter sleigh rides, and lamb barbeques. (These special tours require a minimum of six people.) Older children who are horse crazy may want to participate in the Draft Horse Workshops held for two or three days each spring and fall, where hitching horses and driving are taught. This is a specialized workshop and is appropriate only for kids who love horses (and are accompanied by an adult). The center welcomes school groups of all ages; tours take approximately two hours. The tours are all outdoors, so dress warmly; it gets very cold on the mountainside, even in April. We heartily recommend boots for the farmyard at any time of year.

Facilities: Rest rooms; gift shop, with locally raised lamb products such as sweaters, hats, and gloves; picnic area. Accessibility for wheelchairs is limited; call ahead if this is a problem. This is no place for strollers or pets. There are limited accommodations (one three-bedroom guest house), available by reservation only. Camping facilities for large groups are also by reservation.

Canoe Trips on the Delaware. The Delaware River is the perfect place to canoe: the river is wide and not too fast (it flows at about three miles per hour), the scenery is magnificent, and you can determine the length of your trip. The river is navigable from Hancock, New York, to Dingmans Ferry, Pennsylvania. Sullivan County offers many places to rent canoes. As part of the package, you receive lifejackets, a map, and a pickup service along the river. The canoe outfitters are very accommodating, and there are many places where you can stop and rest or picnic. Anyone who takes a canoe trip must be able to swim; we do not recommend this excursion for children under ten. (Remember, this is river canoeing, complete with rapids and rocks; it is more adventurous than lake canoeing.) The best canoeing seasons are summer and early fall—the water is high enough without being flooded (the Delaware ranges in depth from two feet to fifteen feet). Some essential items to bring on the river: a picnic lunch, liquids, and snacks should be packed in waterproof bags and containers. You should wear sneakers. Cool-weather canoers are advised to wear lightweight woolen clothing—and always bring a change of clothing along in a plastic bag. Sunhats, sunscreen, and sunglasses will make for a more comfortable trip. Don't let all of these warnings frighten you away: if you are new to canoeing, tell the outfitter. They will suggest an appropriate trip as well as show you how to paddle. If you are experienced at paddling your own canoe, call the Upper Delaware River Conditions Information Line ([914] 252–7100) for the latest river conditions before you go. The Delaware River can be dangerous during the spring flood season.

Lander's Delaware River Trips (RD 2, Box 376, Narrowsburg, N.Y. 12764. [914] 252–3925), one of the largest outfitters on the river, offers rentals, overnight camping packages, and car shuttle service. It will even arrange motel accommodations along the river for those who don't want to camp. **Kittatinny Canoes** (Dingmans Ferry, Pa. 18328. [717] 828–2338) is headquartered in Pennsylvania but has six outposts, including four in New York State, along 135 miles of river. It rents canoes and, for the experienced, kayaks. Day trips and quiet water trips for beginners and overnighters and white water for the adventurous can be arranged. It has its own campgrounds along the river (since much of the river land is privately owned, it is sometimes difficult to find camping areas) and offers radio-dispatched vans for pick-ups. **White Water Canoe Rentals** (U.S. 97, Barryville, N.Y. 12719. [914] 557–8178) is another full-service canoe outfitter. For a shorter trip you can start in Barryville and head down into Pennsylvania, following the same route that the old logging rafts used to take. This outfitter can supply box lunches, along with all of your other canoeing needs.

Covered Bridges. Sullivan County is well known for its remaining covered bridges. Resembling small houses, the bridges were thought to have been covered with roofs for two reasons: to protect the timbers and to allow the horses and oxen that pulled the wagons to cross over water without getting frightened. Children will enjoy seeing these remnants of old-time travel, some of the bridges which are still in use. At the Beaverkill State Campground (seven miles northwest of Livingston Manor, on Johnston Hill Road, Beaverkill, N.Y.) the **Beaverkill Bridge,** a lattice-type construction, still spans the Beaverkill River. **Chestnut Creek Bridge** (New York 55 north on Claryville Road) is a 128-foot-long lattice-type bridge built in 1912 over the Neversink River. The **Livingston Manor Covered Bridge** (on County Road 179, north of Livingston Manor) is the country's only remaining example of a Queen Truss bridge. Built in 1860, it spans 103 feet over the Willowemoc Creek. Also in the area is the **Willowemoc Bridge** (on Town Road 18, two miles west of Willowemoc), which hangs over the creek and was built by the same man who constructed the Livingston Manor Bridge. In 1913 the Willowemoc Bridge, which was originally at another site, was cut in half and moved to its present location.

Catskill Fly Fishing Center and Museum. RD 1, Box 130C, Old Route 17, Livingston Manor, N.Y. 12758. (The museum and center are located on the Willowemoc Creek, between Roscoe [Exit 94 from New York17] and Livingston Manor [Exit 96 from New York 17]. [914] 439–4810.) The Museum and Center are open year-round, every day except Thanksgiving, Christmas, and New Year's. Hours: April 1 to October 31, 9 am to 4 pm; and November 1 to March 31, 9 am to 1 pm. Winter hours are Monday through Friday, 9 am to 1 pm. Demonstrations take place on weekends only in the summer. Free. Special group tours are by arrangement.

A special site for fishers of all ages is this beautiful spot on the world-famous Willowemoc Creek. As the birthplace of fly-fishing in the United States, it attracts sportspeople from all over the world to its pristine waters. The center was founded in 1978 as an educational source. Today it carries on the tradition, offering classes in fly-tying and fly-fishing during July and August for eight to ten year olds. Some of these workshops include overnight camping programs on the center's grounds, so Mom and Dad can fish while the kids learn about ecology and biology through hands-on experiments and classes. The museum contains continually changing exhibits on the lore and history of fly-fishing; it has entertained many famous anglers, including former president Jimmy Carter and his wife

Rosalynn. At the streamside site along the Willowemoc, a site manager explains the mysteries of fly-fishing and takes you on a short tour of the grounds. The casting pond and the live trout aquarium are fun stops for younger children. On Broad Street, in Roscoe there are plenty of tackle shops, so you can outfit yourself and the kids for a day's fishing on the Willowemoc River.

Facilities: Rest rooms. The site is not readily accessible to wheelchairs, so call ahead to make special arrangements for fishing. Strollers, too, would not be easy to maneuver.

If you are stopping in Roscoe, try to visit the **O. & W. Railroad Museum** (located in Roscoe at the junction of New York 206 and Old Route 17. [607] 498–4346. Open mid-May to mid-October, Thursday through Sunday, 11 am to 4 pm), housed in a caboose at the site of the old railroad station. There are changing displays of railroad memorabilia, and kids get a chance to walk around an actual red caboose.

Egg University. K. Brand Farms, Glen Wild Road, Woodbridge, N.Y. 12789. (Take New York 17 west to Exit 109 and turn right off the highway; the first left is Glen Wild Road. Egg University is three and one half miles along Glen Wild Road.) (914) 434–4519. Open July and August, Sunday through Thursday, 10 am to noon. Admission. Group rates and tours are available.

This is a working farm, and the program is all about eggs and how they go from chicken to carton. The first stop is the theater, where children can see a short film and slide show explaining the story of eggs and chickens. Then it's off to the chicken house to see how a modern farm feeds and cares for its chickens. There are a hundred thousand live Leghorn chickens here. An elaborate series of conveyor belts moves the eggs to the washing and inspection areas. A demonstration shows how the eggs are candled for grade, packed, and shipped. It's interesting to see that the eggs are not touched by human hands until the carton is opened at home. Kids will be thrilled with their Egg University diploma, ID card, complimentary drink, and freshly laid egg (you can also buy gift-wrapped cartons for friends).

Facilities: Rest rooms; gift shop, which offers lots of egg-related gift items; snack stand. The site is not easily accessible for those in wheelchairs. Strollers are accommodated in the egg house and the theater.

Fishing. There are many fine fishing areas in Sullivan County, and this part of the Catskills offers a broad selection of lakes, ponds, and streams to fish. Brown, brook, and rainbow trout, pickerel, panfish, and bass all lurk beneath the waters, and a skilled fisher of any age can land a big one. Fishing licenses are required for those sixteen and older (and note that these waters are very well patrolled and that the fines can be substantial). You will receive a guide to fishing areas and a rule book when you get your license, which can be purchased at many tackle shops and town halls. Public fishing areas are well marked with bright yellow signs and designated parking areas, so you don't have to go too far off the beaten path for some fishy fun. April 1 marks the opening day of fishing season, and in the Catskills the weather can be anywhere from mild to snowy, so dress accordingly. Sullivan County stocks three lakes: **Mongaup Falls Reservoir** (in Forestburgh, watch for signs), **Lake Huntington** (on New York 52 in Lake Huntington), and **White Lake** (at the junction of New York 17B and New York 55).

Stream and river fishing present another challenge. Kids love casting from the sides of a willow-shaded bank. Try the **Willowemoc River** (Roscoe) and the **Basher Kill Marsh** (County Route 19 and U.S. 209 near Wurtsboro). If the kids have never fished before, you may want to spend the day in Roscoe (see *Catskill Fly Fishing Center and Museum*, earlier in this chapter), which is known as Trout Town. Roscoe is a complete center for tackle, licenses, information, and local fishing streams. One way to almost guarantee a fish is to try your cast at **Eldred Preserve** (New York 55, Eldred, N.Y. [914] 557–8316), a private resort that opens its stocked ponds to the public for fishing. You pay an admission fee as well as by the pound for the fish you catch. This is private property, though, so a fishing license is not required. If you yearn for a real pioneer treat, try some shad fishing on the **Delaware River** (a good access point is New York 97, between Long Eddy and Barryville) in May and June: the run has been fished for over two hundred years.

Fort Delaware Museum of Colonial History. New York, 97, Narrowsburg, N.Y. 12764. (914) 252–6660. Open Memorial Day weekend, 10 am to 5:30 pm; June, Saturday and Sunday, 10 am to 5:30 pm; and July through Labor Day, daily, 10:30 am to 5 pm. Admission (children under six are admitted free when accompanied by two adults). A family ticket for two adults and two or more children is available. Group rates are available.

Relive a part of New York's pioneer history at this re-creation of the first stockaded settlement in the upper Delaware River valley. Visitors are able to see life as it was for the average settler during the mid–eighteenth century: no fancy houses, just log dwellings; an armory; a blacksmith's shop; animal pens; a weaver's shed; and the fort. There are costumed site interpreters around each area to explain the crafts and skills needed to survive in the wilderness. Demonstrations of candle dipping, shingle making, spinning, and musket and cannon firing, and so forth are offered throughout the season. This site will be particularly appealing to young children, who love to pretend that they are living in a wilderness fort in the days before Davy Crockett and Daniel Boone. A rugged historic site, this is not the polished, fancy restoration you see in places like Williamsburg, but this makes it even more appealing to kids. Special events, held every weekend throughout the summer, include Frontier Living Days and a special military encampment, which is staffed by members of the Fifth Connecticut Regiment of Continental Line, a group that re-creates the daily lives of soldiers and their families. Boy Scouts and Girl Scouts should be aware that on a special Scout Day each May, all scouting personnel in uniform are admitted free. Call ahead for the exact date.

Facilities: Rest rooms; gift shop; picnic area outside the fort; snack bar. Call ahead if wheelchair accessibility is needed. Strollers can be managed.

Minisink Battlefield. Minisink Battleground Park, Minisink Ford, N.Y. (Take New York 97 west to Sullivan County Route 168; watch for signs.) For information write to the Office of Public Information, Sullivan County Government Center, Monticello, N.Y. 12701. (914) 794–3000, ext. 225, Parks and Recreation Department. Open May through October daily, dawn to dusk. Free.

This is an excellent place to combine history, nature study, and hiking in a few hours of outdoor fun. The Battle of Minisink took place in 1779, when American rebels were massacred by Mohawk Indians. Kids will be fascinated to know that this area was so wild and inaccessible that the bones of the dead were not collected for burial until nearly fifty years after the battle. Today the site offers three well-marked, self-guided nature trails that weave through the forests. Audio devices tell the story of the park and written trail guides to help you interpret what you see. A small visitors center (which has an irregular schedule) offers detailed information about the battle and the trails, but you don't need this to enjoy the park. The youngest kids will like Battleground Trail (one mile) and Woodland Trail, which wander through wetlands, fern gardens, berry patches, and rock shelters. The trails are not difficult to walk because they are fairly flat, and there are lots of interesting rock formations along the way. Anyone who visits the battlefield will feel that time has stopped. This site is recommended for children ages five and older.

Facilities: Rest rooms. Wheelchairs and strollers cannot be maneuvered through the trails.

Just across the street from the battleground entrance is the **Roebling's Suspension Bridge,** a national historic landmark. Built in 1848 it is the oldest suspension bridge in America and was one of the few bridges to carry a canal aqueduct *above* a river. Its wire cables—still the originals—were spun by hand at the site. The bridge has recently undergone restoration and is open to visitors; kids will enjoy being able to walk or drive across the bridge and into Pennsylvania.

Mongaup Pond State Campsite and Day Use Area. Catskill Park, N.Y. (Take New York 17 west to Exit 96 and go seven miles northeast to DeBruce, then proceed into the state preserve, three miles north of DeBruce; follow the signs to the site.) (914) 439–4233. Open mid-May to Thanksgiving, every day, 9 am until dusk. Admission. Groups are accommodated. Campsites are available by reservation.

Located within the state forest preserve, this 275-acre facility is one of the nicest, most scenic recreational areas in the county for children. A small, sandy beach fronts Mongaup Pond, where you may rent a rowboat, fish, swim, and build sandcastles. Shady areas make this a comfortable beach. When you are tired of water activities, there are hiking and camping to keep everyone busy. The hiking trails are well marked and range in length from under a mile to several miles. This is a fine place to take young children for the day and keep them busy with outdoor activities. There are picnic areas with barbecue pits for day use and complete campsites with hookups for overnight use.

Facilities: Rest rooms; picnic areas; overnight campsites (by reservation only); snowmobile trails.

If you are in the area, the children will enjoy a stop at the **DeBruce State Fish Hatchery** (Mongaup Road, DeBruce; watch for signs [914] 439–4328. Open year-round, daily, 8:30 am to 4:30 pm.) More than five hundred thousand trout are spawned at the hatchery and used for stocking purposes throughout the region. A series of hatching ponds hold the fish. An in-depth tour is available but is recommended for children over ten years of age.

North Branch Cider Mill. Main Street, North Branch, N.Y. 12766. (Take Exit 94 off New York 17 west and follow Tennanah Lake Road into North Branch [the road's name changes, but it still ends up in North Branch].) (914) 482–4823. Open, April through December, daily 10 am to 5 pm. Free. No tours are offered, but groups are welcome to stop.

This is one of the few cider presses still at work in New York State. Although this is not a "site"—at least not in the sense of a restoration—still, a stop here will give kids a chance to see how cider is made. The mill itself is a large, noisy contraption that eats up bushels of apples at a time and presses out fresh, thick, sweet cider; visitors can watch the action from a small viewing area. Sweet and hard cider and apple cider vinegar, along with lots of home-baked goodies, can be purchased inside the mill. Outside there is a large vegetable stand with pumpkins and Indian corn in the fall, Christmas trees in December, and fresh fruits and vegetables in season. The mill really provides a taste of what a rural industry was like a century ago and is an excellent refreshment stop.

Facilities: Rest rooms; gift shop, with lovely country items; picnic area with tables; snack stand. The site is not really wheelchair accessible, but strollers can be wheeled around with ease.

Pick-Your-Own Farms: Sullivan County has many fine farms that welcome visitors to pick their own produce. Because you are doing the work, the prices are usually much lower than those at the markets, and the produce is garden fresh. Prices are set by the pound and will vary with the type of produce you pick. Be sure to dress yourself and the kids in appropriate outdoor clothing, hats included, and to bring along sunscreen for summer afternoons. At the **Bridge Farm** (Fox Mountain Road, Livingston Manor, N.Y. [situated two miles off New York 52 at White Sulphur Springs.] [914] 292–6299. Open June through October) you can pick raspberries, strawberries, beans, cucumbers, and peas. At **Fisher Farm** (Aden Road, Liberty, N.Y. [located four miles east of town: take New York 55 east to

Muhlig Road; proceed north on Muhlig and follow the signs.]
[914] 292–5777. Open September and October) choose your
own pumpkin from the patch and pay by the pound. At Christmastime stop at **Jim Phillip's Country Store** (Dr. Duggan
Road, White Lake, N.Y. 12786. [914] 583–4478. Open December 1 to December 23, daily, 7:30 am to 6 pm), where you
can cut your own Christmas tree. The price is set by size and
type of tree; they provide the saws, but you may bring your
own. **Pine Farm Christmas Trees** (RD 2, Livingston Manor,
N.Y. 12758. [914] 482–4149. Open December 1 to December
24, daily, 9 am to 4:30 pm) has a variety of trees to choose from;
just remember that you have to get the tree into or on top of
your car!

Skiing. For downhill skiers, Sullivan County offers a limited
amount of skiing, but what is available is fine for family enjoy-
ment. At **Big Vanilla at Davos** (P.O. Box 325, Woodbridge,
N.Y. 12789 [off New York 17.] [914] 434–5321. Open from December to March, Monday and Tuesday, 10 am to 4:30 pm;
Wednesday through Friday, 10 am to 10 pm; Saturday, 9 am to
10 pm; and Sunday, 9 am to 5 pm. Lift fee. Group rates are
available) skiers may take advantage of twenty-three slopes, day
and night. There are nine lifts and 100 percent snowmaking
capability on twenty-three trails, a quadruple chairlift, a full-
service restaurant, and a rental shop. Children between three
and six may take part in special full-or half-day children's packages, which include the lift fee, a lesson, rental equipment,
nursery services, and lunch. Older kids are offered a similar
program but with more advanced lessons and more slope time.
The babysitting service is for three to eight years olds; children
must be toilet trained. At seven dollars an hour or thirty-eight
dollars a day per child, this service is rather expensive.) Cross-
country skiing is available, with ten miles of trails plus lessons
and rentals on the site; there is a fee for using the trails.
Guided moonlight tours are available to groups. **Holiday
Mountain** (Box 629, Monticello, N.Y. 12701. [Situated just east
of Monticello, off New York 17.] [914] 796–3161. Open from

December to March, daily, 9 am to 9 pm. Lift charge. Group rates are available) offers both day and night skiing on fourteen slopes and trails. It is the only town-owned ski slope in the region, and it is committed to keeping its prices reasonable for families. Holiday Mountain's snowmaking capability is such that it is open just about all winter. An excellent series of lessons is available that teaches children safe skiing and down-hill racing. The site has a cafeteria, equipment rental, and a lounge. This is not the place to go with very young children who require a nursery, but older kids certainly will enjoy the slopes. One of Holiday Mountain's fun events is its late-February–early-March Winter Carnival, featuring snow softball, snow golf, a ski tug-of-war, hayrides, clowns, a pancake breakfast, and a chicken barbecue.

Good places to go cross-country skiing with kids in Sullivan County are town parks, which offer a wonderful outdoor adventure for an afternoon. **Hanofee Park** (Infirmary Road, Liberty, N.Y. [off New York 52 east.] [914] 292–7690. Open daily, 10 am to 4 pm) has 110 acres of cross-country trails. One nice aspect about this park is that rentals and lessons are available for all ages. Note that the heated trail house is open on weekends only. The trails at **Town of Thompson Park** (Old Liberty Road, Box, 629, Monticello, N.Y. 12701. [Located four and one-half miles past the Monticello Post Office.] [914] 796–3161. Open daily, from dawn to dusk) cover 160 acres of parkland. Skiers must furnish their own equipment.

Sullivan County Museum, Art and Cultural Center. Main Street, Hurleyville, N.Y. 12747. (Take New York 17 west to Exit 100, then take New York 52 east and follow the signs to Hurleyville.) (914) 434–8044. Open year-round, Monday through Saturday, 10 am to 4:30 pm; and Sunday, 1 to 4:30 pm. Closed on legal holidays. Free. Group tours are available.

This small museum contains a great deal of local history and is very accessible to children who want to know what life was like in the country from the nineteenth century to the present. Dioramas with native animals, mining exhibits, railroads, and rafting all create a sense of living history in a not-too-formal museum setting. Old transportation in the form of trolleys and cars is on the site, as is a display of a general store; children may discover the story of one of Sullivan County's polar explorers. The museum shares space with the Catskill Arts Society, which offers changing exhibits by Catskill artists. Classes and special programs are offered for children throughout the year, but call ahead for schedules.

Facilities: Rest rooms. Not accessible to those in wheelchairs; limited access for strollers.

Swimming. There are a few places to swim in Sullivan County, in addition to the numerous lakes in the region, that are particularly good spots for young children. The **Dillon Park Pool** (Dillon Rd. Monticello, N.Y. [914] 794–6130) is open daily from noon to 7 pm from July 4th through Labor Day. **Morningside Park** (Country Route 52 between Fallsburg and Loch Sheldrake [914] 434–8230) is open 10 am to 6 pm every day (8 pm on Saturdays) from July 4th through Labor Day. There is a small charge for swimming in the lake. **Montaindale Pool** (Post Hill Rd., Montaindale, N.Y.) is open from July 4th through Labor Day, daily from 10 am to 5 pm. There is a small use charge. Since hours are variable here it is a good idea to call before going.

Wurtsboro Airport. U.S. 209, Wurtsboro, N.Y. 12790. (Take New York 17 west to Exit 113, then U.S. 209 north two and one-half miles to the airport.) (914) 888–2791. Open year-round, daily, 9 am until dusk, weather permitting. Free for observers; there is a charge for sailplane rides.

Founded in 1927, this is the oldest soaring site in the United States. This is where you and the older kids can take a ride in a sailplane, which is towed aloft by a Cessna tow plane, then released to soar quietly back to earth. For adults and children who have flown before, the silence of a sailplane is relaxing and is probably the closest one can come to flying like a bird. You can either stay on the ground and watch the planes take off and land or sign up for a demonstration flight. The fifteen- to-twenty-minute scenic rides over the Catskills are conducted by FAA-rated commercial pilots who have had lots of experience in this type of flight.

Facilities: Rest rooms; snack bar.

After visiting the airport you may want to stop at the **Canal Town Emporium** (Sullivan and Hudson streets, Wurtsboro, N.Y. 12790. [914] 888–2100. Open year-round, daily, 10 am to 5 pm. Free), a country store in a historic brick building constructed in 1845. Wurtsboro was once an important trading center for the Delaware and Hudson Canal. Today the emporium is a store filled with history as well as enticing country gift items, unusual toys (many handcrafted), and gourmet foods.

Catskill Mountain Railroad. (Route 28, Mt. Pleasant, N.Y. 12457. Twenty-two miles west of Kingston, N.Y. [914] 688–7400.) Open weekends and holidays from Memorial Day weekend through Labor Day, 11 am to 5 pm. Admission. Children under four admitted free. Bus and group tours available by advance reservation; write to PO Box 46, Shokan, N.Y. 12481.

Travel along the scenic Esopus Creek by train. Ride one way or take a six-mile round-trip through the heart of the Catskill Mountains on the historic Ulster and Delaware railroad. Passengers may detrain in Phoenicia to visit shops and restaurants and return on a later train. In the summer train up and tube back down the river (see "tubing" entry).

Facilities: Rest rooms; snack bar; picnic tables; gift shop.

College for Kids. (School of Continuing Education, Ulster County Community College, Stone Ridge, N.Y. 12484. [914] 338–2211.)

Classes are held here year-round and the summer program includes such offerings as puppet making and staging puppet shows, pottery, printmaking, painting, drawing, modern dance, fun with science, songwriting, and acoustic guitar. The classes are divided into four- to six-year-olds, seven- to nine-year-olds and ten- to thirteen-year-olds.

Facilities: Rest rooms; snack bar.

Frost Valley YMCA. Oliverea, N.Y. 12462. (At the junction of New York 28 at Big Indian, and County Route 47 go fifteen miles; watch for signs.) (914) 985–2291. Open year-round. Admission.

This is a perfect place for school groups and families to spend an overnight visit in the country. Frost Valley offers more than forty-five hundred acres of land for hiking, bird-watching, and cross-country skiing (equipment rental is available). A special summer events program has workshops in the arts for all ages. The lodge is built in the elegant style of the older Catskill camps; the cafeteria contains an exhibit that focuses on nature writer John Burroughs. Reservations must be made in advance for overnight stays, since the lodge hosts many school groups, but the site is open all year for day use. Also note that during the winter months Route 47 is difficult to drive after a heavy snowfall, so call ahead if you have any doubts about road conditions.

Facilities: Rest rooms; picnic areas; cafeteria; lodge; warming hut for cross-country skiers. While parents with strollers can use the paths near the lodge, they will have difficulty in the outdoor areas, as will wheelchairs.

Ice Caves Mountain and Sam's Point. New York 52, Ellenville, N.Y. 12464. (914) 647–7989. Open from April 1 to November 1, daily, 9 am until dark. Admission. Group rates are available.

Part of the natural history of New York State, both Ice Caves Mountain and Sam's Point have received national landmark status. You can see five states from the top of the mountain, which is part of a drive-and-walk tour that takes in glacial formations, hidden caves, mysterious rivers, and secret grottos. Children love visiting the Balanced Rock, which will never tilt while they watch it, no matter how long they stand there. At Sam's Point, the tale is told of Trapper Sam, who, in order to escape an Indian war party, leaped over the edge of the mountain and slid all the way down—with a stop or two to disentangle himself from the trees. The nature trails are well marked (this is a self-guided site) and the walkways slope gently so that hikers of all ages can enjoy exploring. Weird formations abound here, as does wildlife, so children can expect to see lots of different sights on even a short walk. The walking and driving tour takes at least ninety minutes. Because you are outdoors most of the time, you should wear comfortable shoes and bring sweaters.

Facilities: Rest rooms; gift shop, with many plastic knickknacks and other amusing items that kids like; picnic area; snack bar. Not wheelchair accessible. And don't expect to use a stroller—the narrow paths and winding stairways are suitable only for walking.

Mohonk Mountain House and Skytop Observation Tower.

Lake Mohonk, New Paltz, N.Y. 12561. (Take I-87 to Exit 18, turn west onto New York 299, and go through the village of New Paltz. After crossing the Wallkill River, turn right onto Mountain Rest Road; follow the signs to the gate.) (914) 255–1000. Open year-round. Admission is charged for day use. Group and children's rates are available.

This magnificent world-famous resort has been owned and operated by the same family for generations. The spirit of the resort revolves around preservation of the twenty-two thousand acres, which are located in the heart of the Shawangunk Mountains. Your first view of the hotel with its turrets and towers and a deep glacial lake reflecting the light of hundreds of windows, will recall Victorian romances. The more than three hundred rooms (half with working fireplaces), gardens, greenhouses, a museum, stables, and modern sports facilities combine to make this a memorable getaway for the whole family. Afternoon tea and classical concerts offer an elegant atmosphere that enthralls kids who are unused to a quieter pace of life. There are walking tours, horseback rides, and extensive cross-country ski tours. In the summer, vast flower gardens scent the air; in the winter, horse-drawn sleighs jingle across snowy roads with their passengers. You can visit Mohonk for a meal, a day, overnight, or several weeks, although restrictions apply to day-use passes. Considering its old-fashioned ambience, Mohonk caters surprisingly well to families. Supervised children's programs are available on weekends year-round and daily in the summer (for overnight guests only). Children are welcome in the dining room when accompanied by their parents; babysitters are available for an extra charge and with advance notice. Mohonk specializes in special theme weekends, some of which are particularly suitable for children. One favorite is Pioneer Weekend, which is usually held in early-March and is devoted to early American skills and crafts. In workshops, children can dip candles, weave, quilt, boil maple syrup, pull taffy, and square dance—and still enjoy everything else that the resort has to offer. Another special weekend is the one before Christmas, when kids under age twelve can stay free if they share a room with their parents. A full schedule of children's events is included. If you need to get away with the kids during the winter try the January Winter Sports Carnival or February's Presidents' Weekend, when there is snow tubing, cross-country skiing, ice-skating on the lake at night, snow sculpture contests, and more.

Facilities: Rest rooms; gift shop; restaurant. For the sports-minded, the following are available, at an additional charge: paddleboats, rowboats, fishing, horseback riding, tennis, ice-skating, and cross-country skiing (rentals are available). The main house is stroller friendly, and there are some paths on the grounds.

Newspaper Tour: The Daily Freeman. 79 Hurley Avenue, Kingston, N.Y. 12401. (914) 331–5000. Group tours by reservation, Monday through Friday, 8 am to noon. Free.

Get an inside view of the exciting, busy, noisy world of newspaper publishing. Visitors will see how the news goes from a story to the newsstand: computers, typesetting machines, presses, layout rooms, and more are covered during this tour, which is led by an experienced newsperson. Children who are studying journalism will get a first-hand look at how computers have changed the news industry and how news is collected, reported, and processed into a paper.

Opus 40 and Quarryman's Museum. 7480 Fite Road, Saugerties, N.Y. 12477. (On New York 212 north of Woodstock; follow the signs.) (914) 246–3400. Open May through October, weekdays except Tuesday, 10 am to 4 pm; and Sunday, noon to 5 pm. Saturday is reserved for special events. Admission (children under five are admitted free). Group tours are available.

This environmental bluestone sculpture rising out of an abandoned quarry covers more than six acres. Opus 40 was built over a thirty-seven-year period by sculptor Harvey Fite. Visitors are astonished by the amount of stone that was quarried, dressed, and moved into place to form the steps and monolith. Children enjoy walking the pathways around the pools, fountains, and crannies. Stones curl around the trees, and wishing ponds abound; it's best to wear rubber-soled shoes for walking. A stop at the Quarryman's Museum offers a look at quarrying equipment and hand-forged "folk" tools as well as a slide show about the history of Fite and Opus 40. Sunset concerts featuring jazz, classical, and folk music are good family outings because they begin in the late afternoon. The site is perfect for picnic dinners.

Facilities: Portable toilets; picnic areas. Strollers can be used along the surrounding grounds, but they can't be used easily on the sculpture itself, which has some bumpy surfaces, steps, and narrow passageways. Wheelchairs will find extremely limited access; not recommended.

Pick-Your-Own Farms. Ulster County offers some unusual farms where you can select or pick everything from strawberries to Christmas trees. Produce is charged by the pound; the cost of a tree is determined by its height. At **Clarke's** (182 Clarke's Lane, Milton, N.Y. 12547. [914] 795–2270), cherries, peaches, pears, and apples are yours for the picking in season. An unusual treat at this farm is scenic tractor rides during the apple harvest. At **Mr. Apples** (Box 98, New York 213, High Falls, N.Y. 12440. [914] 687–9498/0005, open August through harvest season), up to 12 varieties of apples can be picked from the trees by kids. And note that these apples are grown with a minimum of chemicals and are ripened naturally. At **Wilklow Orchards** (RD 2, Box 566, Pancake Hollow Road, Highland, N.Y. 12528 (914) 691–2339, open during autumn harvest season), pick apples and pumpkins that are organically grown. Later in the season youngsters can make Christmas a little more old-fashioned by cutting their own Christmas tree. It's

Christmas trees only at **Stover's Christmas Tree Farm** (Schoonmaker Lane, Stone Ridge, just off Route 209, (914) 687–7512, open early December, Friday through Sunday, 9 am to 4 pm). Here, serious tree-pickers can find Douglas Fir, White Pine, Blue Spruce, and other evergreens ready for cutting. The setting is lovely and kids will enjoy searching for their perfect tree. The saws are provided but, remember: you have to get the tree home yourself.

Rondout Waterfront. One Rondout Landing, Broadway, Kingston, N.Y. 12401. (The waterfront is at the end of Broadway.) Open year-round.

The Rondout area of Kingston served as one of the leading maritime centers in upstate New York during the nineteenth century. Today restored buildings, museums, and ships make this a bustling port once more. At the **Hudson River Maritime Center** ([914] 338–0071. Open year-round. Admission) visitors can see a small museum devoted to the history of sailing on the Hudson River. Children who are interested in old sailing ships will enjoy watching the workers in the boat-building and rigging areas that overlook Rondout Creek. Outside, ships tie up when in port; in the summer visitors are able to view some historically important vessels. In the spring a shad festival revives the importance of this fish to local economies, and in the fall the sloop *Clearwater* ties up here for a one-day pumpkin sale. The center offers an ongoing summertime series of children's crafts and music workshops (ages six to eight) whose themes—mermaids, sailors' valentines, model ships, lighthouses, and so forth—revolve around the rivers and oceans. There is a small charge for the workshops. Across the street from the Maritime Center is the **Trolley Museum** (89 East Strand, Kingston. [914] 331–3399. Admission. Open Memorial Day to Columbus Day, weekends and holidays; July and August, daily, noon to 5 pm. Admission. Special group rates are available). This small museum brings back the days when trolleys clanged along city streets. Housed in an old trolley barn, this no-nonsense exhibit has photos and memorabilia of trolley days plus several trolley cars. The main point of interest at this museum is the short trolley ride that goes alongside the Hudson River, from which you can see the **Rondout Lighthouse.** For children who would like to sail on the Hudson, the **Rondout Belle** (Hudson Rondout Cruises, 11 East Chestnut Street, Kingston, N.Y. 12401. [914] 338–6280. Cruises every day, June to October. Admission. Special school and group rates are available) offers a fascinating lighthouse cruise on a sixty-eight-foot long diesel-powered vessel complete with rest rooms and a snack bar. The tour includes a stop at the only working lighthouse and museum in the county. The cruise itself lasts approximately one and a half hours and leaves from the Maritime Center. No matter what the season, the Hudson River is windy, so bring sweaters and hats. Older kids may enjoy a longer cruise on the *Rip Van Winkle* (Rondout Landing, Kingston. [914] 255–6515, open May to October. Admission. Day cruises to West Point and back depart daily), which heads down the Hudson to West Point and then returns in the late afternoon. There are lots of sights to watch for along the river and you are given two hours to spend at West Point (see pages 34–36).

Royal Kedem Winery. Milton, N.Y. 12547. (Take U.S. 9W; at the blinking light in Milton, turn toward the river and follow the signs.) (914) 795–2240 or 795–2159. Open January 1 to May 1, Sunday only; and, May 1 to December 31, Sunday through Friday, 10 am to 5 pm. Last tour is at 4 pm. Closed on Jewish holidays. Free, but a parking fee of one dollar is charged on Sunday. Group tours are available.

A kosher winery located near the Hudson River, Royal Kedem offers something different from the usual winery tour and is especially nice for children. There is a film about the history of the founding family, which began making wine in Czechoslovakia during the nineteenth century and continued its old-world tradition in New York. Although the grapes are not grown on the site, they are New York State grapes and are processed at the winery into a wide variety of wines. The tour takes you through the winery and ends at a delightful little tasting room located in an old railroad depot. Children enjoy sampling the crackers and Kedem's tasty nonalcoholic grape juice. The history of each wine is discussed.

Facilities: Rest rooms; wine shop; picnic area with tables. Strollers may be difficult to manage in the winery but they are welcome in the tasting room.

Senate House State Historic Site: 312 Fair Street, Kingston, N.Y. 12401. (914) 338–2786. Open April to December, Wednesday through Saturday, 10 am to 5 pm; and Sunday, 1 to 5 pm. Free. Group tours are available by advance reservation.

A site for older children with an interest in history, the Senate House State Historic Site offers two buildings: one, Loughran House, is a modern museum; the second is a seventeenth-century Dutch house where the first New York State Senate met. At Loughran House, a colorful display explains the American Revolution in New York State. In addition, there are many examples of fine New York State art throughout its two floors. Across the site, at the Senate House, visitors are able to experience what an eighteenth-century state senator would have seen during a stay in 1777. New York State's first constitution was adopted there, and the building was witness to the burning of Kingston by the British troops. Outside, a lovely rose garden is delightful in the month of June. During the Christmas season the buildings are decorated as they would have been by both Dutch and English families. Across the street, the **Volunteer Fireman's Hall and Museum of Kingston** (265 Fair Street. [914] 331–2298 or 331–4065. Open April 1 to October 31, Friday and Saturday, 10 am to 4 pm. Group tours are available by arrangement) offers a small display of antique fire equipment, memorabilia, and furniture.

Facilities: Rest rooms; picnic area; information desk. Parents with strollers will have a difficult time with the stairs and in the older Senate House, but they manage easily in the gardens. Limited access for wheelchairs.

Skiing. There are three fine ski centers for kids in Ulster County, and they cater to parents as well. The largest is **Belleayre Ski Center** (New York 28, Highmount, N.Y. 12441. [914] 254-5600. Open Thanksgiving through March, daily, 9 am to 4 pm. There is no charge for the cross-country trails, but a lift ticket must be purchased for downhill skiing. Group rates are available). Belleayre has a terrific, specially designed beginner's circle and T-bar area. There are lots of lessons, play groups, and fun activities for children as well as a nursery for the youngest ones. Ski rentals are available, and a large cafeteria will take care of everyone's need for hot chocolate. Up the road from Belleayre is **Highmount** (New York 28, Highmount, N.Y. 12441. [914] 254-5265. Open in season, weekends only, 9 am to 4 pm. Lift ticket charge. No cross-country trails), a family-oriented ski center that is smaller but considerably less crowded than Belleayre. There is a nursery program that lets the kids get out in the snow on tiny skis and try out a rope tow. Parents can even watch their children's progress from the slopes above on their way back down to the chairlift. Just outside Woodstock is the **Sawkill Family Ski Center** (Jockey Hill Road, Sawkill, N.Y. 12401. [914] 336-6798 or 679-9286. Open weekends and holidays, 9 am to 4 pm. Lift ticket fee). This site offers affordable fun for families who want to try out some skiing for a few hours. Rentals and lessons are available and a cafeteria offers warm treats. The longest run is one thousand feet. There are three slopes and four trails and a 100 percent snowmaking capability, unusual for a smaller ski center.

Swimming. Ulster County's lakes, rivers, and streams offer many places to swim. The **Andretta Recreation Facility** (includes the Kingston city pool, Deitz Memorial Stadium, Lucas Ave., Kingston, N.Y. 12401. There is a small use fee here but the hours vary so it is best to call before going. **Kingston Point Beach,** Delaware Ave. Kingston, N.Y. 12401. [914] 331–1682.) Open June 20 through Labor Day. 10:45 am to 5 pm. There is a small use fee and the beach is on the Hudson River. **Lembo Lake Park** (Routes 44–55, Modena, N.Y. Open July and August every day from noon to 7 pm. There is a fee for use of the lake. In addition to swimming, there is boating, fishing, camping and picnic areas. [914] 883–7135.) **Minnewaska State Park** (Lake Minnewaska, Routes 44–55, New Paltz, N.Y. 12561. [914] 255–6000.) Lake Awosting is free, but swimmers must hike approximately one mile to the swimming area. There is admission to the state park and lake for those who want to visit it as well as swim. **Ulster County Park Pool** (Libertyville Rd., New Paltz, N.Y. 12561. [914] 255–7027.) This Olympic-size pool and kiddie pool are open weekends until the July 4th weekend. Then, open daily, 10 am to 8 pm through Labor Day. There is a small use fee and the pool is surrounded by the dramatic Shawangunk Mountains. The **Village of Saugerties** has a wonderful sandy beach at the bottom of Hill street in town. There is a lifeguard on duty daily from July 4th weekend through Labor Day from 10 am to 6 pm. (914) 246–2321.

Tubing. If you want to go tubing, wait until the mercury hits about ninety degrees and head to Phoenicia, N.Y., to spend the day along the banks of the Esopus Creek. This activity makes for a fun day for older kids (twelve years old and up), who will enjoy bouncing along the rapids in a large inner tube. Although this is a popular sport, there are some caveats: the water must be high; you should wear a life vest, sneakers for protection against glass and rocks, a shirt, and a hat; and never let the kids tube by themselves. This is not an activity for anyone under twelve. The creek can get very crowded on hot weekend afternoons, especially in July and August, the most popular tubing months. There are two different river courses to follow. Tube rentals are available throughout the town—an excellent place to start is **Town Tinker Tube Rental** on Bridge Street ([914] 688–5553. Open daily, 9 am to 6 pm). You can even take a train ride out to the other end of the creek and then tube back to town.

Facilities: There are no local rest rooms here, although some of the tube rental places do have portable toilets.

Tuthilltown Grist Mill. Albany Post Road, Gardiner, N.Y. 12525. (914) 255–5695. Open May 1 to October 31, Friday and Saturday, 10 am to 4 pm. Admission. Group rates and tours available by appointment.

If you combine this stop with the Widmark Honey Farm (see following entry), your kids will have an interesting day learning about food. There is no walking or long tour at the gristmill. Young children will appreciate the turning of the waterwheel, while adults will enjoy the gift shop, which offers a variety of flour ground right there at the mill. (This is the only mill in America that provides grain to Orthodox Jewish kitchens.)

Facilities: Rest rooms; gift shop. Strollers are accommodated here. Not accessible for wheelchairs.

Widmark Honey Farm. U.S. 44–New York 55, Gardiner, N.Y. 12525. (914) 255–6400. *Bear shows:* May to October (call ahead for hours). Tours of the apiary: year-round. Admission. Groups are accommodated.

The bears that live at this farm are not just trained performers, they are family members. This is not a zoo. Watch the black bears dance, wrestle, climb, and even ride a bike during the show. Baby bears are there, too, and the youngest children will delight in their antics. Bears like honey and bees make honey, so be sure to look at the beekeeping exhibit and the apiary, where the honey is produced and processed. The tours are informal. You may be the only ones there early in the season, but don't be afraid to stop by during the week.

Facilities: Rest rooms; gift shop, with lots of honey and honey-related products; picnic area. Stroller and wheelchair accessible.

Kenneth L. Wilson State Park. Wittenberg Mountain Road, Mount Tremper, N.Y. 12457. (Take New York 28 west from Kingston thirteen miles to New York 212; turn right onto 212 and proceed a quarter of a mile to Wittenberg Mountain Road, the first right turn—it is almost directly opposite the bridge. Follow Wittenberg Mountain Road to the park entrance; watch for signs on the right.) (914) 679–7020 or 255–5453 for camping information. Open May through October, daily, 9 am to 5 pm. Use Fee. Groups are welcome. Campsites for overnight stays are available by reservation.

This is a nice, small state park just outside of world-famous Woodstock, so you can enjoy a swim in the morning and a walk through the colorful town in the afternoon. The park has a shallow lake with a lovely sandy beach that will keep toddlers digging for hours. Unfortunately, there is no shade near the beach, so you may want to take a walk on the marked trails in the nearby woods. Wilson Park is excellent for picnics; the mountain views tend to soothe adults.

Facilities: Rest rooms; changing room; picnic area with tables; campsites.

When you are finished at Wilson Park, you may want to stop in the town of the Aquarian Age, **Woodstock.** (Follow Wittenberg Mountain Road east from the park, turn left at the fork, and follow the road to the junction of Wittenberg Mountain Road and New York 212; turn right onto 212 and follow it into Woodstock.) On a summer's day, the village green is always packed with young people. There are lots of colorful characters and interesting shops to be seen along the main street, including an excellent toy store called Tinker Street Toys. And the kids will certainly want an ice cream.

If you are planning to be in Woodstock on a Saturday in July or August, call **The Woodstock Guild,** 34 Tinker St., Woodstock, N.Y. 12498, (914) 679–2079, and inquire about their children's theater and story presentations. The performances usually run from 1 to 2 pm and are held at the Byrdcliffe Barn. Kids, as well as adults, are sure to enjoy the imaginative productions. You can also write to the Guild for their summer schedule.

Woodstock Wonderworks, A Community Playground. Route 375, Woodstock, N.Y. 12498. (914) 679–2316. Open every day year-round from dawn until dusk.

During a five-day period in the spring of 1989, the children of Woodstock, with the help of hundreds of parents, friends, and volunteers, built a remarkable playground. The event itself was similar in spirit to an old-fashioned barn-raising and involved almost the entire community. This wonderland of a playground was actually designed by the children of Woodstock. Robert Leathers, a nationally known playground designer headed up the project (he has helped over 400 communities in the United States build creative play spaces). A multilevel, wooden structure, the playground includes a castle maze, space tunnel, dragon slide, Viking ship, haunted house and more, all designed to stimulate a child's imagination. This is a stop that shouldn't be missed if you are traveling through Woodstock with young children.

Facilities: Rest rooms (open only during school hours during the week); picnic tables; wheelchair accessible areas.

James Baird State Park. Freedom Road, Pleasant Valley, N.Y. 12569. (Go one mile north of New York 55 on the Taconic State Parkway.) (914) 452–1489. Open year-round, daily, 6 am to 10 pm. Free. Group tours are available.

A complete outdoor entertainment center, this park has a fifty-meter swimming pool, volleyball courts, baseball field, tennis courts, hiking trails, camping sites, golf course, and—an unusual offering—a full-service restaurant. There are special programs during the summer months for children. Concerts, nature programs, and a puppet theater make this park a great excursion for families. In the winter cross-country ski trails are open (but you must bring your own equipment). Dutchess County is well known for its forests and woodlands. This park is in the center of the county and is easily accessible to travelers.

Facilities: Rest rooms; changing room; picnic areas; restaurant; snack bar; pool; campsites (by reservation only). Wheelchair accessible.

Bardavon Opera House Children's Theater. 35 Market Street, Poughkeepsie, N.Y. 12601. (914) 473–2072. Open year-round; performance times and offerings vary. Admission by ticket; prices vary. Group tours are accommodated by special reservation. Group discounts are available.

This is one of the last (and best) old-time opera houses that once operated as the cultural center of almost every small town and city in America. Built in 1869, Bardavon still operates as a lively theater and performing arts center. It has a history of fine entertainment: past performers have included Mark Twain, Sarah Bernhardt, Ethel Barrymore, and Milton Berle. The theater was refurbished in the 1920s and today it offers audiences a wide range of nationally known performance groups and soloists. A perfect place to introduce young people to the glories of entertainment, Bardavon's Young People's Theater program is busy all year. In the past, life-size puppet shows, incredible magic shows, plays, ballets, and musicals have entertained youngsters. The selection of shows appeals to many different age groups, and Bardavon does note which performances are appropriate for various age groups. The emphasis at Bardavon is on learning through entertainment, so even though every performance is fun, there also is usually a chance for children to meet the performers after the show and to learn firsthand about the wonders of theatrical entertainment.

Facilities: Rest rooms. The theater is wheelchair accessible and there are specially designated seats for the handicapped, but you should call ahead about this service. Hearing-impaired children are able to rent lightweight headphones. Adults who plan to accompany a group to Bardavon should inquire about the special offerings, such as theater tours and question-and-answer sessions with the performers. (Call [914] 473–5615 for information).

Culinary Institute of America Cooking Courses. U.S. 9, Hyde Park, N.Y. 12538. (914) 452–9600. Open for spring and fall sessions. Courses are held on Saturday morning and run for four weeks. Tuition for classes is fairly steep, so a child should be interested in cooking. Registration is by phone or mail.

This institute is one of America's premier schools for the fine culinary arts. Set overlooking the Hudson River, the school site was formerly a seminary. Visitors are welcome to walk around the campus and dine in the restaurants (only St. Andrew's Cafe does not require reservations). In keeping with its educational goals, the school offers a wide variety of classes for the public, and among them are some fun workshops for kids. In Kids Culinary College 1, younger kids from eight to eleven spend time with professional cooks, who demonstrate and explain the art of making pizza, bread, salads, and other exciting kid foods, such as breakfast items. Older cooks (twelve-to fifteen-year-olds) will want to sign up for Kids Culinary College 2, which teaches the basics of good cooking to budding chefs and lets the participants develop their own menus.

Facilities: Rest rooms; wheelchair accessible.

Hudson River Tours. A day on the Hudson River in summer and early autumn can be a treat for the entire family and a rare way to see the region. Lighthouses, mansions, bridges, and beautiful riverscapes pass before you, almost close enough to touch—children who love the water won't want to leave the boat! The tours are always personalized, and the kids will usually get a chance to meet the captain and hear some river tales or explore the nooks and crannies of the boat. Cruises are available between May and October. Prices vary according to length and type of cruise. Call ahead for schedules as well as for children's and group rates. There are two excellent river tour operators in Dutchess County. **Riverboat Tours** (P.O. Box 504, Pleasant Valley, N.Y. 12569. [914] 473–5211) offers daily sightseeing tours, and brunch and dinner cruises. Cruises leave from the Rinaldi Boulevard dock in Poughkeepsie on delightful double-decker boats that chug up and down the river on various-length tours. Strollers are accommodated on the ships, and there are snack bars and rest rooms. **Shearwater Cruises** (RD 2, Box 329, Rhinebeck, N.Y. 12572. [Head south from Rhinebeck on U.S. 9 and follow the signs to Staatsburg.] [914] 876–7350) is located at Norrie Point in Staatsburg, New York. This cruise operator offers two-hour, half-day, and full-day tours of the Hudson River, some complete with gourmet lunches and dinners. We recommend that you plan your cruise around the age of your child: two hours on the river for younger kids is often more than enough, while older children might enjoy half a day's adventure. Experienced sailors may want to inquire about renting a boat from this company, especially if the whole family likes to travel at its own pace.

Ice-skating at the McCann Ice Arena in the Mid-Hudson Civic Center. Civic Center Plaza, Poughkeepsie, N.Y. 12601. (In downtown Poughkeepsie; follow the signs from U.S. 9.) (914) 454–5800. *Rink:* Open September through March, Monday, 11 am to 1 pm; Wednesday, 11 am to 1 pm, 4:30 to 6 pm, and 7:30

to 9 pm; Friday, 8 to 9:30 pm; Saturday, 2 to 4 pm; and Sunday, 3 to 5 pm. Admission. There is no children's rate, but there are group rates for fifteen or more.

This indoor rink is part of the Mid-Hudson Civic Center, a recreation, entertainment, and convention center that offers a variety of programs year-round. It's one of the best places in the Hudson Valley to ice skate indoors. Kids will enjoy the large skating area, the skating music, and the bustling ambience. Parents can watch from the sideline seats or grab a pair of skates for themselves.

Facilities: Rest rooms; concessions and snack bar; skate and locker rentals. The parking in downtown Poughkeepsie can be tight, so we recommend parking in the lot across the street from the center (there is a parking charge).

Locust Grove. P.O. Box 103, 370 South Road, Poughkeepsie, N.Y. 12602. (914) 454–4500. Open Memorial Day weekend through September, Wednesday through Sunday, 10 am to 4 pm (last tour is at 3 pm). Admission (children under seven are admitted free). Group tours are available.

This charming house, in the style of an eight-sided Italian villa, served as the summer home of inventor and painter Samuel Morse in the 1840s. Most children know that Morse developed the telegraph and Morse code, but almost everyone is surprised to learn that Morse was also a famous painter; several of his canvases are on display throughout the house. In the basement area there is an extensive display of telegraphs, from earlier models to the later machines. A tour of Locust Grove shows life in the mid–nineteenth century, complete with fine examples of artwork, furniture, and even a billiard room. The house is interesting for children who enjoy history, but the tour is recommended only for older children. There are changing displays from the Martha Young collections, which have included toys, dolls, and clothing. Outside, the grounds have been restored with beautiful plantings, flower-filled urns, and an extensive herb garden. Also, a series of hiking paths is accessible, where children who like the outdoors can walk through ravines and around ponds.

Facilities: Rest rooms; gift shop; picnic area with tables; hiking paths. Wheelchairs cannot be accommodated in the house but may be able to manage in the garden area. Nor is the house stroller accessible.

Mills-Norrie State Park and Mills Mansion.
U.S. 9, Staatsburg, N.Y. 12580. (914) 889–4646 or 889–4100. The park and mansion grounds are open all year, but hours vary with the season. *Park:* Open at 8 am, May through October; and at 9 am, November through April. Camping (by reservation only) is from the first Friday after May 10 to Sunday before October 31. *Mills Mansion:* Open from mid-May to Labor Day, Wednesday through Saturday, 10 am to 5 pm; and Sunday, 1 to 5 pm; and from Labor Day to the last Sunday in October, Wednesday through Saturday, noon to 5 pm; and Sunday, 1 to 5 pm. Open on Independence Day and for special events until Christmas. The park and house tour are free, but there are charges for camping and for golfing. Groups are accommodated in the mansion by reservation only.

This unusual combination of state park and historic mansion is situated on more than nine hundred acres of land along the Hudson River. Day-trippers will enjoy all of the outdoor activities of a park, with a few extra attractions. There are hiking trails with lovely river views and a mile-long physical fitness trail that is popular with all ages of athletes and is a good family activity. If you want to picnic, the bluffs on the river offer a chance to sit and watch the ships and boats running up and down the Hudson. Fishing can be done from any area of the park where there is access to the Hudson River; however, the Mills-Norrie Marina (which is private) is not open for fishing. In the winter groomed cross-country ski trails snake around the park, and the golf course and Mills Mansion grounds are renowned for their sledding hills, a sport that has been popular in the area for almost three hundred years. The park also contains a small environmental museum with several displays of local

animals and plants. Special educational programs are offered
here during the summer; in the past these have included a visit
from Smokey the Bear, puppet shows, and classes in birds,
plants, and astronomy. One night each week is family film
night. These programs are in the late afternoon and evening,
and campers, junior naturalists, and visitors are welcome to attend.

Since kids love to camp, you may want to plan ahead for an
overnight stay in the park. There are both campsites and cabins, but reservations are necessary at this popular site. Flush
toilets, washrooms, and showers are centrally located, and the
cabins lie along the major hiking trail. Kids can play in the
nearby playground. The park also has two nine-hole golf
courses.

Mills Mansion is a Greek Revival glory that dates back to
the mid–nineteenth century. The furnishings and decorations
display the wealth of the Hudson River families at the turn of
the century. While adults and older children will enjoy the
short house tour, younger children will prefer to stay outside in
the park. There are, however, special events at the mansion
throughout the year that appeal to all ages. Everything from
square dances to banjo bands and Scottish tatoos, jazz ensem-
bles, and troubadors have appeared at the mansion, which also
extends its tour hours on concert days. During holidays plan to
visit and glory in the elaborate arrangements of greens and
flowers, a huge Christmas tree, and so forth, which recall celebrations past at a grand mansion.

Facilities: Rest rooms; picnic areas. The clubhouse at the
golf course contains a restaurant that is open to the public for
lunch and dinner from early April to early November; it is not
wheelchair accessible. Nor is the mansion. There is some
wheelchair accessibility within the park, but access is limited in
some areas due to unpaved walks. Strollers can be used on the
paved walkways in the park, but you will have to carry them
upstairs in the mansion. Campers should note that campsites
offer a table and bench at each site, while the cabins have bunk
beds, cookstoves, refrigerators, electricity, and running water.

The park begins accepting reservations on January 1 of the camping year, so you must plan ahead if you want to stay overnight. Applications may be obtained by writing to: Park Manager, Mills-Norrie State Park, Staatsburg, N.Y. 12580. A boat-launch ramp on the Hudson River at the marina is open from May to October, daily, from 8 am to 8 pm; there is no charge for launching your boat, but there is a docking charge.

Old Rhinebeck Aerodrome. U.S. 9, Rhinebeck, N.Y. 12572. (Take U.S. 9 north from Rhinebeck to Stone Church Road and watch for the signs.) (914) 758–8610. *Museum:* Open May 15 through October, daily, 11 am to 5 pm. Air shows are held only on Saturday and Sunday at 2:30 pm (pre-show activities begin at 2 pm). Admission (children under six are admitted free, and there is a reduced admission price for six to ten year olds). Group rates are available by advance reservation on Saturday only. Ten percent discount for fifteen or more people.

We cannot recommend this site enough: it's colorful, corny, exciting, and full of activity, especially during the shows. Founded by Cole Palen, this is America's original living museum of old and restored airplanes. It recaptures the thrill of flying when the Red Baron and barnstorming were popular. The tour guides are enthusiastic experts on the finely restored airplanes, which are housed in several hangars. The walking tour highlights Fokkers, Sopwith camels, and Curtiss airplanes, as well as old engines and many other small planes. Be sure to attend one of the weekend air shows, when the air hums and whines with planes, and the crowds cheer on the heroes and the bad guys. On Saturday the pioneer era of airplanes is highlighted, with demonstration flights of old planes, and on Sunday the battles of World War I are reenacted, complete with full costumes, a parade, and the best villains in the Hudson Valley. The planes are either original aircraft or powered with original engines of the period. Palen, who flies each weekend, makes the audience feel that each show is especially for them. There are announcers who describe the overhead antics— aerial bombing, acrobatics, fly-bys and comedy routines (the same heroine has been rescued hundreds of times from the burning building!). Brave souls can schedule barnstorming rides in a 1929 open-cockpit biplane before or after the shows at an extra charge. The air shows are viewed from an outdoor stand, and we heartily recommend hats in the summer and jackets in the fall.

Facilities: Rest rooms; picnic tables; free parking. Snacks are available. The area is navigable for wheelchairs and strollers.

Pick-Your-Own Farms. The lush Hudson River valley has been home to farms for more than three centuries, and Dutchess County boasts some of the best pick-your-own produce. Each of the following farms provides containers for the fruits and vegetables for a small fee. After you pick the produce, the farms weigh it and you are charged by the pound. Prices vary, but they are almost always a great deal less than you would pay for comparable produce in the supermarket. Since you will be out under the hot sun, dress accordingly in the summer months. At **Greig Farms** (New York 9G north from Red Hook to Pitcher Lane; watch for signs. [914] 758–1911 or 758–5762. Open May through October; call ahead for crop conditions and hours) you will find one of the largest pick-your-own farms in the region. With acres of strawberries, blueberries, raspberries, peas, asparagus, apples, and pumpkins, there is almost continuous picking all growing season. This lovely site has mountain views, and just up the road there is a magnificent herb garden where you can stop for refreshments. Older children will enjoy walking around the gardens, especially in June and July, when the flowers are at their most colorful. One warning: bees like berries, and although honeybees are not considered aggressive, they are around, so anyone who is allergic to or just plain scared of bees should be aware. **Henry Dykemans** (In Pawling, N.Y., at the junction of New York 22 and Route 20. [914] 855–5166 or 832–6054. Open May 1 to November 1, every day, 10 am to 6 pm) lets you pick your own strawberries in June and take a hayride to the pumpkin patch in October. **Johnson Farms** (Carpenter Road, Hopewell Junction, N.Y. [914] 221–7940 or 221–7948. Open June and July, daily, 8 am to 8 pm) has strawberries, snap peas, and raspberries for the picking. (914) 897–4377. **Fishkill Farms** (on East Hook Cross Road, Hopewell Junction, N.Y. Open after Labor Day for pick-your-own apples and pumpkins, daily, 9 am to 5:30 pm) has more than a dozen varieties of apples for the choosing as well as large pumpkins for Halloween. The farm store is well stocked with old-fashioned cider and doughnuts, a traditional treat in this area since the seventeenth century, in addition to some more modern specialties, such as cheese and homemade fudge. A historic site for picking apples, peaches, pears, and pumpkins is **Montgomery Place Orchards** (On River Road, at the corner of New York 9G New York 199; River Road is the last right turn before the Kingston-Rhinecliff Bridge, just outside of Rhinebeck. [914] 758–5461. Open mid-June to late-November, 10 am to 6 pm). After gathering your produce you may want to see the Montgomery Place mansion and grounds (there is an admission charge), although we recommend this stop for older children with an interest in history. Kids are encouraged to play on the grounds. Parents with strollers will have a tough time on the graveled paths. The admission seems a little steep for just a quick visit.

Poughkeepsie Journal Tours. 85 Civic Center Plaza, Poughkeepsie, N.Y. 12601. (914) 454–2000, ext. 252. Tours are offered Monday through Friday, 10 am to 4 pm, by reservation. Suggested age for the tour is eight and up. Free. Groups of up to twenty are welcome; smaller family groups will be accommodated.

This newspaper, founded in 1785 by Nicholas Powell, is the oldest paper in New York State and the fourth oldest in the country. The paper is located in Poughkeepsie, the county seat, which was settled in 1687 by the Dutch. Today it is housed in the last fieldstone structure authorized built by Franklin D. Roosevelt under the Public Works Administration. This paper has reported such notable events as the ratification of the Constitution and the death of George Washington. The tour begins at a mural—a wall-sized painting that depicts people from the history of newspapers and printing as well as those who were involved with the *Poughkeepsie Journal*, such as Mark Twain. Visitors then proceed to the pressroom, typesetting section, advertising room, and newsroom, where they have a chance to talk about newspapers with people who love journalism. This is an excellent tour for children who want to know how and why a daily newspaper is put together. Knowledgeable guides answer questions. Teachers should ask about the special Newspapers in the Classroom class, which illustrates how newspapers can be incorporated into schoolwork.

Facilities: Rest rooms. Wheelchairs have access to certain areas. Stroller-bound babies and toddlers will be bored with this tour.

Franklin Delano Roosevelt Home and Library Museum and Val-Kill. U.S. 9, Hyde Park, N.Y. 12538. *Museum:* (914) 229–8114. *Home* and group tour arrangements: (914) 229–9115. Open year-round, except major holidays, daily, 9 am to 5 pm; closed Tuesday and Wednesday from November to March. Admission (children under twelve are admitted free). Group tours are available; there is no charge for school groups. *Val-Kill:* Open April 1 to October 31; daily 10 am to 5 pm accessible by shuttle bus only from the Roosevelt Home site. Val-Kill is also open in November, December, and March, but access is by private vehicle only. There is an additional charge for the bus. Only groups of ten or more are accommodated for tours in January and February by advance notice.

This site, part of the Roosevelt family estate, is composed of several smaller areas: Franklin Roosevelt's boyhood home, the first presidential library, and the Roosevelt Museum, which contains memorabilia from both the president and the first lady. Because it is sometimes difficult to introduce children to recent history, especially political history, this site is highly recommended as a place to start. All through the museum and house are photos, exhibits, and personal items that recall one of the most vibrant (and troubled) periods in American history. The museum houses an extensive collection of "Rooseveltiana," from model ships to books, manuscripts, and clothing. Here is the letter from Einstein to Roosevelt that led to the development of the atomic bomb, part of the president's collection of naval artifacts, and some toys of the famous Scotty, Fala. Inside the house, younger visitors will see how a child of their own age lived a century ago. Toys, portraits, and even the stuffed birds that Franklin collected help to make a president seem more real to children. Outside, the magnificent grounds contain rose gardens, stables, a nature study area, and the graves of Franklin Delano and Eleanor Roosevelt. (If you do walk in the nature area, watch for poison ivy and stay on the trails.) For those children who want to know more about Eleanor Roosevelt, a visit to Val-Kill, her permanent home after Franklin's death, is enjoyable. A twenty-minute film traces her life, and a tour of the house and gardens is included. During December, Val-Kill is decorated for Christmas (but you can get there only by private vehicle).

Facilities: Rest rooms; gift shop. The museum is accessible to those in wheelchairs, but there is limited accessibility in the home and at Val-Kill. Strollers can be managed around all of the sites.

Sports Nine, Inc., Splashdown. RD 1, Box 178, U.S. 9, Fishkill, N.Y. 12524. (914) 896–6606. Open May to September, daily (call for hours). Admission. Groups are welcome by reservation.

Water parks are a wonderful break from sightseeing in the summer, especially when the younger children start getting hot and tired. This park has three huge water slides, a small slide for younger visitors, play pools, and water playgrounds. Also on hand is a miniature golf course.

Facilities: Rest rooms; locker rooms; picnic area; snack bar. The site is wheelchair accessible. Strollers are welcome.

Stony Kill Environmental Center. New York 9D, Wappingers

Falls, N.Y. 12590. (914) 831–8780. Grounds: open year-round, daily, dawn to dusk. Orientation building hours: Monday through Friday, 8:30 am to 4:30 pm; also open for special weekend programs. Free. Groups are limited to ten people and are by advance reservation only.

For children who enjoy the outdoors or who are studying the environment and nature, this 756-acre site offers a wide variety of habitats for local animals and plants. Rolling meadows, woodland areas, ponds, and swamps attract lots of wildlife, which can be observed from the network of hiking and walking trails that run through the site. There are three major trails, ranging from one-half mile to two miles in length, all of them marked and self-guided: the Verplanck Farm Trail lets children learn about farming techniques and crops in season; the Twin Trunks Trail lets children learn about farming techniques and crops in season and shows typical habitats (forests, swamps, and fields) in the Dutchess County area; and the Sierra Trail offers a good hike for older children in warm weather and fine cross-country skiing in the winter. Snowshoes can be rented in the winter for use on the trails. Also located on the site is the Farm Education Area, which has a nineteenth-century barn and real livestock (note that this area is open to the public by appointment only, so call ahead if you want to see the cows). Kids can feed the ducks on the pond or watch migrating birds in the birdwatching area. Because the emphasis at this site is on outdoor life, and we think that unless the kids are interested only in seeing an environmental site, this trip should be scheduled to coincide with one of the center's many special weekend programs. At the Annual Fall Harvest Festival there is sheep shearing, pony rides, and exhibits of unusual breeds of cattle and goats. In January the barn at the Family Farm Discovery Tour is opened and the animals can be fed by kids. Life on a nineteenth-century working farm is explored, too, through talks, tours, and even some food tastings. Also in January, an annual Sleigh Rally is held at the site. Antique horse-drawn sleighs and cutters right out of a Currier and Ives print are exhibited by their proud owners. At driving contests at the

center, live commentary kee[...]
ages. The interpretive building [...]
hibits is open, so you can warm your [...]
outdoors, so dress very warmly and bun[...]
There are also snowshoe hikes schedule[...]
winter (when the weather cooperates) and a pr[...]
for youngsters and adults on how to tap your own [...]
and produce your own maple syrup.

Facilities: Rest rooms; designated picnic areas. The b[...]
ing is wheelchair accessible. The site is not stroller friendl[...]
along the trails. Bring your own cross-country skis; there are
extensive trails, but no rentals.

Swimming. Dutchess County has several places to swim. However, many of them are open to town residents only. The following spots are open to the public and provide an oasis in which to relax after touring the county's marvelous sites on a hot summer day. The **J. H. Ketcham Memorial Pool,** Mill St., Dover, N.Y. (914) 877–3701, is open daily from noon to 6 pm during July and August. A small entrance fee is charged. The lake in **Edward R. Murrow Park,** at the intersection of Lakeside Drive and Old Route 55, Pawling, N.Y. is open to the public in July and August from 10 am to 7 pm on weekdays, until 8 pm on weekends. An admission fee is charged. The **Town Pool** on East Market Street, Rhinebeck, N.Y. 12572, is open daily in July and August from 1 to 7:30 pm. A use fee is charged.

Taconic State Park: Rudd Pond and Copake Falls. Millerton, N.Y. 12546. (Located two miles north of the village of Millerton on New York 22.) (518) 789-3059. Open year-round, daily, dawn to dusk. A day use admission is charged per vehicle.

There are two sections to this huge park: the southern area takes in Rudd Pond and the northern area contains Copake Falls. A wonderful place to take the kids swimming, Rudd Pond is seventy-five acres in size and has a beautiful sandy beach with lifeguards and rowboats for rent on a large, crystal-

u do need a New
of sixteen. Camp-
vations are neces-
mall pond (but no
the smallest water
ion. A nature center
by rangers for the
ctivities, such as pup-
throughout the sum-
rs will enjoy the wild
wn equipment, but the
rming hut.
; picnic areas; snack bar;

*the action interesting for all
which also houses small ex-
le up the youngsters is all
throughout the
gram in March
maple trees
ild-*

Webatuck Craft Village k 55 at Webatuck Road,
Wingdale, N.Y. 12594. (914) 832 5464. Open year-round except February, Wednesday through Saturday, 10 am to 4:30 pm;
and Sunday, noon to 4:30 pm. Admission is charged for some
festivals. Groups and educational tours are by appointment.

Webatuck is nestled in a idyllic setting along the Ten Mile
River. The craft shops offer retail items along with the chance
to watch the craftspeople in action. Glassblowing, furniture
making, blacksmithing, weaving, and stained glasswork are all
demonstrated and explained by the artists. Children also can
enjoy and participate in special festivals held April through October. If you want to spend the day, try to coordinate your visit
with the Festival of the Great Outdoors in April or with the
Nature Festival and the Medieval Fair, both held in September.

Facilities: Rest rooms; picnic area; restaurant; gallery with
changing exhibits. Parents with strollers or wheelchairs will
find them difficult to navigate around the grounds and small
buildings; some buildings have steps, and the terrain is hilly.

Wilcox Park. New York 199, Stanfordville, N.Y. 12581. (914)
758–6100. The park grounds are open year-round, but its facili-

ties are open from Memorial Day to Labor Day weekend, daily, 10 am to 8 pm; and in the winter from 10 am to 4 pm. Admission.

This is one of the nicest parks to take young children to, with its small lake and sandy beach area. Paddleboats are a popular rental item for older children, and when the water fun wears off, there's miniature golf and a special children's playground to keep the kids occupied. The hiking trails vary in length, so even the youngest in your party will enjoy taking a nature walk, where you might come across deer and raccoon. A winter visit will provide skiers with many cross-country trails, which are maintained and marked by the park, as well as sledding hills; bring your own equipment.

Facilities: Rest rooms; bathhouse; picnic area with tables; snack bar. Campsites are available (electric and water hookups) by reservation.

Wing's Castle. RD 1, Box 167, Millbrook, N.Y. 12545. (Go north on U.S. 44 to County Route 57, then go west three miles to Bangall Road and turn right; Wing's Castle is half a mile up the road on the left.) (914) 677–9085. Open May 31 to October 31, Wednesday through Sunday, 10 am to 5 pm. Reservations are advisable. Admission (children under twelve are admitted free). Group tours are available by appointment.

This unique castle-in-progress has been under construction for the last twenty years. Visitors can see this fieldstone edifice on a guided tour conducted by owner and builder Peter Wing. He and his wife Toni have used salvaged materials from antique buildings to create this unusual structure, and which includes arches, cupolas, and towers (which they have dubbed "Recycled Americana"). An antique ship has been used as a balcony in the house and Victorian birdbaths are used as sinks, and children will delight in the "cauldron" bathtub, complete with terracotta fountain. Young visitors will view the whole house as something out of a fairytale as they visit the many rooms and the grounds. You may even be lucky enough to meet the giant macaw, the castle's mascot. The castle is crammed full of antiques, bric-a-brac, and collectibles, with carousel horses and suits of armor vying for space with stained glass windows and military weapons. The details will keep everyone on the tour visually entertained, and Peter Wing is only too happy to answer any and all questions about the castle, which is scheduled to have a moat and its own set of ruins. Some new special children's events are offered each summer. In the past these have included a children's version of a Shakespearean play, with the castle as a backdrop. This is a perfect place to have a picnic and enjoy some offbeat culture.

Facilities: Rest rooms. Call ahead if wheelchair accessibility is a concern. Strollers may find it difficult to maneuver here.

If you are in the area for the day, after visiting the castle stop by the **Trevor Teaching Zoo** (Millbrook School—go six miles east of Millbrook on U.S. 44 to Millbrook School Road. [914] 677–8261. Open every day during daylight hours. Admission. Groups are welcome by appointment. The zoo is not wheelchair accessible, but strollers can manage on the paths. This small zoo is a part of Millbrook School's curriculum, and visitors are welcome. On the four-acre site you will see hawks, badgers, snakes, deer, and other local and exotic fauna. A one-and-a-quarter-mile self-guided nature walk takes you through the zoo, so the very young might tire before seeing the whole site. It is the only zoo in the region.

American Museum of Fire Fighting. Harry Howard Avenue, Hudson, N.Y. 12534. (Located next to the Firemen's Home.) (518) 828–7695. Open April 1 to October 31, Tuesday through Sunday, 9 am to 4:30 pm. Free. Group tours are available.

Children of all ages will appreciate an hour spent in this museum, which is packed with colorful equipment and art of the fire fighter's trade. As you step into the large display room called the Engine Hall you will discover more than two dozen pieces of antique fire engines, pumpers, and trucks, all in fine condition and, of course, most of them painted bright red. The exhibit contains samples of equipment dating back to the early–eighteenth century, when fires were fought by hand and with limited water sources. The walls of the museum are lined with old fire banners and lovely paintings that were used by the various companies in parades and at festivals. The fire fighter is remembered in paintings, advertisements, statues, helmets, and the elaborate fire horns that were carried during processions. Each display is clearly marked, and there are often lots of fire buffs around to answer your questions and relay fascinating tales.

Facilities: Rest rooms.

Clermont. County Route 6, Germantown, N.Y. (Located just off New York 9G; watch for signs.) For information write to Clermont State Historic Park, RR 1, Box 215, Germantown, N.Y. 12516. (518) 537–4240. Open Memorial Day to Labor Day, Wednesday through Saturday, 10 am to 5 pm; and Sunday, 1 to 5 pm. (The grounds are open year-round from dawn to dusk.) Free. Group tours are available.

This is the ancestral home of the Livingston family in America, established in 1686 and in use by the same family until the 1960s. Chancellor Robert Livingston was a signer of the Declaration of Independence and a supporter of Robert

Fulton and his steamboat. Adults and older children will enjoy a tour of this elaborately restored house, which overlooks the Hudson River and is filled with magnificent eighteenth- and nineteenth-century antiques. Special events for children are offered throughout the year. There is something going on just about every weekend: early-spring sheep shearing, revolutionary war encampments, brass band concerts, steamboat displays and exhibits, autumn hayrides, and a pumpkin-painting festival are some examples. The site is also a perfect place to picnic or barbecue (cooking stations are available). School tours are welcomed all year, and there are special tours offered at Christmastime to see the elaborately decorated house.

Facilities: Rest rooms; picnic area with tables and barbecue pits. Pets are allowed in limited areas if leashed. There are paths, but you may have a problem with a stroller or wheelchair on the lawn.

Coach Farms. Near Pine Plains, N.Y. (Call ahead for directions.) (518) 398–5325.

Children who are involved with agricultural organizations (4-H, Girl Scouts, Future Farmers of America) will find this tour fascinating. You have to call ahead for tour arrangements, which are for groups only and are by special reservation. Visitors have a chance to see how goats are raised and can see parts of the cheese-making process, from milking to production. We emphasize that the tour is technical and is for interested young people only, but we highly recommend that teachers and parent leaders of such groups arrange for a visit. This small farm is a family-run operation, so there is a personal touch throughout the tour.

Facilities: Rest rooms; food specialty shop stocked with goat's milk products and local items. The tour is indoors, and walking is involved. You should not have any problems with a stroller. Not wheelchair accessible.

Dinosaurs at Louis Paul Jonas Studios. RD 4, P.O. Box 193, Hudson, N.Y. 12534. (The studio is on a small back road outside of Hudson in the hamlet of Churchtown; they recommend calling ahead for detailed directions and an appointment.) (518) 851–2211. Open year-round. Free.

Louis Paul Jonas Studios is an unusual find: they were responsible for the huge lifelike dinosaurs that stalked the 1963 World's Fair, and they are still producing dinosaurs of all sizes for display and museum use. A tour shows children how a dinosaur is constructed. There are several smaller versions to see—the type of lizard depends on the current project in the works. This is an excellent outing for school groups.

Facilities: Rest room.

Lake Taghkanic Park. New York Route 82 at the Taconic State Parkway, eleven miles south of Hudson. (518) 851–3631. Open year-round. Free.

This park is a delightful getaway year-round: there is camping, fishing, swimming, and hiking in the summer; cross-country skiing and ice-skating in the winter; birdwatching, exploring the woods, and participating in one of the park's many special events or programs during the rest of the year. Children will love the workshops that tell all about the animals that can be found in this region. Other program topics include astronomy, puppets, Smokey the Bear, and dinosaurs. At the nature center, children can examine the live displays, which offer fish, small animals, and reptiles from the park itself. This is a fine place to camp overnight or just for a short visit to get a taste of the great outdoors.

Facilities: Rest rooms; picnic area with tables; snack bar; campsites. Pets must be kept leashed and are restricted to special areas; call ahead if you have any questions. The site is a park; strollers may not be appropriate in certain areas. The nature center is wheelchair accessible.

Pick-Your-Own Farms. Columbia County offers kids a chance to see lovely farmland, horse farms, and other open country spaces. We recommend a stop at one of the pick-your-own farms for the freshest produce available. Remember to bring along sunscreen and a hat and to wear comfortable outdoor clothing suitable to the summer sun. Your harvest will be weighed (and you will be charged) by the pound. It is advisable to bring along your own containers, but you can buy them for a nominal fee at most pick-your-own farms. The following farms welcome kids and adults. **Miller Orchards** (County Road 19, Livingston, N.Y. [off U.S. 9, one-quarter mile from the Adventist Church]. [518] 851–7470. Open September to November, daily) has apples and pears only. **Golden Harvest Farms** (U.S. 9, Valatie, N.Y. [one mile north of the junction of U.S. 9 and New York 9H]. [518] 758–7683. Open August through November) also has apples and pears. **Hotalings Farm** (New York 9H, Claverack, N.Y. [two miles north of town]. [518] 851–9864. Open year-round) has tours all year, but you can pick cherries in June and July and apples in September and October. At **Loveapple Farm** (New York 9H, Ghent, N.Y. [six miles northeast of Hudson]. [518] 828–5048. Open June through December) you can pick apples, cherries, nectarines, peaches, pears, and plums in season. **Miller's Willow Spring Farm** (County Road 10, Linlithgo, N.Y. [between U.S. 9 and New York 9G, three miles south of the Rip Van Winkle Bridge]. [518] 828–5624. Open May through October) has the following harvests in season: apples, blackberries, cherries, peaches, pears, plums, raspberries, corn, and pumpkins.

Shaker Museum. Shaker Museum Road, Chatham, N.Y. 12037. (In Chatham, go to the East Chatham Post Office and turn left; follow County Road 13 south to the museum.) (518) 794–9100. Open May 1 to October 31, daily, 10 am to 5 pm. Admission. Group tours and rates are available.

This Shaker museum is not as well known as its larger Massachusetts counterpart (see pages 177–78), but it does offer children a unique look at some old tools, farm equipment, and inventions of the Shakers, a sect that flourished in New York during the nineteenth century. The walk-through exhibits, including displays of Shaker baskets, clothing, and a large offering of woodworking tools, are well marked. Younger children might be uninterested in the static displays, but most older children (ages seven and up) will enjoy the story of the Shakers in the New World. There are some special events for children during the year: on July Fourth a flag-making workshop is offered, along with a luscious strawberry shortcake breakfast and old-time musical entertainment. In the fall, apple harvests are turned into apple pies, juice, and other tasty "exhibits" for children's delection. This museum is an enjoyable introduction to an often neglected part of America's social history.

Facilities: Rest rooms; gift shop; picnic area with tables; snack bar. Strollers are welcomed here and are easily maneuvered through the exhibits. Limited wheelchair accessibility.

Skiing: Catamount Ski Area. New York 23, Hillsdale, N.Y. 12529. (518) 325–3200. Open weekends and holidays, 8:30 am to 4 pm; and weekdays, 9 am to 4 pm. Night skiing: Wednesday through Saturday, 3:30 to 10 pm. Charge for lift ticket (children five and under ski free when accompanied by a ticketed adult). Group rates are available.

When you ski at Catamount you can see three states—New York, Massachusetts, and Connecticut—from the top. There are twenty-five slopes and trails, seven lifts, and snowmaking on 90 percent of the mountain. This is a busy, full-service ski area, with all of the amenities. The terrain really varies there, so skiers of all ages and skills can have fun. A full children's ski program is offered, too. The Kitten Corral, for ages four to six, includes a full day of nursery time, skiing, and lunch in a supervised area. Other classes are available for children six to thirteen who want to learn to ski or to improve their skills. The nursery will care for children ages two to six from 8:30 am to 4 pm while parents enjoy the slopes. There are even special weekday discounts that, with the purchase of a lift ticket, include a full day of free nursery care.

Facilities: Rest rooms; ski shop; picnic area with tables; restaurant; snack bar; full equipment rental; nursery.

Carson City. New York 32, Catskill, N.Y. 12414. (518) 678–5518. Open from mid-May to June 20, weekends only, 9:30 am to 6 pm; June 20 to Labor Day, daily, 9:30 am to 6 pm; Admission (children under three are admitted free). Group tours and rates are available.

This is a place that sophisticated older children should avoid but that younger kids will absolutely adore. Carson City is one of the largest reproductions of an old Western town in the country, and a day here is packed with action and fun. Skilled performers reenact a full slate of jailbreaks, gunfights, bank robberies, and saloon fights. On the less active side there are also cancan dancers, trick horseback riding, magic shows, and native American dancing. Take a stagecoach or a train ride—but watch out for robbers, who might even steal your gum (yes, that masked man was Jesse James!). The actors are all in period costume, and the surroundings look like an old *Gunsmoke* set. There's noise and action aplenty, and even a carriage museum with sleighs and horse-drawn vehicles on display. Stop in at the gift shop, where Western goods are sold, or have a snack at—where else?—the Chuckwagon (bring a picnic lunch if you think you won't be in the mood for franks and chili). Parents should note that they can make arrangements for birthday parties at Carson City. And although the initial entrance fee may seem rather steep, remember that the continual entertainment and live shows will keep the kids amused all day. Please note: parents who are concerned about exposing their children to guns and gunfights may want to skip this site.

Facilities: Rest rooms; gift shop; picnic area; snack bar. Strollers will be troublesome in the graveled areas. Some wheelchair accessibility.

Catskill Game Farm. Game Farm Road, off New York 32, Catskill, N.Y. 12414. (Take New York 32 and watch for the signs.)

(518) 678–9595. Open April 15 to October 31, daily, 9 am to 6 pm. Admission; there are additional charges for the train and amusement rides. Group tours and rates can be arranged.

This is one of the oldest game farms in the country; its more than two thousand animals and birds make it a place to spend an entire day. Lions and tigers and bears entertain all ages, and not to be missed are the special shows, which include dancing elephants, juggling monkeys, and bicycle-riding bears. The petting zoo has friendly deer and llamas that can be fed by hand if you purchase crackers. (Very young or small children may feel overwhelmed by the loose animals that crowd around people who have food in their hands.) The petting zoo has lots of small baby animals, such as pigs and lambs, that can be bottle-fed. A train takes visitors from the petting zoo to the bird house, a trip that delights small children. Although the admission charge to the Game Farm is on the high side, the site is enormous, and a family could easily spend the entire day there. After the children tire of the animals and the show, there is an amusement park with rides and a playground with lots of sand.

Facilities: Rest rooms; gift shop; picnic areas; snack bars. The paved pathways and stroller areas make this an excellent place for moving about with infants. Wheelchairs can manage well on the paths.

Catskill Reptile Institute. New York 32, P.O. Box 134, Catskill, N.Y. 12414. (518) 678–5590. Open May 15 to September 15, daily, 10 am to 6 pm; and during the rest of the year, weekends, noon to 5 pm; and weekdays by appointment. Admission. Group tours and rates are available.

This small museum offers children a unique chance to see snakes and lizards from around the world in a safe, educational environment. All of the dangerous reptiles are either behind glass or kept at a safe distance, but you can touch "safe" snakes under the watchful eye of your guide. You can even have yourself photographed with a friendly reptile. A tour is offered at no extra charge (the average tour is ninety minutes in length); shorter tours are available for those who have younger children. The snakes (more than one hundred of them) and reptiles that live here include cottonmouth moccasins, copperheads, and lizards as well as more exotic species such as cobras, fer-de-lance, African puff adders, gaboon vipers, and the eighteen-feet-long African rock python. In the summer there are outdoor shows with a question-and-answer format that are geared toward children. A new addition is a nature park, which has mountain lions, bobcats, bears, parrots, and a walking trail. (Quiet visitors may even get a chance to hear an American diamondback shake its rattles.) It's a nice place for kids to learn that snakes aren't at all slimy to the touch!

Down the road from the Reptile Institute is the **Mystery Spot** (New York 32, between Cairo and the Catskill Game Farm. Open daily during the summer and weekends in the spring and fall, 10 am to 9 pm), one of those old-time roadside attractions that are part silly, part amusing. The "spot" consists of an old house in which everything is topsy-turvy. Water apparently runs uphill, gravity goes wild, pendulums swing in a mysterious fashion, and you can sit on the wall. The tour lasts approximately thirty minutes. Although adults might not be enchanted by this attraction, children will never forget it (the site was once featured in a *Life Magazine* article).

Adjacent to the "spot," the **Mine 'N Find Gem Mine,** Route 32, Cairo, N.Y. 12413, (518) 622–3637, will delight kids who love "jewels" of all kinds. Some of the stones to be discovered in this "enriched field" include sapphires, rubies, topaz, and amethyst. (Same hours as Mystery Spot.)

Facilities: *Reptile Institute:* Rest room; gift shop. Strollers are welcome. *Mystery Spot:* Rest rooms; gift shop; game room. Limited stroller and wheelchair accessibility.

Junior Speedway. Route 32, Cairo, N.Y. 12413. (518) 622–3330. Open: May, June, and Labor Day through Columbus Day weekends only from noon to sunset; July through Labor Day, daily from 10 am to 10 pm.

This mini-amusement park has go-carts, a miniature golf

course, baseball batting cages, and a game room to entertain kids of all ages. The four- to nine-year-old set will enjoy the battery-operated jeeps and roller racers (boards with roller skate wheels that can be steered).

Facilities: Rest rooms; snack bar; gift shop; picnic tables.

North and South Lakes. New York 23A to County Route 18 (O'Hara Rd.), Haines Falls, N.Y. 12436. (518) 589–5058 or 943–4030. Open late-May to early-December, daily, 9 am until dusk. Admission, with an extra charge for camp sites. Group rates are available by reservation.

This multi-use campground and recreational area offers breathtaking scenery and a multitude of activities. You can swim in a mountain lake with a clean, sandy beach, hike, fish, and boat (you can rent a boat). For active kids, a short hike through the woods will bring you to Kaaterskill Falls, one of the highest falls on the East Coast and one that is associated with many native American legends. The drive up to the site is along a beautiful winding road, and even on popular weekends in the summer, there's enough room at both lakes for everyone. For those who want to spend the night under the stars, there are campsites for rent and hookups for your recreational vehicle. The area is clean, safe, and well maintained, making for a nice overnight visit for nature lovers. Be warned, however, that you should make reservations for the campsites early in the season. If you do decide to take a hike around the lakes, keep your eyes open for the "lost treasure of Rip Van Winkle." This consists of a gem-encrusted ebony ninepin that will go to the finder of a stone inscribed with Rip's initials. Whoever finds the treasure stone, which is located on public land somewhere in Greene County, can claim the treasure. This is a unique chance to kids to participate in a real treasure hunt. For further information about the treasure write to: The Kaaterskill Foundation, P.O. Box 551, Catskill, N.Y. 12414.

Facilities: Rest rooms; changing room; lockers; picnic area with tables; snack bar; campsites.

Palenville Interarts Colony: New York 23A, Palenville, N.Y. (Follow the signs.) Open July through mid-September; show times and workshop schedules vary, so call ahead. For schedules write to P.O. Box 59, Palenville, N.Y. 12463. (518) 678–3332; in New York City call (212) 206–7564. Admission. Group rates are available.

Set on a private sixty-five-acre estate, the colony is also located at the site of one of the first American arts colonies, where Thomas Cole and Frederic Church worked and visited. Since 1983 the colony has been home to the Bond Street Theatre Coalition, which each summer presents an astounding assortment of actors, singers, mimes, jugglers, dancers, and performers. The group favors work that incorporates folk roots and ethnic traditions, so you may see a Chinese acrobat as well as a champion boomerang thrower. The circus arts are highlighted through workshops and performances; in fact, the whole village of Palenville gets involved. Every Saturday morning at 10 am there is a children's show featuring magicians, clowns, storytellers, stilt walkers, and more. The opening ceremonies are usually circus oriented, and you actually get a chance to learn juggling or how to walk a tightrope. Bring a picnic and enjoy the open spaces; if you want, stay for one of the unique evening shows, which present acts and companies from all over the world and which are usually appealing to all ages.

Facilities: Rest rooms; picnic area with tables. Some accommodations are available, reservations have to be made in advance; the accommodations also offer both regular and vegetarian meals. Accessible to wheelchairs and strollers.

Skiing: Cortina Valley. New York 23A, Haines Falls, N.Y. 12436. (518) 589–5600. Open early-December to the end of March, weekends, 9 am to 4 pm; and weekdays, 10 am to 4 pm. Night skiing: Wednesday through Saturday, 5 to 10 pm. Group rates are available. Lift ticket charge (children six and under ski free if accompanied by a paid adult).

Several excellent ski areas in Greene County offer both downhill and cross-country facilities. Cortina Valley is a family-oriented ski center with eleven trails, two lifts, and a towrope. The slopes cater to beginners, intermediates, and experts. A play-learning school caters to the youngest skiers (six and under). For those who don't ski at all there is a nursery (children must be over eighteen months old). Special-events weekends revolve around such events as tree trimming and the learn-to-ski race-off. Parents should note that a really worthwhile feature at Cortina Valley is the ski instruction for hearing-impaired children.

Facilities: Rest rooms; ski shop; picnic area with tables; restaurant; snack bar; equipment rentals.

Skiing: Hunter. New York 23A, Hunter, N.Y. 12442. (518) 263–4223. Open November to April, daily, 9 am to 4 pm. Charge for lift tickets. Group rates are available.

This is the granddaddy of the Catskill ski areas, a huge, busy ski center that is challenging to professionals as well as young skiers. This "snowmaking capitol of the world" has more than forty-four slopes and trails that can be covered with manufactured snow. It also has a full program for children: the Peewee Program is a combination nursery–ski school for the three to four year old. The Frosty Ski Program, for ages five through nine, is a full-day program that includes lift ticket, equipment rental, lessons, and lunch (this fills up quickly during holidays, so make reservations in advance). The ski schools operate only on weekends and during holiday weeks. Hunter is not cheap: lift tickets are among the most expensive in the region, with children age five and under paying six dollars for a lift ticket and six- to twelve-year-olds paying twenty-two dollars a ticket. However, with its snowmaking capacity, you will always be able to ski at Hunter and no guesswork is needed when planning a trip.

Facilities: Rest rooms; snack stand; restaurant; gift and rental shop.

Skiing: Windham. New York 23, Windham, N.Y. 12496. (518) 734–4300. Open late November to mid-April, weekends and holidays, 8 am to 4 pm; Monday through Friday, 9 am to 4 pm. Charge for lift ticket (children age six and under ski free when accompanied by a ticketed adult; during the nonholiday weeks, junior skiers age twelve and under ski free when accompanied by a ticketed adult). Group rates are available on weekdays only.

With its wonderful mountain views and complete snowmaking facilities, Windham is another fine ski area in the Catskills that caters to both children and adults. The new base lodge, opened for the 1989–90 season, offers the expanded Children's Learning Center, one of the most elaborate centers in the northeast. Up to 130 children from six months to seven years old can be accommodated in the 6,000 square foot space. There is a terrain garden for ski training, heated floors, an arts and crafts area, kitchen, and all kinds of educational toys. The Smokey Bear Ski School is an exciting learn-to-ski program for four- to seven-year-olds. Young skiers will begin their lessons with stationary exercises and video ski cartoons if they have never been on the slopes before. A full-day session includes two lessons, lunch, lift ticket, and nursery supervision; a half-day session is also available. Instruction is made fun through the use of games and activities, and children can return to the nursery for hot chocolate and a rest period whenever they are cold and tired. But note that these sessions are very popular, so you must reserve a space for your child. For nonskiing children from six months to seven years old there is a complete baby-sitting service with supervised activities. Junior development programs, for novice to expert skiers ages five through seventeen, are also offered on weekends. There are twenty-seven trails, with three triple chairlifts, two double chairlifts, and one pony lift. One-third of·the trails are suitable for novice skiers. Note that the disabled ski program at Windham accommodates children as young as five years old and handles all types of disabilities.

Facilities: Rest rooms; cafeteria and restaurant; gift and rental shop.

Cross-Country Skiing. Cross-country skiers will want to visit the following ski centers, all of which offer equipment rental and lessons. All open as soon as conditions are suitable, from December to March. At **Hyer Meadows Cross Country Ski**

Area (Onteora Road, off New York 23A, Tannersville, N.Y. 12485. [518] 589–5361) there are thirty-three kilometers of groomed trails, and guided tours can be arranged. **White Birches** (two and a half miles off New York 23, Nauvoo Road, Windham, N.Y. 12496. [518] 734–3266) is another area that grooms its trails and has warming huts. **Winter Clove Inn** (see entry below) has extensive trails (fifteen kilometers) and lovely vistas and is open to day visitors.

Winter Clove Inn. Winter Clove Road, Round Top, N.Y. 12473. (518) 622–3267. Open year-round. Group rates are available.

This inn is located in Winter Clove, a deep valley that holds the winter snows until spring. A family vacation resort, it has been run by the same family for four generations. Guests are housed in an old-fashioned (but comfortable) lodge with a large porch, complete with rockers, on which to spend a summer's evening. Indoor and outdoor pools, tennis courts, volleyball courts, a golf course, and a bowling alley are all on the premises, so that everyone will be able to find something fun to do in the country. There is a beautiful natural pool with a waterfall, where guests are welcome to swim, and movies are shown each week. Meals are served family-style and everything is home cooked and hearty. The kids will love the horse-drawn hayrides and picnics that are offered throughout the summer and fall. In the winter you can rent equipment and cross-country ski along well-marked trails that meander in and out of the Catskill Mountain State Park. Or take the sleigh rides drawn by Belgian horses in the winter, participate in maple syrup making in the spring, and just toss a few leaves around in the fall. A unique feature of the inn is the use of llamas to carry trail equipment and snacks on the organized hikes. The kids will adore them.

Facilities: The Winter Clove Inn has complete facilities as well as: a bowling alley, a baby-sitting service, a gift shop with Winter Clove maple syrup, a golf course, and hiking trails. This is really a full-service family resort that has reasonable prices and welcomes children of all ages. Limited access for wheelchairs; steps lead to the main entrance and to activity areas.

Zoom Flume Aquamusement Park. Shady Glen Road, East Durham, N.Y. 12423. (518) 239–4559. Open from Memorial Day through June, weekends only, 10 am to 7 pm, weather permitting. Open daily, June 24 through Labor Day, 10 am to 7 pm. Admission. Reduced admission for children under eight. Group rates are available.

Located in a historic Catskill canyon, visitors to this wet site will find beautiful scenery (it has been featured on national television) as well as lots of fun. A series of giant waterslides—the Raging River Ride and the Zoom Flume—lets you skid your way down through the glen on tubes, while bumper boats and waterfalls let you enjoy staying in the pool all day. Young kids will love the Soak-a-Buddy, where you can drench one another with buckets of water. If you want to stay dry there are the mountain coasters (a sort of flat scooter that winds its way down a track) and the moonwalk, where kids can bounce and jump to their heart's content. A suspension bridge, which gives you a view of the whole park, takes you over to the snack bar. And if you still have the energy, there are nature trails, games of skill, and a playground. This is a nice place to spend the day, since visitors of all ages will have a good time in the water, and there is enough to please everyone, from the youngest child to the adult.

Facilities: *Zoom Flume:* Rest rooms; changing rooms; lockers; picnic area with tables; snack bar/restaurant. Stroller and wheelchair accessible on boardwalk paths only.

There are a few other things to see and do in East Durham; we recommend calling for hours before you go. The **Butterfly Art Museum** (Wright Street. [518] 634–7759. Open seasonally through August) is a private collection of mounted butterflies from all over the world. This may interest youngsters who like insects. The **Durham Center Museum** (New York 145. [518] 239–8461. Open Memorial Day to Labor Day) is another small, private museum that has native American artifacts, fossils, minerals, and railroad relics. **Supersonic Speedway** (New York 145. [518] 634–7200. Open May 1 to Columbus Day, daily, 10 am to 10 pm) lets older children have fun with go-carts, hitting balls in a batting cage, and other sports.

Bobcat Ski Center. Gladstone Hollow Rd., Andes, N.Y. 13731. (Located 2.5 miles off Route 28 on Gladstone Hollow Rd. Follow signs. [914] 676–3143.) Open Friday through Sunday and holiday weeks only, 9 am to 4 pm. Charge for lift ticket. Children under the age of five ski free. Reduced rate available for five- to sixteen-year-old skiers. On Fridays, two skiers are admitted for the price of one ticket. There are discount tickets for adult, junior, and student groups of twenty or more, including one complimentary ticket per twenty paid. There is a reasonably priced learn-to-ski package which includes lift ticket, rentals, and a beginner lesson.

Bobcat's value for the money make it a wonderful place for family skiing. There are eighteen trails (nine expert, seven intermediate, and two novice), with a vertical drop of 1,050 feet and top elevation of 3,345 feet. This is a low-key ski area that doesn't attract the huge crowds usually found at many other Catskill ski areas. Babysitting services are available upon request.

Facilities: Rest rooms; lockers; cafeteria; lounge; equipment rental; ski school.

Delaware County Historical Association. New York 10, Delhi, N.Y. 13753. (607) 746–3849. Open from late-May to late-October. Summer hours: Monday through Friday, 10 am to 4:30 pm; and weekends, 1 to 4:30 pm. Call for spring and fall hours. Admission. Group tours and rates are available.

Kids who love the past will enjoy becoming a part of it when they visit this historic site. The Frisbee House, which is on the grounds, was the birthplace of Delaware County's government, but the house is much more than dry history. Inside, kids will get a chance to see a children's room from the mid–nineteenth century as well as a selection of old toys, clothing, furniture, and even pictures of the family who used to live there. If a site interpreter is working in the kitchen, children are usually welcome to try their hands at peeling apples and cake baking using the old wood-burning stove. Out in the barn, a permanent exhibit called It's A Fine Growing Time introduces viewers to the rhythm and patterns of farm life in the last century. A dog churn (run by a dog walking on a treadmill) is fascinating, as is the extensive collection of wagons and farming tools, such as rakes, flails, and apple presses. Also on the grounds are a gun shop, a one-room schoolhouse, a tollhouse, and a small family cemetery. Young nature lovers will enjoy walking the short trail that begins at an old farm path and winds down to Elk Creek. Plants and flowers are marked; lucky observers may even spot a raccoon or two. Even the youngest visitors will be able to complete this trail, so don't hesitate to take the walk, especially in the summer. Special events at the site are well suited to children's interests. Farm Festival and Home and Hearth Day re-create mid-nineteenth-century activities, including hayrides, apple bees, and taffy pulls, while entertainment abounds on Tavern Day and at Children's Fair, when singers and dancers may get youngsters to join in on old-fashioned songs. Because many of these special events depend on the weather, call ahead for a complete schedule. Teachers may want to ask about the I Worked Like Fury program, which allows school groups to spend a day in a one-room schoolhouse.

Facilities: Rest rooms; gift shop, stocked with many old-fashioned children's toys; picnic area with tables. Pets are not allowed. There are gravel paths for walking, but strollers will be difficult to maneuver and touring the buildings requires walking up and down stairs. Limited wheelchair accessibility.

Delaware and Ulster Rail Ride. New York 28, Arkville, N.Y. 12406. (Mailing address: P.O. Box 243, Stamford, N.Y. 12167.) For recorded schedules call (in New York State) 1-800-356–5615 or (outside New York State) 1-800-642–4443; for general information and special arrangements call (607) 652–2821. Open Memorial Day weekend, July 3 and the day after Labor Day through October 31, weekends only, and July

4 through Labor Day, Wednesday through Sunday. Special fall and winter rides are also available; call ahead for a schedule. All trains depart from the depot at 10:30 am, 12:15 pm, 2 pm, and 3:45 pm; each trip lasts one hour. Admission (children under five ride free). Group rates are available.

All aboard for a ride on the old Doodlebug, a self-propelled mail and freight car that was used more than sixty years ago on the Catskill railroad lines. Painted bright red, the car is one of several pieces of old railroad stock that have been restored to use and now provide fun rides for all ages. Even the youngest child will be delighted with the whistles, the bells, and the clickety-clack of the train as it weaves its way through meadows and up mountains. Along the way, the friendly train crew points out interesting sites and tells stories of what travel was like before the automobile. Try to visit the D&URR on a special-events weekend that caters to kids. Sometimes, costumed train robbers will stop the train and holdup the crew and the passengers. Other days, fiddlers and storytellers entertain passengers with their songs and tales. During the fall there are teddy bear rides, pumpkin events, and even moonlight rides at night.

Facilities: Rest rooms; picnic area with tables; snack caboose. The D&URR has a unique train-related gift shop, where kids can buy everything from an engineer's hat to train whistles. Also in the depot, you can sit on benches and watch a slide show about the Catskill Mountains while waiting for your train to depart. Wheelchair accessible. Strollers are accommodated.

After the train ride, cross the street and visit the **Auto Memories Museum** (County Route 29. Open late June through October. Admission is by donation), where a changing exhibit of more than forty vintage cars, including a steam-powered locomobile, captivates kids. Back on New York 28, directly across from the D&URR, look for **Church Street Station** (Church Street. [914] 586–2425. Open spring through fall, daily, depending on the weather. Admission. Strollers are fine, but call

ahead if wheelchair accessibility is required), where a miniature golf course dotted with windmills, covered bridges, and
giant pigs keep company. Visit the replica of the old train station or hit a hole-in-one on the nineteenth green and set a
model train in motion. The trout pond is a great place for kids
to spend an hour trying to hook the big one (no license is required). There's a batting cage with pitching machine and a
putting green for adults, which makes this a nice stop after
riding the D&URR.

Edge of the Mountain Indian Museum. Oquaga Lake Road,
Deposit, N.Y. 13754. (607) 467–3757. Open Memorial Day
through mid-October, daily; and late-October through late-
May, weekends (also open weekdays by appointment only).
Call ahead for hours. Free. Group tours are available.

This small museum is perfect for children who are studying
native Americans in school. Curator Martha Juttner, a self-
taught authority on Indian peoples, enjoys introducing young
visitors to the world of both local and distant tribes. Her collection is housed in a room next to her home, and the artifacts
include tools, jewelry, masks, rattles, and dolls that were used
in rituals by many different tribes. If you are near Deposit (an
old rafting town on the Delaware River), the kids will appreciate seeing this collection.

Hanford Mills Museum. East Meredith, N.Y. 13757. (The museum is located at the intersection of Delaware County routes
10 and 12, ten miles east of Oneonta.) (607) 278–5744. Open
May 1 through October 31, 10 am to 5 pm. Admission. Group
tours and rates available.

Once a busy, noisy sawmill and gristmill, this pastoral site
has been restored to its original use, and visitors are able to
watch as water power is harnessed once again to produce wood
products. Situated alongside a serene millpond, the buildings
reflect the pace and industries of a century ago. A ten-foot waterwheel is still used to make the machinery run, and the
Kortright Creek and the millpond are harnessed to provide

power. Visitors are guided along a series of wooden catwalks that take them through the pulley room, the wheel room, and the woodworking room, where craftspeople are usually busy making decorative spindles and gingerbread for houses. The staff is friendly and will answer questions about the procedures, and the tour will interest adults as well as children, who never seem to tire of watching the waterwheel and hearing its roar. Outside, there are more woodworking machines and a barn, which houses displays of farm equipment. Hanford Mills is well known for its special children's events. On July 4, an old-fashioned Independence Day celebration is re-enacted with traditional music, games, and rides. Another popular, although noisy, event is the Antique Engine Jamboree, when dozens of collectors bring their steam and gas engines and visitors can watch (and listen) as pistons, gears, and pulleys work with Rube Goldberg–like precision.

Facilities: Rest rooms; gift shop, with children's games and books as well as many local food products; picnic area with tables (the pond is a lovely place to have lunch, but bring your own, as there are no restaurants nearby). There are gravel paths, but it would be very difficult to maneuver a stroller inside the buildings. Not accessible for wheelchairs. Pets are not allowed.

Roundup Ranch. Wilson Hollow Road, Downsville, N.Y. 13755. (607) 363–7300. Open year-round, to paying guests only. Call for rates (which include three meals per day).

For youngsters who are horse crazy, a stay at this family-style resort would be worthwhile. There are two thousand acres to explore and a wide range of activities in which to participate. Horses are the main attraction here: there are indoor and outdoor riding rings, trail rides, and lessons available. Rodeos, with good, authentic cowboys, are held each Saturday night from May to September. In addition to riding, there is swimming in indoor and outdoor pools, golfing, fishing, tennis, square dancing, and, in the winter, cross-country skiing and ice-skating. The ranch has sixty guest rooms, but it never seems crowded. Children are welcome; in fact, there is a special children's dining room and a full program of activities for kids. School groups are welcome to spend the day (students can enjoy a full day of riding and two meals for less than thirty dollars each).

Facilities: Rest rooms; gift shop, specializing in western gear for cowboys and cowgirls of all ages; picnic area.

Roxbury Arts Group. Main Street, Roxbury, N.Y. 12474. (607) 326–7908. For a summer schedule, call ahead. (See Calendar of Annual Events for a complete listing of special events.) Admission is charged for some activities.

This is not a specific site, but the Roxbury Arts Group sponsors some excellent children's programs throughout the summer. The Metawee River Arts Company performs outstanding plays based on stories found in folklore and myths of other countries. The company is renowned for using giant puppets, colorful costumes, and elaborate masks to tell its tales; shows have included stories about the wild man of medieval myth and the ring dove of India. At the Roxbury Country Fair, held on Saturday during the Labor Day weekend, children will love the chance to make cornhusk dolls, churn butter, paint their faces, listen to storytellers, watch clog dancers, and sing along with folk musicians. A special children's tent is set up each year, so all of these activities are available within a few feet of one another. Parents will enjoy the craft show and the food, including a popular barbecued chicken.

Facilities: Rest rooms; picnic area with tables. Although there are no walks, you should be able to navigate with a stroller or a wheelchair. The plays are held in various localities, but these areas are always roped off and have plenty of room for kids to run and play. Pets are allowed if leashed.

Skiing: Deer Run Resort. New York 10, Jefferson, N.Y. (Mailing address: Box 251, Stamford, N.Y. 12167.) (607) 652–7332 or (in New York State) 1-800-252-7317. Open from the first week in December through the last week in March, Monday and

Tuesday, 10 am to 6 pm; Wednesday through Friday, 10 am to 10 pm; Saturday, 9 am to 10 pm; and Sunday, 9 am to 5 pm. During holiday weeks, open daily, 9 am to 10 pm. Charge for lift tickets. Special group rates for the Learn to Ski Program are available.

Deer Run is a year-round resort complete with all of the amenities: swimming, bowling, horseback riding, and fishing. In the winter the ski slopes and trails come alive with more than fifteen trails, three lifts, and more than forty kilometers of trails that lead through beautiful Catskill scenery and over-looks. Ski instruction and equipment rental are available for all ages, and there are guided cross-country ski tours along the old logging trails. Night skiers will enjoy schussing down the lighted slopes, but if you and the kids don't want to ski, there is an indoor pool to relax and splash in. Children can also take part in the special activities, such as games and art projects, that are overseen by a children's director. There is a special full-day program called the Button Buck, which includes in-struction, lunch, and ski time. This program is for five- to twelve-year-olds and runs from 10 am to 4 pm for an inclusive fee of thirty-five dollars.

Facilities: Rest rooms; picnic areas; snack bar; restaurant. An excellent full-service nursery operates daily from 9 am to 5 pm. There is an hourly charge for this service, and children must be at least two years of age. Lodging is available at Deer Run's motel, but you must call ahead for reservations during ski season.

Skiing: Plattekill Mountain Ski Center. Roxbury, N.Y. 12474. (Follow the signs from New York 30 to Plattekill.) (607) 326–7547. Open November through March, daily, 9 am to 4 pm. Lift ticket fee. Group rates are available.

This center has special offerings for young skiers. Kids learn while playing at the Round-Up Ski School, which has lessons for five- to ten-year-olds of all skill levels including ad-vanced and racing. Snacks, warming breaks, and lunches (when required) are offered. The children are always under adult supervision. For young kids (ages one through five) who don't ski, there is a staffed nursery in the lodge. You are charged by hourly, half-day, and full-day rates, with a discount if you have two kids in the nursery. Outside on eighteen slopes, novices to expert skiers will find challenges. There are three lifts and 90% snowmaking capacity. Plattekill is a really nice ski center that is never too crowded and that offers a relaxed, family atmosphere.

Facilities: Rest rooms; cafeteria; bar; rental/repair shop; ski school; ski shop; and nursery (open seven days a week for one- to five-year-olds). Nursery services are available on an hourly or daily basis. Overnight accommodations in nearby inns, bed and breakfast homes, and motels, not at the site.

Boat Tours. Cooperstown, New York, lies at the foot of Otsego Lake, and there is no better way to see the lake and the surrounding landscape than from the water. Lake tours take you past scenes from James Fenimore Cooper's novels, Kingfisher Tower (a small water tower from the nineteenth century built in the shape of a castle), well-manicured lakeside estates, Sunken Island (which disappears when the water is high), and James Fenimore Cooper's home. Older children will love the stories of pioneers and native Americans told by the boat guides. We recommend that you bring along hats and even sweaters, especially if it is a breezy day. All boat tours leave from the bottom of Fair Street in Cooperstown, near the Baseball Hall of Fame. We recommend that you call these places ahead of time, especially if you are not certain of the weather conditions. **Lake Otsego Boat Tours** ([607] 547–8238 or 547–6031) has one-hour tours on a fifty-five-foot yacht built in 1912 for one of the area's wealthy families. Tours run from Memorial Day weekend through mid-October; from Memorial Day weekend through June and Labor Day to mid-October they run weekdays at 1:30 and 3 pm and weekends at 1:30, 3, and 4:30 pm. From July to Labor Day they run daily at 10 and 11 am and at 1, 2, 3, 4, and 6 pm. **Classic Boat Tours** ([607] 547–6031) has one-hour tours aboard two classic boats, 1902 and 1912 launches. These beautiful boats may even make older children feel that they have been whisked back in time, when sport boating was only for the rich.

Christmas Shops. There are two unusual holiday shops in Otsego County that help to make Christmas sparkle for many months and will get kids (and adults) into the holiday mood. **Butternut Barn**, Allen's Lake Rd., Richfield Springs, N.Y. (Go one-quarter mile east of Richfield Springs on U.S. 20 and turn right on Allen's Lake Road; the shop is five hundred feet up the road on the right. [315] 858–0964. Open April through December, daily, 10 am to 6 pm; and January through March, weekends only, 10 am to 6 pm), located in a 150-year-old carriage barn, stocks lots of handmade treasures. Throughout the year, special celebrations such as County Homespun Days in the spring and the October Scarecrow Contest (kids can make and bring their own scarecrow) make a stop here fun for children. For the month of December, dozens of trees, ornaments, wreaths, and handmade holiday gifts, including dolls, toys, and decorations, fill the barn. Holiday goodies are offered to visitors, and kids will love picking out gifts for that special friend. Another nice stop is **Christmas House at Meadow View Farm** Robinson Rd., Mohawk, N.Y. (Take New York 167 north from Richfield Springs and go one mile past the Russian monastery up Robinson Road. [315] 866–2595. Open April through December, daily, 10 am to 5 pm.) This mansion was built in 1790, and today it houses lots of rooms filled with more than twenty decorated Christmas trees, dolls, music boxes, and more. Although there are many fine (and expensive) gift items here, the kids will enjoy picking out an ornament and seeing more Christmas trees in one place than anywhere else in the county. On your way up to Meadow View Farm you will pass a **Russian monastery.** Although there are no guided tours of the site, visitors are welcome to walk along the monastery's paths and enjoy the views.

Cooperstown Famous Family Campground. RD 3, Box 281, Cooperstown, N.Y. 13326. (Take New York 28 south from Cooperstown, turn right onto County Route 11, and go four miles; watch for the signs.) (607) 293–7766. Open May through September; call ahead for exact dates and times. Fee.

This is a large (one-hundred-unit) campground that offers a lot for the family that likes to camp out. The campground is only minutes from Cooperstown, so you can enjoy the outdoors and still visit all of the museums, but once you have seen the surrounding sights, there are lots of things to do at this campground. For example, there are free pony rides for the kids, hayrides on summer evenings, and a small working farm that lets the early risers help milk the cow every morning, feed the chickens, and visit with the animals. Fishing ponds are on the site, and you can take a dip in the pool after a long day. Younger hikers will enjoy the short, marked nature trail, the miniature golf course, the paddle boats, and, for those rainy days, the recreation hall. This is a busy campground, as you may imagine, but it is one of the few that has so much to do in such a small area. Because of its proximity to Cooperstown, the campground may fill up quickly on summer weekends, so call in advance.

Facilities: Rest rooms; store; showers; launderette.

Farmer's Museum and Village Crossroads. P.O. Box 800, Cooperstown, N.Y. 13326. (Located on Lake Road, one mile north of Cooperstown.) (607) 753–5500. Open May through October, daily, 9 am to 6 pm. The museum is also open on a limited schedule during April, November, and December; call ahead for hours. Admission. Group rates and tours are available by reservation.

Although this "village" looks as if it has been in Cooperstown forever, it was really assembled during the last fifty years by importing buildings from across central New York State. Split rails and stone fences guard the landscape, sheep and geese run wild, and children always have a wonderful time in this nineteenth-century setting. You enter the site through a huge stone barn that houses several exhibit halls, each worth the price of admission by itself. Downstairs there is a re-creation of an old curiosity museum, an early type of exhibit hall that catered to American naivete. Here is the Cardiff Giant, a huge stone carving that was considered the greatest hoax of its time. The so-called giant was buried by night and then dug up by an enterprising farmer–con artist who then publicized it as a petrified giant of biblical times. (P. T. Barnum eventually bought the giant.) Other curious exhibits include rocks, paintings of murders, and nineteenth-century scientific discoveries. In the next hall an exhibit entitled Past Times lets kids see how their counterparts of the past spent their leisure time. Sleds, kites, hot-air balloons, and games are all on display. There is sometimes a photographer on hand who will take a picture of your children in old-fashioned dress. Kids who wonder about farm and pioneer life will enjoy the main hall, where the story of everyday life is told through easy-to-understand displays that include farm tools, kitchenware, clothing, wagons, and samples of crops such as corn and barley. Museum interpreters are often demonstrating their skills during the warmer months, so you might learn how to make a broom or weave a bedspread.

Outside in the village, there's lot to see and explore, and the buildings house enough to keep all ages interested, since most of the self-guided tour stops have costumed guides on hand. There is a printer's shop, where much of the village's printing is still done, a doctor's office, an herb garden, a blacksmith shop with a working smith, a tavern, a church, and more. Farm animals are always around—these may include chickens, cows, and even a patient pair of oxen. Special weekend events such as cider pressing and sheep shearing are held during summer and fall; a stop at the village green may result in all the kids getting together to walk on stilts or roll a hoop along the grounds. You can spend several hours here, and all ages should be intrigued, but this is a walking tour, so the youngest may need a stroller. There is even a winter weekend for parents and children: participants "live" in a nineteenth-century farmhouse for a day, cooking their food in the open fireplace, playing games, and doing chores.

Facilities: Rest rooms; gift shop; picnic area with tables; snack stand. The paths can be navigated by wheelchair, but call ahead if handicapped access is required. Parents with strollers will be able to manage here.

Just across the street from the Farmer's Museum is the **Fenimore House Museum** (Route 80, [607] 547–2533. Hours are the same as the Farmer's Museum's. Admission), which houses one of the most outstanding collections of folk art in the United States. Although we don't recommend this as a stop for younger children, older kids who enjoy art will love the colorful, exciting folk art, through which they can relate their own world with the world of the past. There are carvings, weather vanes, quilts, portraits, toys, and more on display here, with enough famous paintings (such as the *Peaceable Kingdom*) to please adults as well.

Firehouse Museum. U.S. 20 and New York 80, Springfield Center, N.Y. 13648. (The museum is located in back of Burger World.) (315) 858–2342. Open year-round, daily, when the restaurant is open (the hours vary with the season). Free.

This small, unusual museum, really part of a catering hall, is a fire engine lover's delight. The museum started as a private collection, and when the Burger World restaurant added the catering hall, the owners decided to add a special touch with the firehouse memorabilia. The walls are lined with hundreds of antique toy fire trucks dating from the 1890s, including many hook-and-ladder trucks and some rare child-sized pedal toys. Outside, there are picnic tables near the restaurant and a large pond with ducks waiting to be fed by young visitors.

Facilities: Rest rooms; small gift shop (in the museum); fast-food burger restaurant; picnic tables. Wheelchairs can move around the restaurant area; the exhibit is stroller friendly.

Fly Creek Cider Mill and Orchard. Goose Street, RD 1, Box 38, Fly Creek, N.Y. 13337. (Fly Creek is located on Route 26, eight miles from Cooperstown; follow the signs from U.S. 28.) (607) 547–9692. Open Labor Day weekend to December, daily, 10 am to 5 pm. Free.

This site offers visitors a chance to see apple cider produced as it was a century ago. It is one of the oldest water-powered mills in the state. Built in 1856, the mill is still worked with a 1924 tractor and an 1889 hydraulic apple press, and the apples are grown in the surrounding orchards. Cider samples are offered to visitors, and each weekend after Columbus Day there is a big Applefest at the mill, with baked goods, crafts, and of course, apples and apple cider for sale. The mountain views are lovely in autumn, but the Applefest is too late in the season for a fall foliage tour. You may want to combine a stop at the mill with a day in Cooperstown (see related entries).

Facilities: Gift shop; rest rooms. Strollers and wheelchairs may have a difficult time in the mill.

If the kids want to go horseback riding, a stop at **Windsong Stables** (in Fly Creek, off County Route 26. [607] 547–8740. Open year-round. Fee for rides) is just perfect, especially in the summer. Besides horseback riding, sometimes the staff loads up a wagon for hayrides through the countryside. The stables are open daily in the summer, from dawn to dusk; call ahead for riding reservations. There is also a tack shop. Windsong Stables is a vacation resort, too, with fishing, swimming, boating, and hiking on the premises. Cross-country skiers will enjoy using the groomed trails that run through the property.

Gilbert Lake State Park. Oneonta, N.Y. 13820. (The park is located between New York 205 and New York 51, twelve miles northwest of Oneonta.) (607) 432–2114. Open year-round; open from Memorial Day to Labor Day, daily, 8 am to 6 pm; and the remainder of the year, daily, dawn to dusk. Small use fee. Groups and camping are by reservation only.

This large (sixteen-hundred-acre) state park is located in one of the loveliest areas of central New York State. Lush forests and open meadows surround Gilbert Lake, where kids will enjoy boating and swimming along a sandy beach. In the park there are children's play areas as well as several marked nature and hiking trails to tempt the adventurous. A special summer recreation program often includes storytellers, puppet shows, films, and more to entertain the youngsters. Camping is available on the site, in either campgrounds or cabins, but we warn you: the cabins are assigned by lottery each January, so if you want to get in on the contest, you have to plan ahead. The action at this park doesn't stop at Labor Day: cross-country skiing, ice-skating, sledding, and snow-tubing are all popular in the winter.

Facilities: Rest rooms; picnic areas; snack stand in the summer. The beach is wheelchair accessible, with a ramp down to the lake, and several of the bathrooms have access as well. Strollers are not recommended here.

Glimmerglass State Park. RD 2, Box 580, U.S. 20, Cooperstown, N.Y. 13326. (The park is located on County Route 31, seven miles north of Cooperstown, on the east side of Otsego Lake; watch for signs to Kabosus Road.) (601) 547–8662. Open year-round, daily, 9 am to 5 pm, for day use. Small use charge. Groups are welcome by reservation; camping is by reservation only.

James Fenimore Cooper called Otsego Lake "Glimmerglass" because of its serene beauty, and this lovely park certainly lives up to the name. You can swim and fish from lakeside spots, watch the sailboats go by, or enjoy some time with the kids in the playground areas. The six hundred-acre park has hiking trails as well as a short nature trail for younger naturalists. A picnic area is complete with fireplaces and even covered pavilions for bad weather, but we must warn you: because of the small number of campsites (only thirty-six) and the popularity of the lake, this campground fills up quickly in the summer. Even day-trippers should bring along portable chairs and tables. Still, the lake and the views make this park well worth the trip. If you are in Cooperstown during the winter months, there is a lot to do at the park. Five kilometers of trails snake throughout the park. The skiing is free, but you must bring your own equipment. When there is enough snow on the ground, kids will enjoy the snow-tubing offered on weekends (the tubes are free), and ice-skating is allowed on the lake (bring your own skates).

Facilities: Rest rooms; picnic areas with cooking fireplaces; snack stand; playground; campsites. On winter weekends, the rest rooms are open and there are hot drinks and snacks for sale. Those in wheelchairs and parents with strollers will find some limited-access areas in the park.

Maple Farm Tours. Otsego County is well known for its high maple syrup production, and there are many farms throughout the county that invite visitors to stop by and watch the sap being boiled down into syrup. The saphouses are usually small affairs that are steamy, hot, and sweet; there is nothing like the taste of warm maple syrup to make you and the kids feel like spring. Tours consist of a stop in the sugarbush (the maple trees) and a visit to the saphouse and, sometimes, the candy-making area. The tours are usually very informal, and we suggest that you have boots and a hat on before venturing out into the March woods and mud. The following farms offer tours in maple sap season, which usually runs from March to mid-April; because the sap run varies greatly from year to year, however, we suggest that you call before you go. In general, these farms are open every day during sap season: **Earl Aldrich and Sons** (New York 205, Oneonta, N.Y. [two miles north of New York 23]. [607] 432–5539. Open year-round for retail sales); **W. C. Arnold and Son** (New York 51, Burlington Flats, N.Y. [three miles north of town at the junction of Routes 19 and 51]. [607] 965–8944. Open year-round for retail sales); **Brodies Sugarbush** (Westford, N.Y. [Take New York 165 to County 34 and procede one mile up the road; watch for signs.] [607] 264–3225. Open year-round for retail sales); **Fassett Brothers** (U.S. 20, East Springfield, N.Y. [nine miles east of Richfield Springs.] [607] 264–8484. Open year-round for retail sales); **Brian Hackley** (Unadilla Forks Road, West Winfield, N.Y. [South of U.S. 20 between West Winfield and Bridgewater.] [315] 855–4138. Open year-round for retail sales); **Stannard's Maple Farm** (Stannard Hill Road, Roseboom, N.Y. [one mile from the post office in Roseboom; watch for signs.] [607] 264–3090. Open March and April only); and **Tyler Maple Farms** (Route 36, Westford, N.Y. [607] 638–9474. Open year-round for retail sales).

National Baseball Hall of Fame. Main Street, Cooperstown, N.Y. 13326. (607) 547–9988. Open year-round, daily, except Thanksgiving, Christmas, and New Year's Day. Hours: from May 1 to October 31, 9 am to 9 pm; and from November 1 to April 30, 9 am to 5 pm. Admission (children under seven are admitted free and there is a young-adult price). Group rates are available with advance reservation. A combination ticket is available in conjunction with the Farmer's Museum and the Fenimore House Museum (see the Farmer's Museum listing).

This is it: *the* mecca for all baseball lovers. Three floors are filled with thousands of pieces of baseball history, memorabilia, clothing, photos, cards, and equipment. Younger baseball fans will not want to leave. From the time you enter, where the hand-carved lifelike wooden statues of Babe Ruth (including his locker, uniform, and bat), Ted Williams, and other greats greet you, until the time you leave, everything you see will be related to great (and not-so-great) moments in America's favorite pastime. Pictures of the current players and uniforms from all of the major league teams in the Baseball Today room will gain the attention of young fans, as will the large baseball gum and tobacco card collection on display. The Hall of Fame gallery holds the plaques of the inductees (new ones are voted in every year), and there is a section devoted to the early Negro leagues. In a state-of-the-art theater, in the new wing, a short film explains all about the excitement and tradition of baseball. Kids who love numbers will enjoy the Great Moments room, which is filled with memorabilia and displays concerning the records set by the greatest players. There is also a chronological history of baseball that runs year by year to the present and contains many bats, balls, and gloves that were involved in the greatest plays. The museum's video machines let kids call up information on the Hall of Fame members. There are even displays about women in baseball, umpires, and the World Series. Throughout the summer a series of baseball films are screened in the Library Building, which faces Cooper Park. The National Baseball Hall of Fame is a comfortable museum, especially during a hot summer's afternoon, but be warned: it is always crowded on the Fourth of July, and in early-spring, when the Hall of Fame induction is held, you cannot get near the building, so call ahead if you are planning a trip and you think it may coincide with the induction celebrations.

Facilities: Rest rooms; gift shop, with lots of baseball memorabilia. The museum has wheelchair access; strollers are manageable as well.

Right next door to the museum is the **Doubleday Batting Range** ([607] 547–5168. Open Memorial Day weekend to Labor Day, daily, 10 am to 5 pm; and post–Labor Day to Columbus Day, weekends only, 10 am to 5 pm. Admission), which is not connected with the Hall of Fame but is an interesting commercial stop for baseball-hungry kids. There, you can use the same pitching machines used by the pros, check your pitching speed with radar, and have your photo taken in your favorite team's uniform.

Just off Main Street on Pioneer Alley, young baseball and softball lovers will adore the **Cooperstown Bat Company** (Mailing address: P.O. Box 415, Cooperstown, N.Y. 13326. [607] 547–2415. Open May to June and September to October, Monday through Saturday, 10 am to 5 pm; and July and August, Monday through Saturday, 10 am to 5 pm and 7 to 9 pm; and Sunday, noon to 4 pm. Free). This company specializes in making custom and fine bats and bat accessories, such as display racks. They issue commemorative bats, personalized bats, and autographed bats. Each bat is handmade, and you may see them working on a custom order if you stop in during the summer.

National Soccer Hall of Fame. 5–11 Ford Avenue, Oneonta, N.Y. 13820. (From New York 28 in Oneonta, watch for Ford Avenue junction and follow the signs to museum.) (607) 432–3351. Open June 1 to September 30, Monday through Saturday, 9 am to 7:30 pm; and Sunday, noon to 7:30 pm; and October 1 to May 31, Monday through Friday, 9 am to 5 pm; Saturday, 10 am to 5 pm; and Sunday, noon to 5 pm. Closed

Thanksgiving, Christmas, and New Year's Day. Admission. Group rates are available by advance reservation.

The history of soccer in America goes back to the 1860s and is filled with memorable moments and interesting personalities. The story of the sport is preserved in this museum, where photos, trophies, uniforms, and other soccer memorabilia are displayed. The museum will delight soccer aficionados of all ages, but a stop here is not recommended for toddlers or very young children. There are glass showcases filled with soccer equipment and photos that tell many stories, from the World Cup to the best goal tenders, the history of soccer, and soccer clubs in America. In June, during National Soccer Hall of Fame Week, players are honored with induction ceremonies, games, and special events. Throughout the summer you can watch one of the many games and tournaments played on site, and in the winter there are indoor activities for children as well as adults, including films and clinics. You may want to call before visiting, however, to see what events are planned. If you have a soccer lover at home, you may want to ask about the summer soccer camps that are sponsored by the museum.

Facilities: Rest rooms; gift shop. There is some access for wheelchairs; strollers can be maneuvered easily.

Pick-Your-Own Farms. Although much of Otsego County is dairyland, there are several pick-your-own vegetable and fruit farms that you can visit with the kids. Be sure to wear comfortable clothes, and bring sunscreen and a hat. You may bring your own containers or purchase them at the farms. Produce is weighed and paid for by the pound, but the cost is usually much lower than supermarket prices and the food is fresh. **Jamaica Dream Farm** (New York 7, Maryland, N.Y. [one mile west of town or three miles west of the Schenevus exit on I-88]. [607] 638–9785. Open May through October, daily, 10 am to 5 pm) has beans, peas, pumpkins, and tomatoes in season. **Paul Lhommedieu Farm** (U.S. 20, Richfield Springs, N.Y. [four miles west of the junction of Routes 28 and 20]. [315]

858–0214) is open as a roadside farm stand from June through March, but strawberries may be picked in June only. Call ahead for a crop report before you make the drive. **Snowden Hill Farms** (Raymond Fish Road, Hartwick, N.Y. [two-thirds mile north of the junction between New York 205 and New York 80; watch for the signs]. [607] 293–7959. Open May through October) has corn, pumpkins, and strawberries for picking in the appropriate seasons.

Bramanville Grist Mill Museum. Caverns Road, Bramanville, N.Y. (The museum is located one mile off New York 7.) (518) 827–5247 or 296–8448. Open May, June, September, and October, weekends only, 10 am to 5 pm; and July and August, Thursday through Tuesday, 10 am to 5 pm. Admission. Group tours are available by reservation.

This charming, bright-red working museum is a restored 1816 gristmill that still grinds corn with a water-powered millstone. There are three floors of exhibits here, all related to the history and art of milling, including stone dressing (preparing the stones for milling) grinding, and waterwheels. There is a short tour of the site, plus the miller in charge will answer questions about the works of the mill. Children will enjoy watching the wheels go around and listening to the rush of water as it pours into the mill through the elaborate series of gutters and races. Outside, there is a lovely picnic area along the millpond. A series of short hiking paths lead along the mill race. The overshot waterwheel located at the side of the mill is just as entertaining as the mill itself for younger visitors.

Facilities: Rest rooms; picnic area with tables. Not suitable for wheelchairs or strollers, although the mill grounds do have paths.

Cobleskill College Agricultural Tour. New York 7, Cobleskill, N.Y. 12043. (518) 234–5011. Open year-round, 10 am to 5 pm; call in advance for a guided tour, although a self-guided tour can be done at any time. Free.

Cobleskill College is part of the State University of New York (SUNY) system, and it contains more than fifty buildings over a 550-acre campus, including a 300-acre working farm. Cobleskill has a national reputation as a fine agricultural college. A tour of the campus will introduce children to the workings of a modern farm. Tour stops include a visit to the Beef

Barn, where there is cattle; a greenhouse with crops and flowers, a plant science building, a horse barn, and a dairy barn. Kids love the farm machinery on display, especially the tractors. Although this is a walking tour, children as young as four should be able to manage it easily. There is a small fishery and wildlife museum on the campus with displays and exhibits of local plants and animals, but the museum is open only when school is in session (so it is closed during the summer and holiday weeks). Because many of the tour stops are actual work areas, you may have a chance to see milking or harvesting in progress, but what you see depends on the season and the time of day. The campus is lovely, and this is a nice stop for kids interested in farm life. Note that there is a touch-and-see nature trail on the campus that was designed especially for the visually impaired; ask on the campus for directions to the trail.

Facilities: Rest rooms; gift shop (in the student center); picnic area. Wheelchairs and strollers are manageable on the campus.

Fox Creek Flea Market. New York 443, West Berne, N.Y. 12023. (The market is ten miles east of Schoharie on New York 443; watch for signs.) (518) 872–2510. Open Memorial Day weekend through September, Sunday only, 9 am to 6 pm. Admission only on holiday weekends.

If you've been wanting to stop at a flea market but were afraid the kids wouldn't be interested, a stop at Fox Creek will change your mind. This flea market has everything there is to be found, from fine antiques to kitsch, along with plenty of entertainment for the kids. Rows of dealers' tables (up to two hundred dealers may be there) are set up both outside and inside, and the market is held rain or shine. There are plenty of things for kids to look at, eat, and buy. There are also some permanent exhibits that, while not of museum quality, are fun enough to please the younger flea-market goer. The display of hand-painted Easter eggs is fascinating. One tree alone holds more than nine hundred eggs, each set into nursery rhyme and historical settings. It's the largest display of its kind in the

United States. There is an exhibit of old-fashioned hob-
byhorses, carriages, and wagons, plus a Yesteryear Museum
with a blacksmith shop, a one-room schoolhouse, and costumed
mannequins. A small zoo holds ponies, goats, and exotic birds,
and there is often entertainment on hand. Parents should note
that an auction is also held at noon; kids can attend if they are
quiet, but we don't recommend it for children.

Facilities: Rest rooms; picnic area; snack stands. The site is
wheelchair and stroller accessible. Because you will spend a lot
of time outdoors there in the good weather and there is little
shade, a hat is necessary.

Howe Caverns. P.O. Box 107, New York 7, Howe's Cave, N.Y.
12092. (Take Exit 22 from I-88 and follow the signs.) (518)
296–8990. Open year-round, daily, 9 am to 6 pm, except
Thanksgiving, Christmas, and New Year's Day. Admission.
Group rates are available by advance reservation.

One of the oldest caves for tourists in the Northeast, Howe
Caverns has been introducing people to the underground since
the nineteenth-century. Discovered by a local farmer in 1842,
today you can still see what millions of years have created underneath your feet. The tour begins with an elevator ride from
the visitors center. The elevator descends 156 feet to the sub-
terranean walkway that takes you through the colorfully lighted
caves. The temperature is a constant 52 degrees year-round; it
is both eerie and fascinating in the caves. Children will enjoy
seeing the Bridal Altar, with its heart-shaped stone (more than
two hundred marriages have taken place here); some unique
wall formations, including the Old Witch; the Chinese Pagoda
in the Titan's Temple; and the Stone Organ, which emits
strange sounds. But the best part of the tour is the boat ride on
the river, where the guides will turn off the lights and let you
experience total darkness (the caves are all brightly lighted otherwise). You should bring a sweater, because it is damp in the
caves and the tours last an hour and a half. In general, kids
enjoy the rock formations and tunnels, but anyone who is claus-
trophobic may want to wait on the surface. If you visit in the

winter, spend some time on the cross-country ski trails, which are some of the most extensive in the county and are quite scenic with their overviews of the lovely Cobleskill Valley. There are twenty kilometers of groomed trails that range from novice to expert. The trails open at 9 am; rentals are available for adults and children. Overnight accommodations are available at the motel on the site.

Facilities: Rest rooms; three gift shops (they have wonderful fudge for sale); picnic area with tables; snack bar; restaurant; motel. The caves are neither wheelchair accessible nor stroller friendly.

Iroquois Indian Museum. North Main Street, Box 158, Schoharie, N.Y. 12157. (The museum is located on Cavern Road, three miles east of Cobleskill off New York 7.) (518) 234–2276. Open May, June, September, and October, Tuesday, Wednesday, Friday, and Saturday, 10 am to 5 pm; and Sunday, noon to 5 pm; and July 1 to Labor Day, daily except Thursday, 10 am to 5 pm. Admission (kids under eighteen are admitted free if accompanied by an adult). Group rates and tours are available by reservation.

This colorful museum is housed in a temporary structure while the new main building is erected, but it contains a marvelous collection of ancient and modern Iroquois art and artifacts. The Iroquois, an American Indian confederacy consisting of the Mohawks, Oneida, Onondaga, Cayuga, Seneca, and Tuscarora, were the most powerful tribe in the region. The self-guided museum tour takes visitors through a series of displays, which include an archeological dig, Iroquois creation myths, crafts, and artwork. There are shelves and displays filled with beadwork, basketry, paintings, soapstone carvings, cornhusk weavings, and costumes. Silver glints in another section, while in another there are ceremonial objects such as pipes and clothing. Changing exhibits have highlighted, for example, living Iroquois artists and their works. A visit here on a summer weekend will often include the delights of a traditional storyteller or dollmaker. The gift shop deserves special men-tion because it stocks only Iroquois arts, crafts, and publications; nice gifts can be found for all ages and budgets. School groups may request special programs about the modern Iroquois. A new museum building is under construction, so we suggest that you call ahead to find out which site is operative.

Facilities: Rest room; gift shop. The museum is wheelchair accessible; strollers are manageable.

New York Power Authority Visitors Center. New York 30, North Blenheim, N.Y. 12131. (Watch for the signs on New York 30.) (518) 827–6121 or (607) 588–6061. Open year-round, daily. Hours: late-June to Labor Day, 10 am to 7:30 pm; and post–Labor Day to mid-June, 10 am. to 5 pm. Free. Group tours are available.

The New York Power Authority Pumped Storage Project is just across the reservoir from the Visitors Center and although it isn't open to the public, the Visitors Center is. A small energy museum there is a fun, hands-on experience especially for children ages eight to twelve. Throughout the self-guided tour (you can request a guided tour), there are lots of hands-on energy exhibits to try: spin a wheel to make electricity; fire a water pistol to turn the pistons and measure the water's force; touch a computer screen and answer questions about modern energy use. There are also some interesting fossils that date back 380 million years and were discovered during the excavation for the power project. A short film explains how pump storage works: they pump the water uphill during the day and drop it through tubes into turbines at night to produce a clean, recycled source of energy. Parents should note that this is one museum where the kids can make noise and play with the exhibits and not have a guard reprimand them. And there is a lovely picnic area overlooking the reservoir. Special events weekends are held monthly and include a variety of indoor and outdoor activities for the entire family. Past Winter Festivals have offered ice- and chain-saw sculpting, live wolves, make-your-own birdfeeders, snow-tubing, hayrides, and cross-country skiing.

Facilities: Rest rooms; picnic area with tables.

If you are in the area, there are several other places of interest. **Lansing Manor House** is located right next to the Visitors Center. (Open from Memorial Day to Columbus Day, 10 am to 5 pm; closed Tuesday. No wheelchair accessibility. Free.) This eighteenth-century home, once owned by a prominent Schoharie County citizen, has been restored to its original grandeur. There are guides to take you through the house. At **Minekill Falls Overlook** (New York 30, between Mine Kill and Blenheim. Open daily, weather permitting, 10 am until dusk. Free) you can park and walk along a path to the overlook, where the falls drop dramatically to the stream. This is not a good walk for the youngest sightseer, however, since it is uphill on the way back and is about a quarter-mile trek. If you want to picnic at an unusual site, try the **longest single-span covered bridge in the world,** which is located just north of the Power Authority entrance in Blenheim (the bridge will be on your right). The remains of a **petrified forest** (the oldest known fossils in the world) are found on County Route 342 off New York 30 in Gilboa (watch for the county road markers). The forest is really only a pocket-sized park, but there is a bronze marker at the site and it is an unusual stop for kids who are interested in the days of dinosaurs.

George Landis Arboretum. Esperance, N.Y. 12066. (From the center of town, follow the signs to the arboretum.) (518) 875–6935. Open April to October, daily, 9 am until dusk. Free. Group tours are by reservation.

This sixty-acre arboretum is home to hundreds of rare shrubs and trees from around the world. Founded in 1951, the site contains plantings, gardens, and pathways that are lined with trees from Russia, Japan, China, and elsewhere. The short walking paths are well marked, as are the plants, so you will enjoy spending an hour or so identifying trees with the kids. It's really peaceful and lovely on a warm afternoon. The kids will enjoy running around and letting off some steam. The arboretum offers special children's workshops in botany and nature studies throughout the summer, but you should call ahead for the latest schedule.

Facilities: Rest rooms; picnic area. This site is not recommended for wheelchairs or strollers.

Mine Kill State Park. New York 30, Blenheim, N.Y. 12131. (518) 827–6111. Open year-round, daily, 8 am to dusk. Summer pool hours: July and August, daily 10 am to 6 pm. There is a small day-use fee spring through fall for the park.

This excellent day-use park (no overnight camping is allowed) has not really been discovered, so it is often quiet, even on holiday weekends. Located on the Schoharie Creek, which is part of a reservoir system, the park overlooks the water and offers dozens of hiking trails, covered picnic areas, and other seasonal delights. The summer offers pool swimming (complete with locker rooms), snack bars, and sunbathing areas. A boat launching ramp for the reservoir is open from May through Labor Day, and there are cross-country skiing and snowmobile trails in winter. Kids will enjoy walking the trails, which wind down through the forest to the water's edge.

Facilities: Rest rooms; locker room; picnic areas with tables; snack bars. Limited wheelchair accessibility.

Old Stone Fort. North Main Street, Schoharie, N.Y. 12157. (Watch for signs on New York 30.) (518) 295–7192. Open April 30 to Memorial Day and Labor Day to October 31, Tuesday through Saturday, 10 am to 5 pm; and Sunday, noon to 5 pm; and Memorial Day through Labor Day, daily, 10 am to 5 pm. Admission (children under five are admitted free). Group tours may be arranged by advance reservation.

The Old Stone Fort is a marvelous museum complex that will give young visitors a glimpse into Schoharie County's past. There is the fort itself, which withstood an attack by the British during the American Revolution in an unsuccessful attempt to rout two hundred settlers. It's done up in the old curiosity style: rows of glass cases alternate with open exhibits of some odd, quirky items. An old hand-pump fire wagon from the eighteenth century is there—it is the oldest one in America—as are foot warmers, farming tools, bear traps, musical instruments, and lots of other items. There are specimens from a nearby fossil forest and tools from prehistoric cultures, along with a complete one-room schoolhouse and a British cannonball that was fired in 1780 in an attempt to gain control of the fort. Also in the complex is the William Badgley Museum (just across the street) which houses a re-created blacksmith shop, farm equipment, and the car owned by the first female mayor in New York State. There is a small burial ground outside the fort with lots of early tombstones, including an unusual glass marker. Kids will like the unstructured feeling to the museum and the jumble of collections there. Stone Fort Days, held the first weekend of October, features lots of costumed militiamen and camp followers who reenact revolutionary war skirmishes. The music, old-fashioned food, and camp reenactments will please children of all ages, and we suggest that, if possible, you coordinate your trip with this weekend.

Facilities: Rest rooms; small bookshop. The site is not wheelchair accessible. Those with strollers may be able to manage, but there is a staircase.

Pick-Your-Own Farms. Schoharie County is famous for its farms (which, as a matter of fact, produce a lot of vegetables for baby food companies), and you can take advantage of the harvests by picking your own produce. Wear hats in the summer and don't forget the sunscreen. Bring your own boxes or baskets for picking or buy the containers at the farms. **Bohringer's Fruit Farm** (New York 30, Middleburgh, N.Y. 12122 [one and a half miles south of town]. [518] 827–5783. Open June through December) has strawberry picking in June, but you must call ahead for crop reports. They also have nectarines, peaches, plums, and apples, all grown in their orchards. **Sharon Orchards** (45 Chestnut Street, Sharon Springs, N.Y. 13459 [two miles southwest of Sharon Springs on County Road 55]. [518] 284–2510. Open year-round for tours. Free) is open for pick-your-own apples in September, although their farm stand and tours are available all year. **Pick a Pumpkin Pumpkin Patch** (Esperance, N.Y. 12066. [Take I-88 to the Central Bridge, go two miles north, and follow the signs to the patch.] Open September through November. Free tours) has pumpkins and corn for the picking. **Westheimer's Carrot Barn** (New York 30, Schoharie, N.Y. [One mile north of Schoharie.] [518] 295–7139. Open from April to December. Call ahead for picking hours, as they vary according to crop and season) is run by Dr. Ruth's cousins. This huge barn complex is really a farm stand that sells a lot of local produce—including, of course, carrots—by the ounce or by the barrel, but you can pick your own raspberries, asparagus, beans, and rhubarb. In the shop you may find lettuce, apples, onions, turnips, potatoes, and more, along with local honeys and maple products. A bakery and coffee shop have freshly baked carrot cake, and there is even a small carrot carousel for the children. The place is bustling with farm activity and is colorful, with lots of carrot and cartoon cutouts on the walls. It's a nice country refreshment stop for all ages.

Putnam Maple Farm. Beard's Hollow Road, Richmondville, N.Y. 12149. (Take I-88 to New York 7 south, which becomes Beard's Hollow Road; follow the signs. [518] 294–7278). Open from Thanksgiving to Christmas (gift shop only), March, and April, Thursday through Sunday, 10 am to 5 pm. Free. Group tours are by advance reservation.

We suggest a visit to this farm during the sap season, from mid-March to mid-April, when the sweet clouds of steam from the saphouse show that maple syrup is on its way. Putnam's is one of the largest producers of maple products open to the public during the season. Located in the valley of Beard's Hollow, once a large rural community, the maple farm gives tours of the kitchen, where maple products such as syrup, candy, and cream are produced (sample tastings are included!). Outside, in the saphouse, you will watch as the clear sap is boiled down in huge wood-fired evaporators. The sugarbush (the trees where the sap is tapped) is just outside the buildings, so kids will have a chance to watch the entire process, from collection to candy. There is a really unusual and enjoyable plus at Putnam's: on Sunday during the sap season they hold old-fashioned pancake breakfasts, complete with pancakes, sausages, apple sauce, and, of course, maple syrup. Because the sap season varies, however, you must call ahead about the breakfasts.

Facilities: Rest rooms; gift shop, with many maple products. This stop is not suggested for those in wheelchairs or parents with strollers, so call ahead if these are required.

There are other maple syrup producers and saphouses in Schoharie County, but many are run on an intermittent basis; however, the following farms are open every year. The **Buck Hill Farm** (Fuller Road, Jefferson, N.Y. 12093. [Take New York 10 to Jefferson and watch for signs to the farm.] [607] 652–7980. Open year-round, but weekends are best. Free tours) has a complete maple production setup, including a candy-making area. There are tours of the sugarbush, saphouse, and shop during maple season and they will even mail any gifts you buy. **Maple Hill Farms** (Grovenors Corners Road, Cobleskill, N.Y. 12043 [three miles northeast of town at the junction of Crommie Road and Grovenors]. [518] 234–4858. Open daily in March, April, and December, and weekends other times of the year. Free tours) also stocks a full line of maple products, and they offer short tours of the farm as well.

Secret Caverns. Cavern Road, P.O. Box 88, Cobleskill, N.Y. 12043. (The caverns are located five miles east of Cobleskill, between New York 7 and U.S. 20 on Cavern Road.) (518) 296–8558. Open every day, April 15 through November 1. Hours: May, June, and September, 9 am to 6 pm; July and August, 9 am to 8 pm; and October and November, 10 am to 5 pm. Admission. Group rates and tours are available by advance reservation.

This is a totally different underground experience when

compared with Howe Caverns (see earlier listing for that site). The two cave companies have been competing for years, and Howe wins hands down as the more sophisticated tourist attraction. However, if you and the older kids are looking for somewhat more adventure and Tom Sawyer–style exploration, then by all means, stop at tiny Secret Caverns (don't bring younger kids unless they like to walk). The half-mile tour beings not with an elevator ride but with a walk down more than 130 steps to the cave floor. Then you trek alongside the underground river to see lighted wonders such as Alligator, the Cavern's Monster, City of the Future, and Wonderland. (City of the Future was once known as City Hit by Atomic Bomb, but public sentiment forced a change.) The rock formations are all lighted and there is a wonderful misty one-hundred-foot waterfall that is very impressive. Kids will love the stalagmites and stalactites (stalac*tites* stick *tight* to the ceiling walls—that's how you tell the difference) and the colorful wall deposits, called flowstone. The caverns are a constant fifty degrees, so bring along a sweater for the forty-five-minute tour.

Facilities: Rest rooms; motel. This site is not wheelchair or stroller accessible.

Max V. Shaul State Park. New York 30, Fultonham, N.Y. 12071. (Watch for signs.) (518) 827–4711. Open year-round, 8 am until dusk. Use fee is per vehicle. Group rates and camping are available by advance reservation.

This small, wild park is only fifty-seven acres, but it packs a lot into its space. The park sits along the Schoharie Creek, which is renowned for its fishing, and is the perfect recreational stop for a summer's day when you are traveling with kids. Campsites are available for overnight use—they have a joint ticket with Mine Kill State Park for campers (see separate listing earlier in this chapter)—and there are barbecue pits for day-trippers as well. Short nature trails filled with ferns, plants, and birds let you take a quiet walk through the woods with the kids. The park also has playgrounds, and movies are offered on Friday evening in the summer. Cross-country ski trails are open in the winter, but you must bring your own equipment. We recommend this park as a nice stop for a picnic or to get away from the summer tourist bustle at some of the larger parks in the region. If this park doesn't suit you, try going north another mile or so on New York 30. You'll find a charming picnic and rest stop along the creek on your right.

Facilities: Rest rooms (wheelchair accessible); picnic areas; playgrounds; nature trails; campsites.

ALBANY, SCHENECTADY, & RENSSELAER COUNTIES: THE CAPITAL REGION

Albany Institute of History and Art. 125 Washington Avenue, Albany, N.Y. 12210. (518) 463–4478. Open year-round, Tuesday, Wednesday, and Friday, 10 am to 4:45 pm; Thursday, 10 am to 8 pm; and weekends, noon to 5 pm. Closed on major holidays. Free. Group tours are by reservation.

This museum was founded in 1791 as a repository for science and history materials. Today it is housed in an elegant building that offers something of interest to all ages. The main floor contains many rooms filled with Hudson River valley furniture, art, and documents dating from the seventeenth-century founding fathers and mothers, who were Dutch. Colorful, large pieces of furniture, such as the handpainted *kas*, "wardrobe," offer attractive windows to the past. Older kids, especially those who have read about Peter Stuyvesant and Henry Hudson, will enjoy seeing the paintings, coins, weapons, and other artifacts that were new when New York State was very young. Upstairs there are several art galleries with fine collections of glassware and ceramics, but it is the basement rooms where even the younger kids will be astounded. The favored stop is the Egyptian room, which houses mummies (nicknamed by local schoolchildren) of people and animals, along with many smaller items from pharaonic tombs. There are also some statues and examples of tomb wall paintings, and although the room is quite small, the exhibit is packed with an *Indiana Jones* feeling. Changing exhibits throughout the year have included Japanese art, the history of family life in Albany, and Hudson River artists. Special programs and workshops for families and children are a regular part of the museum's offerings. Kids may be able to make their own Valentines, try their hand at creating some Egyptian art or painting Easter eggs, or take part in a Mother's Day treasure hunt. Teachers should note that special lectures can be arranged for classes if reservations are made in advance.

Facilities: Rest rooms; gift shop; restaurant. There is handicapped accessibility; parents with strollers may have to climb some stairs.

Just down the block from the institute is the **Harmanus Bleeker Center** (19 Dove Street, Albany, N.Y. 12210. [518] 465–2044 or 463–4478. Open Wednesday through Friday, 9:30 am to 4 pm; and Saturday, noon to 3 pm. Closed holiday weekends. Small fee for classes), the applied arts division of the institute, where kids can take creative arts classes in painting, printmaking, movie discussions, and other areas. The center even sponsors a greeting card design contest. It's a nice stop if you are going to be in the area for a few days.

Amtrak Train Station. Herrick Street, Rensselaer, N.Y. 12144. (The station is just over the Dunn Memorial Bridge.) (518) 462–5763. Open year-round, daily, 7 am to 11 pm. Free (but there is, of course, a charge for train rides).

Kids love trains, and there is a conveniently located station in the capital region where you can take a short train ride to Saratoga Springs, Schenectady, Hudson, or Rhinecliff. The views along the Hudson River are magnificent any time of year, especially when there are boats and ships chugging up and down the river, but the foliage makes for a really spectacular trip in autumn. Even if you don't take a train ride, you can watch the trains come and go from the observation area near the tracks. The kids will enjoy getting up close to the tracks, seeing the bustle and color of train crews, and hearing the whistles and bells. Note that you should time your visit before or after the morning and evening rush hours.

Facilities: Rest rooms. Wheelchairs may be accommodated on trains but call in advance for assistance.

Behind-the-Scenes Tours. Several local companies offer tours of their factories, which range from costume-making facilities to cannon production lines. Since companies seem to prefer taking around groups rather than families or individuals, we recommend that you call ahead to make plans for a tour and to get specific directions to the site. Wheelchair accessibility and stroller use can be a problem at some commercial sites, so call if this is a concern. **The Costumer** (1020–1030 Barrett Street, Schenectady, N.Y. 12305. [518] 374–7442. Open year-round, weekdays, 10 am to 6 pm; and Saturdays, 10 am to 5 pm. Groups and individuals must make arrangements in advance for a free tour. Not wheelchair accessible) is a real treat, and children age six and over will be delighted with the magnificent costumes and mascots here. You can watch while costumes are manufactured for an array of cartoon-type characters. On display are costumes for Michael Mouse, the Smurfs, and a character similar to Big Bird. In a magic shop, demonstrations are given for groups, and the gift shop is filled with all kinds of special tricks, makeup kits, and gadgets. Food lovers will enjoy a tour of **Freihofer's Baking Company** (Prospect Road, Albany, N.Y. 12206. [518] 438–6631. Wheelchair accessible), which has free tours for both groups and individuals, but reservations must be made in advance and children must be age seven or older. The tour includes a look at how bread is made, from beginning to end. The mixing process of the dough in the large commercial mixers is noisy fun for the younger set. Watch hot dog and hamburger buns being shaped, taste the bread, and, at the end of the tour, receive a free box of Freihofer's chocolate chip cookies.

Watervliet Arsenal (Route 32 and 9th Street, Watervliet, N.Y. 12189–4050. [Take I-87 to the Watervliet exit and get on Broadway, then take New York 32 and follow the signs.] [518] 266–5805 or 266–5868. Open Tuesday through Saturday, except holidays, 10 am to 3 pm. Free. Wheelchair accessible) does not offer tours of the arsenal itself (for security reasons), but its museum is an unusual stop for children six and over. The museum traces the history of cannons in the United States. Several fascinating examples of guns and artillery are on display, including one of George Washington's cannon and several Civil War cannons. There are also photos and a video on the cannon-manufacturing process. Outside you'll find a full-size tank on display. The museum itself is one of the few cast-iron buildings still in existence. Although not for everyone, many older children are interested in military history and will enjoy this stop. **Proctor's Theater** (432 State Street, Schenectady, N.Y. 12305. [518] 382–3884. Open year-round, daily except holidays, 9 am to 5 pm. Free. Tours are for groups only. Reservations are required) has backstage tours. You will get a glimpse of the inside world of the theater, including dressing rooms, scenery areas, lighting, and a small memorabilia display.

Older children who are interested in planes will enjoy a complete tour of the **Stratton Air National Guard Base** (Schenectady County Airport, Scotia, N.Y. 12302. [518] 381–7431. Open year-round, Monday through Friday, 7:30 am to 4 pm. Free. Tour arrangements are by advance reservation. Wheelchair accessible). The highlight of the visit is being able to go inside one of the aircraft, but you will also see the firehouse, fire trucks, and even the life-support systems that are used in the event of a plane going down. A slide presentation of Antarctica is shown (this military base supports other bases throughout the world), followed by a question-and-answer period. **WMHT Television** (17 Fern Avenue, Schenectady, N.Y. 12306. [518] 356–1700. Open year-round, 9 am to 5 pm. Free. Tours are by appointment and are for groups of kids ten and older) gives hour-long tours of its master control room, working studios (where you may see a program being produced), and graphics room (where animation is demonstrated and explained). At the end of the tour you get a chance to see yourself on television. A guide describes the entire production process. Kids who are really interested in television production and who live in the area may want to ask about the volunteer opportunities the studio offers to kids.

Biking. There are a couple of excellent places to go bicycling in the capital region. If your kids don't have a place to bike that is free of traffic, try **Erastus Corning Riverfront Preserve Park** (Take the Colonie Street exit from I-787 and follow the signs to the bike path). This park's bikeway runs parallel to the Hudson River, so you'll have the additional fun of watching the boat traffic go by as you bike. This is also the start of the **Mohawk-Hudson Bikeway** (Open year-round. Free), a fifty-five-mile long bike path that links the counties of Albany and Schenectady and runs near the Hudson and Mohawk Rivers. Many access points, parking areas, and rest stops, with rest rooms and picnic areas, are located along the bikeway. You don't have to bike the full length of the bikeway. In the winter cross-country skiing, snowshoeing, and hiking are allowed along the length of the path. For a complete tour map of the bikeway write to: Riverspark, 97 Mohawk Street, Cohoes, N.Y. 12047, or call (518) 237–7999.

Central Park. Fehr Avenue, downtown Schenectady. (The park is located off State Street [New York 5].) (518) 382–5151. Open year-round, daily, dawn to dusk. Free.

This 372-acre city park, complete with lake, playing fields, swimming pool, tennis courts, and playgrounds, is a gem. Young children will enjoy feeding the numerous ducks (bring your own bread), the toddler playground with smaller equipment, the train ride, and the swimming pond. Older kids will like the boats that can be rented for rides on the pond. Visitors of all ages will be delighted by the exquisite rose gardens, where more than forty-four hundred rosebushes bloom in a three-acre garden. Be sure to visit in June, when the gardens are at their peak.

Facilities: Rest rooms; picnic area; snack bars. Those in Wheelchairs can manage on the pathways, as can parents with strollers, but there is no wheelchair access to the rest rooms.

Children's Theater. Children's theater is alive and well in the Albany region, and there are two outstanding performing arts centers that have special children's programming. Because each season is different, you must call ahead to find out the performance schedules and prices. The **Empire State Institute for the Performing Arts (ESIPA)** (Empire State Plaza, Albany,

N.Y. 12223. (518) 443–5222. [To find the plaza, take the Empire Plaza exit from I-787; the plaza is bound by Swan, Madison, State, and Eagle streets.] Open year-round) is housed in one of the most unique theater buildings in the world: the Egg, as it is affectionately known, is a half-round building placed on a pedestal, and it is sure to intrigue adults and children alike. There are two theaters inside, plus a wraparound lounge that offers an excellent view of the Plaza. Children's programming in the past has included *The Pied Piper, Peter Pan, Sicilian Marionettes,* and *Once Upon a Mattress.* In addition to the shows, there is a series of slide shows and talks about the making of a theatrical production that is certain to enchant a star-struck adolescent. These are offered on Thursday at noon, prior to the opening of each season's productions. The presentations are free and are located at the main theater lobby. **Proctor's Theater** (432 State Street, Schenectady, N.Y. 12305. [518] 382–3884 or 346–6204 [box office]) was completed in 1926 and is furnished in the gilt and marble grandeur of old vaudeville. There is a full season of theater, year-round, for all ages, including holiday presentations like *The Nutcracker, A Christmas Carol,* and the Christmas show, which is the upstate answer to Radio City Music Hall (the screen is the largest in the Northeast outside of Radio City). Later in the season watch for the famous magician Harry Blackstone, who does all of those traditional magician's tricks, like sawing a lady in half and making things appear like, well, . . . magic. On Thursday there are silent films accompanied by Wurlitzer organ music—great fun for older kids. A film festival each summer offers some children's films, too, and there is a complete selection of children's theater programs year-round.

Crailo. 9½ Riverside Avenue, Rensselaer, N.Y. 12144. (From Albany or I-787, take U.S. 20 east to Rensselaer. At the first traffic light, turn right and go one and a half blocks to the site.) (518) 463–8738. Open April to December, Wednesday through Saturday, 10 am to 5 pm; and Sunday, 1 to 5 pm. Closed Monday and Tuesday *except* Memorial Day, Independence Day, and Labor Day. Free. Groups are accommodated by advance reservation only.

Crailo was a Dutch home built in 1705 by the Van Rensselaer family. It soon became the center of a vast manorial estate that contained more than fifteen hundred acres of land. Although the building has undergone many changes through the centuries, serving at various times as a fort—there are even two gun ports, which were cut into the walls when the building was used as a fort in the 1700s—a home, a boarding school, a church rectory, and even a cinder block factory, today the restored building contains exhibits concerning the history of Dutch culture in the Hudson River valley. Through displays of art, furniture, and other items, young visitors can see how the Dutch lived, slept, worked, and ate (school groups can arrange for a cooking demonstration). While the museum is lively enough, very young children will not be entertained unless they have a strong interest in history or in everyday life of long ago. If the weather is warm, don't forget to step out into the herb garden. It was there, tradition has it, that in 1758 a British surgeon composed a funny song about American soldiers and then set the words to an old drinking tune. The result is still sung, and it is known as "Yankee Doodle."

Facilities: Rest rooms. The site is only partially accessible to wheelchairs. Parents using strollers will have a hard time in the house.

Empire State Plaza. Albany, N.Y. 12223. (To find the plaza, take the Empire Plaza exit from I-787; the plaza is bounded by Swan, Madison, State,and Eagle streets.) (518) 474–5877. Open year-round, daily. Free. Group tours are by reservation only.

The Empire State Plaza consists of a series of office and cultural buildings along a glorious mall that has achieved world renown as an outdoor arts center. Although there are many buildings, indoor snack areas, and gift shops, the plaza is really an urban park, indoors and outdoors—a park for all seasons. It is a great place to take the children because there's lots to do year-round and there is enough open space so that kids will keep themselves entertained. Scattered across the plaza, or the esplanade, are a series of reflection pools, where kids are allowed to ice skate in the winter. Roller skates are for rent for skating on the walkways in the summer. Along the mall there are plantings, modern sculpture, fountains, waterfalls, and an excellent play area known as the Children's Place, complete with outdoor activity areas, a sandbox, and a separate toddlers' area. Next to the play area is an environmental sculpture called the *Labyrinth,* where you can sit on benches and take a break from the walk. The New York State Vietnam Memorial is in the courtyard in the Justice Building. This quiet park contains memorial panels to the people who served in the war from New York State. Inside the concourse you will find fine examples of modern art, which are on permanent display and will serve to introduce older kids to colorful canvases by great masters. For a bird's-eye view of it all, head for the observation deck in the Corning Tower. (Take the elevator to the forty-second floor. The deck is free and is open from 9 am to 4 pm every day.) You can see the Catskills, the Adirondacks, and the Berkshire Mountains on a clear day. At the end of the mall, near the huge stairway that leads up to the New York State Museum, concerts and special events are held throughout the summer, among them, an Independence Day celebration, a Tulip Festival, a Snow Expo, and a Northeastern Wildlife Expo. From early-May to mid-November (on Wednesday and Friday from 11 am to 2 pm, near the State Capitol Building in the South Mall; [518] 457–1762), farmers participate in the Empire State Plaza Farmers Market. There, trucks and tables are filled with fresh fruits, vegetables, and herbs from local farms. Kids will love sampling whatever treats are available. (Note that there are separate entries in this chapter for the New York State Capitol and the New York State Museum, which are also located in the Empire State Plaza.)

Facilities: Rest rooms; gift shop; three cafeterias; restaurant; pushcart food concessions; rental for ice- and roller-skating. There are many shops inside the concourse. The plaza is wheelchair accessible and stroller friendly.

Five Rivers Environmental Center. Game Farm Road, Delmar, N.Y. 12054. (The center is seven miles south of Albany, off New York 443 in Delmar; watch for signs.) (518) 457–6092 or 453–1806. Open year-round, dawn to dusk. *Interpretive center:* Open April through October, Monday through Saturday, 9 am to 4:30 pm; and Sunday, 1 to 5 pm; and November through March, Monday through Saturday, 9 am to 4:30 pm. Free. Groups are accommodated by reservation only.

A unique nature center, Five Rivers offers a wide variety of programs, hikes, and tours for all ages of children. Named after the five large rivers nearby, Five Rivers is a great place to spend hours exploring the outdoors on a nice day. A series of self-guided nature trails are specially designed for younger children. Wooden walkways let you explore pond areas, trees, marshes, and woodlands, and there are free guide brochures for each walk, which run in length from an eighth of a mile to two miles. A special feature is the cassette tapes and players that can be borrowed for each walk, offering a recorded explanation of what is seen at each numbered point of interest. The trails include stops at beaver dams, woodlots, orchards, fields, wildflower meadows, and streambanks, and the tapes tell you about erosion, animal habits, and ecosystems. There is even an herb garden where you can spend time identifying the herbs and their history and uses. Inside the interpretive center, kids will see exhibits about local wildlife and fauna, including many touchable samples something that is rare among museums; Archimedes the owl is a special favorite with the kids. Many special events are held in the center throughout the year. Week-long Family Fun programs run all summer and offer guided walks, projects, and birdwatching. The center participates in the annual New Year's Day bird count for the Audubon Society, and you are welcome to head out with your binoculars and help out. In the winter there is maple sugaring, snow tracking, and learning about signs of the season; in the fall there are walks in the wetlands and nature's harvest workshops; spring and summer bring animal identification, pond visits, and tree identification classes. While you are at the center, don't forget to ask for copies of the nature worksheets and game pages for the kids to use on the trails. The center also offers large-print guides for the visually impaired.

Facilities: Rest rooms; picnic area. There is a lot of wheelchair access both inside and outside the interpretive center (the Woodlot Trail is wheelchair accessible), and the site is stroller friendly (at least along most of the wooden trails).

Grafton Lakes State Park. Box 163, Grafton, N.Y. 12082. (The park is on New York 2, fourteen miles east of Troy.) (518) 279-1155. Open year-round, dawn to dusk. Small use charge in the summer only.

This state park offers a complete selection year-round of sports and outdoor activities for all ages. We recommend this as one of the best parks in the Albany area for a day trip, since the kids will be kept busy there and parents will enjoy the beautiful lakes and forests. The park is more than two thousand acres in size, and it contains a full range of playgrounds, ball fields, and tennis courts. There are four lakes, but swimming is permitted only at Long Lake, which has some lovely sandy beaches and is wheelchair accessible. There are boat rentals available or you can bring along your own canoe or sailboat. Three out of the four lakes are stocked with trout, bass, and pickerel, so be sure to bring the kids' poles along (you do need a license for fishing there). A nice touch at this park is the short (three-eighths-mile) nature trail, a self-guided walk using a brochure through forest, pond, and wildlife habitats. (Pick up the brochure at the beginning of the path.) Throughout the summer special events are offered—shows, games, storytelling, and more. In the winter there are special warming huts, complete with toilets, so that you can cross-country ski, ice skate, and sled in comfort (but you must bring your own equipment).

Facilities: Rest rooms; lockers (at the poolhouse); picnic areas; snack bars (in the summer only). This is a park, so strollers can be maneuvered in some places but not in others; the same applies to wheelchairs, although the bathrooms and the lake are accessible.

Hoffman's Playland. U.S. 9, Latham, N.Y. 12110. (the park is located one mile south of the Latham Circle Mall.) (518) 785–3842. Open April through September, daily 10 am to 5 pm. Admission. Group discounts are available.

This thirty-five-year-old amusement park is a tradition in the Albany area: it is not crammed full of the latest technology, but it offers a nice place to escape with kids two years old and up for an afternoon of fun and rides. There are fewer than two dozen rides there; these include a carousel, boats, bumper cars, a ferris wheel, helicopters, a train, a small roller coaster, and a caterpillar. Older kids have a few rides of their own, such as the Tilt-a-Whirl, the Scrambler, and the Paratrooper. A large arcade has some more up-to-date entertainments. There is a miniature golf course adjacent to the site as well (there is an additional charge for this). This is a small, clean, enjoyable park that is nicely landscaped and offers a welcome exchange from the mega-amusement parks.

Facilities: Rest rooms; gift shop; picnic area. A snack bar is next door at the miniature golf course. The site is wheelchair accessible and stroller friendly.

Hudson River Cruises. Several companies offer trips up and down the Hudson River, but most of them are not geared toward children. We did find two, however, that offer weekend and luncheon cruises that welcome families and are not too long in length. **Dutch Apple Cruises** (1668 Julianne Drive, Castleton, N.Y. 12033. [The boat, docks in downtown Albany at Broadway and Quay streets, Port of Albany.] Open May 1 through November 1, daily, with 11 am and 2 pm excursions. Admission [children under five are free]) offers daily narrated sightseeing tours that are two hours long and come complete with a double-deck ship, snack bars, and rest rooms. On the tour you will see old Dutch mansions, tiny hamlets, and ocean-going vessels in the Port of Albany. Afterward, you may want to check with the Port of Albany office of information ([518] 445-2599) and ask whether any U.S. Navy ships are in port and offering tours. **Captain J. P. Cruise Line** (278 River Street,

Troy, N.Y. 12180. [518] 270–1901. Open from late-April to October. Admission [kids under twelve are free]. Group tours are by reservation) has special family tours on Saturday at 12:30 pm and Sunday at 3:30 pm on a six-hundred-passenger Mississippi paddlewheeler. The tour heads down the Hudson past the Port of Albany, where you can watch the large ships as they unload their cargoes. Live music is provided on the cruise and kids will enjoy the sing-a-longs. There is also a Saturday afternoon cruise on the old locks of the Erie Canal (this cruise boards at 11 am, and a buffet lunch is provided). The boat actually enters the working locks of the canal, so you can watch as the boat is raised and lowered to different levels.

Ice-Skating. The capital region offers some excellent places, both indoor and out, to go ice-skating. While outdoor rinks and skating ponds have been indicated under the appropriate park or site, there are a few other places that should be mentioned. Most of the indoor rinks offer rentals, but at outdoor sites you usually have to bring your own skates. Because the hours at skating areas are notoriously unpredictable and inconsistent, you must call before you go. On Clinton Avenue in Albany, try **Swinburne Park Skating Rink** ([518] 438–2406. Admission. Rentals are available), which is considered to have the best skating surface in the city; and **Empire Plaza Ice Rink** (at the Empire State Plaza, just beneath the Capitol. [518] 474–6647. Free. Rentals are available). Schenectady offers **City Center Rink** (bound by Center, City, Jay, and State streets. [518] 382–5104. Admission. Rentals are available) and **Achilles Rink** (Union College Campus. [518] 370–6134. Admission). Another area rink is The **Clifton Park Arena** (Vischers Ferry Road. Clifton Park [off New York 146]. [518] 383–5440. Admission. Rentals are available), which is the newest in the region.

Junior Museum. 282 Fifth Avenue, Troy, N.Y. 12182. (From I-87 take the downtown Troy exit and make an immediate right onto U.S. 4; go north to 106th street and turn right onto Fifth Avenue.) (518) 235–2120. Open year-round, Saturday through

Wednesday, 1 to 5 pm. Closed on major holidays. Donation requested. Groups are scheduled by appointment.

This is a fun museum housed in an old firehouse and filled with lots of hands-on experiences for even the youngest children. There are live animal exhibits, including ones of snakes and bees, and a marine tank filled with such watery denizens as crabs, turtles, and starfish. Young historians will enjoy the reproduction of a nineteenth-century settler's cabin, complete with furnishings such as a hay-filled mattress and a butter churn (which you are allowed to touch). Other exhibits include a chance to stand in a dinosaur's shoes—really the footprints of a brontosaurus. There is a small planetarium on the site, too, where shows of seasonal interest about the skies are offered, including "Songs of the Night," a slide and sound show about a beaver pond. If you are traveling, the best time to visit the museum is during a weekend workshop (these are generally scheduled every weekend). The workshops may offer potato printing, ice-cream making, mobiles, silhouette cutting, a chance to make your own stuffed animal—and they are usually free.

Facilities: Rest rooms. There is wheelchair access; those with strollers can manage there.

New York State Capitol. The capitol is located at the Empire State Plaza. For tour information write to: Visitor Assistance, Room 106, Empire State Plaza, Albany, N.Y. 12242. (Take the Empire Plaza exit from I-787; the plaza is bound by Swan, Madison, State, and Eagle streets, and the capitol is located on State Street, at the northern end of the plaza.) (518) 474–2418. Open year-round, daily, 9 am to 4 pm, with tours given on the hour. Closed Thanksgiving, Christmas, and New Year's Day. Free. Group tours are available (for groups of more than ten) by advance reservation.

The New York State Capitol building is considered to be one of the loveliest government buildings in the world, and rightfully so. Built between 1867 and 1899, the intricate carvings and decorative motifs are still as fresh and fascinating as they were almost a century ago. The tour is designed to introduce children to the workings of the state legislature; along the way they are able to see architecture, art, and perhaps even some real-live lawmakers at work. Surprisingly, some of the most fun art can be found on the famous staircases. The Senate Staircase is also called the Evolutionary Staircase because of the wonderful carvings of animals that decorate its sides, from single-cell animals to lions. The Great Western Staircase is the most elaborately carved one; it is also known as the Million Dollar Staircase, both for the cost that went into its construction and for its wealth of carvings (in fact, many of the carvings are of famous people, and the stonecarvers added their own portraits as well). The East Lobby holds changing exhibits in addition to a fine permanent collection of flags that date back to the Civil War. Older kids will enjoy watching the lawmaking process from the Senate galleries (this is only when it is in session, so you may want to call before you go to see when sessions are taking place). There is enough to see for all ages. The capitol is always buzzing with activity, so this is not a boring tour. Outside there are two parks, at either end of the building, that offer magnificent flower gardens and a great spot for picnic lunch and rest.

Facilities: Rest rooms; cafeteria. Wheelchair accessible. Strollers are welcome, but there are stairs.

New York State Museum. Empire State Plaza, Albany, N.Y. 12230. (Take the Empire Plaza exit from I-787; the plaza is bounded by Swan, Madison, State, and Eagle streets.) (518) 474–5843. Open year-round, daily, 10 am to 5 pm. Closed Thanksgiving, Christmas, and New Year's Day. Free. Group tours are available by advance reservation.

This is by far one of the best places to take kids in the Albany region. The changing life and history of New York State over the centuries is shown in a series of realistic, lifelike dioramas. Mastodons, wild birds, bears, deer, and other wildlife are all shown in their natural habitats, while street scenes of old New York show pushcarts, subways, fire engines, and shops of the past. The most popular stop for younger kids is the original "Sesame Street" set, complete with a continuously running video filled with Oscar the Grouch, Kermit, the Count, and Big Bird. A separate native American section has displays of the everyday lives of various New York tribes; a Gems of New York exhibit will dazzle even the littlest rockhound. The Dino Den Discovery Room is a play space with a dinosaur theme, and it's a good place to take a break. Changing exhibits offer some seasonal specialties, such as a miniature railroad at Christmas. Special events have included a movie festival and a holiday-break week during winter school recess, complete with puppet shows, workshops, and more.

Facilities: Rest rooms; gift shop, which offers an excellent selection of educational toys and books; cafeteria. Wheelchair accessible; stroller friendly.

Pick-Your-Own-Fruit Farms. Albany County is well known for its strawberry and apple harvests, and there are several farms where you are welcome to pick your own produce. Remember to dress for outdoor work (hats, long sleeves) and bring along the sunscreen. You pay for the produce by the pound, plus a small fee for containers if you don't bring your own. Still, this fresh harvest costs much less than the same fruit at a farmstand or the supermarket.

Strawberries can be picked in late May and June at: **Altamont Orchards** (Dunnsville Road, Altamont, N.Y. [on New York 397, one mile south of U.S. 20]. [518] 861–6515) also gives kindergarten and first-grade school tours of the orchard (by appointment); **Dan Marquardt** (County Road 406, South Westerlo, N.Y. [one-half mile from the junction of New York 32 and County Road 406]. [518] 966–8536); **Lansings Farm Market** (Lishakill Road, Colonie, N.Y. [between Consaul Road and New York 7]. [518] 869–6906); and **Le Vies Farm** (Maple Road, Voorheesville, N.Y. [on New York 85A, between New Scotland and the town of Voorheesville]. [518] 765–2208).

Apples are an autumn attraction in September and October at the following farms (but beware—sometimes it only takes a few minutes to fill a basket, so you may want to plan to do something else with the rest of your day): **Goold Orchards** (1297 Brookview Station Road, Castleton, N.Y. [518] 732–7317) is a particularly good farm stop, since school and group tours can be scheduled to see the old-fashioned cider press, cold storage areas, and oak racks. Two other stops for pick-your-own apples are **Indian Ladder Farms** (New York 156, Voorheesville, N.Y. [two miles west of town]. [518] 765–2083); and **Orchard Hill Organic Farm** (County Road 202, Guilderland Center, N.Y. [take New York 146 to County Road 202 and go south two miles]. [518] 465–8593).

Scotia-Glenville Children's Museum. Mailing address: 102 North Ballston Avenue, Scotia, NY. 12302. (518) 346–1764. The museum schedule changes constantly, so you must call to find out where it is planning to make a stop. Program fees. Groups can arrange for museum programs by calling the above number.

This truly is an unusual children's museum: you don't go to it, it comes to you, in the form of a bus and tote bags filled with materials and projects. Founded by three women who believe that museums should offer touching and participatory exhibits, the museum travels around the region. If you are a teacher or a leader of a children's organization, you can arrange to have your own museum for a day. The museum has such traveling programs as What is a Bird's Nest, Beautiful Insects, Iroquois Castles Revisited, the Ancient Art of Shadow Puppetry, and Create a Movie. But the exhibits are more than just displays, since kids are encouraged to become involved as geologists, explorers, musicians, and artists. The workshops are designed for class-sized groups, but the museum also makes stops throughout the upper Hudson Valley region, and some of its programs are offered on weekends and vacations at schools, community centers, and parks. Our best advice to you is to call the museum and find out where it is going to be in the near future; the kids will love it.

Schenectady Museum and Planetarium. Nott Terrace Heights, Schenectady, N.Y. 12305. (The museum is located just off New York 5 in the downtown area.) (518) 382–7890. Open year-round, Tuesday through Friday, 10 am to 4:30 pm; and weekends, noon to 5 pm. *Planetarium:* Saturday and Sunday, 2:30 and 3:30 pm shows (open to children over five and adults only). Special young people's shows at the planetarium are on Sunday at 1:30, for children two years old and over. Admission. Group tours are available by reservation.

This museum of science, industry, and arts is a wonderful stop even for very young children. The Nature Room gives kids the chance to touch displays of various plants and minerals. A large section of the museum is devoted to industrial displays (pulleys, generators, and so on) that demonstrate how things work; the kids can try out all of the various gadgets themselves. There is a great deal of information about local industry, including a miniature railroad exhibit and a special exhibit honoring Thomas Edison, who had roots in the Schenectady area. There is also an unusual and extensive selection of "exploration boxes," which are filled with stones, animals bones, and shells and which can be touched or examined through special lenses. An ongoing display of optical illusions has been designed to let children explore the ways in which we see the world. In addition to changing exhibits in the art gallery, the museum contains one of the largest costume collections on the East Coast. Exhibits may include anything from Victorian wedding gowns to men's antique hats. Preschoolers will appreciate Life in the Longhouse, an exhibit that allows them to pretend they are native Americans. For most children, the chance to visit a hands-on-oriented museum is a real treat, and this one is excellent. The planetarium shows are really good, too, adding to the excitement of this special museum.

Facilities: Rest rooms; gift shops, one of which features local crafts. The museum is partially wheelchair accessible; strollers are manageable.

If you are in the Schenectady area, you may want to take a self-guided walking tour of the historic **stockade district,** one of the region's most extensive collections of eighteenth-century architecture. The tour brochure may be obtained from: Schenectady County Historical Society, 32 Washington Avenue, Schenectady, N.Y. 12305. (518) 374–0263. Older children with an interest in architecture will enjoy this tour. The stockade area contains many interesting shops and eateries. Also, make sure the kids see *Lawrence the Indian*, a statue in the village square that memorializes one of the earliest friends of the settlers.

John Boyd Thacher State Park. New York 157, fifteen miles southwest of Albany. (518) 872–1237. Open year-round, 8 am to 10 pm in the summer, otherwise, 8 am to 6 pm. Free, except for a small parking charge from Memorial Day to Labor Day.

Thacher Park is unusual in one respect: it is one of the largest fossil-bearing areas in the world. Many Indian artifacts have been discovered there as well. The park is well equipped for a day of fun: extensive hiking trails leading to the Helderberg Escarpment overlook; the Indian Ladder Geological Trail, (for young hikers at least age eight and over), where fossils and arrowheads abound; an Olympic-sized swimming pool; playgrounds; and tennis courts. It's nice to note that several of the picnic areas are wheelchair accessible, as are the rest rooms and the pool. In the winter there are ten kilometers of groomed trails that are especially designed for novice skiers. Heated bathrooms and shelters make sledding and skiing especially comfortable at this park.

Facilities: Rest rooms; picnic areas; snack bars (in the summer only). Handicapped accessible.

Washington Park. Madison Avenue, Albany, N.Y. 12210. (The park is between State Street and Madison Avenue.) (518) 434–4181. Open year-round, daily, dawn to dusk. Free.

This park has served as a gathering area for the public since the seventeenth century, and it is still one of the most beautiful parks to visit in any city, in any season. The five-acre lake has paddleboats for rent, and ducks that always enjoy a handout or two. There are several small play areas throughout the site, some of which include play equipment designed for toddlers. The park hosts special events throughout the warmer months, including the Albany Tulip Festival in April, which takes advantage of the colorful flower plantings throughout the park and is highlighted by costumed performers. A free outdoor summer theater series offers fine family entertainment with shows like *Annie* and *Camelot* being performed throughout July and August. Children love to watch the horse-drawn cabs that are available for hire, and the rose gardens offer a perfect spot to rest. In the winter, ice-skating is allowed on the lake, while the trails and hills come alive with cross-country skiing and sledding (bring your own equipment). Be sure to plan a stop in Washington Park, especially if you are going to spend the day taking in the other Albany sights. The park is a gracious, quiet, and restful place for kids to refuel.

Facilities: Rest rooms; picnic areas; small snack stand (which operates at the bathhouse near the pond in the summer). Wheelchair access can be a problem here, but strollers are manageable on some of the paths.

Alpine Meadows. New York 9N, Greenfield Center, N.Y. (Alpine Meadows is located just outside Saratoga Springs; watch for signs.) (Mailing address: 494 Broadway, Saratoga Springs, N.Y. 12866.) (518) 893–2591. Open during ski season, weekends only, 9 am to 4:30 pm; and Christmas and Presidents' Day weeks, daily, 9 am to 4:30 pm. Admission (children five and under ski free). Discount lift tickets for families and group rates are available. An all-day lift ticket costs half the price of other ski areas.

This family-style ski center is a real find for those who are tired of paying outrageous prices for a day of skiing. There are ten trails and three T-bars, with the longest run being 1½ miles. Of course, the trails are geared for novice and intermediate skiers—although there are four expert runs—but if you want to teach your kids to ski and you don't want to drop one hundred dollars for the day, try this ski center, which is only fifteen minutes from Saratoga Springs. Those who have a child old enough for the slopes and one still in diapers may want to take advantage of the nursery, which charges a very reasonable per-hour fee.

Facilities: Rest rooms; base lodge with fireplace and restaurant; beer and wine bar; equipment rental; ski lessons; nursery, with babysitting services available for children two years and over.

Breakfast at Saratoga Racetrack. Union Avenue (New York 9P), Saratoga Springs, N.Y. (For information in months other than August or call: New York Racing Association, P.O. Box 187, Jamaica, N.Y. 11417. [718] 641–4700, Ext. 475.) (518) 584-6200 (August only). Open only during August; breakfast is served from 7 to 9:30 am. Free, but there is a charge if you buy breakfast. Group rates and reservations are available.

Breakfast at Saratoga Racetrack has been a tradition for

more than a century, when ladies and gentlemen were brought by elegant carriages to the trackside tables. Today you can still enjoy the combination of breakfast and an exciting look at thoroughbred horses as they work out each morning at the racetrack. Children love to watch the horses gallop around the track. A trackside announcer explains which horses are working out and who is riding them. The breakfast, called the Saratoga Sunrise, is simple, but there is a selection of the traditional fare, and if you want, you can bring your own food and sit at a picnic table. Each morning, a starting gate demonstration is held. This shows how horses are loaded into the gate and how they must wait for the bell and the cry "And they're off!" before they take off around the track. Adults may want to sneak away to one of the handicapping seminars (also free), which explain the mysteries of picking the winner. After dining, take a free tour of the paddock area, where the horses live during their stay at the track. Visitors ride through the area on small "people trains" from which they can see the grooms, owners, trainers, and jockeys as they go about the very busy, and expensive, routine of caring for racehorses. Note that you must be eighteen to place a bet; and you have to leave the track area after breakfast and before the track reopens for the races.

Facilities: Rest rooms; gift shop; picnic area with tables. The breakfast area is fine for strollers and wheelchairs, but do not attempt to take one on the paddock tour.

The Casino, Congress Park, and the Springs. Broadway and Circular Street, Saratoga Springs, N.Y. 12866. (518) 584–6920. Open year-round, but hours and days vary during winter months and the racing season (August), so call ahead. Admission.

When Saratoga was the Queen of Spas, the very elegant would take the waters at the local springs and then walk in Congress Park. In the evening, the casino (located in Congress Park) would open for gambling and dining, and both the infamous and the famous, such as Lillian Langtry and Diamond Jim Brady, would attend. Today's visitors can still enjoy the same peaceful atmosphere, which is enhanced by recent restoration projects. A walk through the park will bring you to hidden pools and fountains surrounded by flowers. (Our favorite was two puffy-cheeked creatures who spew water at each other across a small pool.) At the lake, parents can sit and watch the kids feed the ducks or play along the graveled paths. Just outside the park, look for the famous **Saratoga flower beds,** which are planted in the shape of horses and horse-shoes. (The city even has its own watering trucks, to ensure fresh flowers all through the summer.) The red brick casino contains a charming museum that offers vignettes of early Saratoga life, costumes, toys, a gambling room, and various small collections of everything from rocks to Chinese shoes. Across the street from the casino, on Spring Street, is one of the original Saratoga springs, where you can take a cup of natural water for whatever ails you.

Facilities: Rest rooms; gift shop. Strollers are perfect for the park, but there is a very steep flight of stairs up to the casino museum. Not accessible to wheelchairs.

National Museum of Dance. South Broadway, Saratoga Springs, N.Y. 12866. (518) 584–2225. Open summer, Tuesday through Sunday; and fall, Thursday through Sunday. Call for hours (note that there are evening hours during July). Admission. Group tours and group rates are available.

Balletomanes and children who are fascinated by dance will undoubtedly want to spend an hour in this museum. Changing exhibits focus on the history and glamour of dance in America, as told through photos, videos, costumes, and music. But the highlight of the museum for youngsters comes during the month of July when the New York City Ballet is in residence at the Saratoga Performing Arts Center (see individual listing for the center, late in this chapter). Dance Behind the Scenes, offered to all ticketholders ages five to fifteen, takes young people on a rare backstage tour of the theater before and after dance matinees. Unfortunately, these tours are limited to twenty children each and reservations must be made in advance (call the number listed above). In December, an old-fashioned family Christmas celebration sponsored by the museum offers a puppet show, sleigh rides in the spa park, songs, bells, and delightful snacks for the lucky children who attend. This is also by reservation; we recommend calling at least two weeks in advance.

Facilities: Rest rooms; excellent children's gift shop. Stroller friendly; limited access for wheelchairs.

National Museum of Racing. Union Avenue, Saratoga Springs, N.Y. 12866. (518) 584–0400. Open year-round. Hours: Labor Day to Memorial Day, Tuesday through Saturday, 10 am to 4:30 pm; and Memorial Day to August; Monday through Saturday, 10 am to 4:30 pm; and Sunday, noon to 4:30 pm. Racing season hours: Monday through Sunday, 9:30 am to 6 pm. Closed New Year's Day, Easter, Thanksgiving, and Christmas. *Museum shop:* Monday through Saturday, 10 am to 4:30 pm; and Sunday, noon to 4:30 pm. Admission (children under five are free).

The National Museum of Racing has been updated into one of the most technologically advanced sports museums in the country, and it will entertain any child who has ever shown an interest in horses. The first stop should be the film *Race America*, which introduces the viewer to the excitement of a day at the races: noise, music, movement, and color all rolled into one, with lots of visuals and not too much information to confuse younger viewers. In the museum galleries, hands-on exhibits let the viewer participate in such activities as walking through a starting gate, watching a jockey go through a race, and listening to commentaries of famous trainers and jockeys. An elaborate display of costumed mannequins will show nineteenth-century Saratoga at its most elegant, and there is a reproduction of a famous horse portrait painter's studio. Throughout the year, special films and talks are offered, many of them specifically aimed at children.

Facilities: Rest rooms; gift shop (this is one of the best shops for horse lovers, with gifts for all ages). The museum is stroller friendly, air-conditioned, and one of the most comfortable places to visit during those hot Saratoga summers.

Pick-Your-Own Farms. Saratoga County has long been famous for its horses, and for its Hand melons (sweet summer cantaloupes) but there are also farms that offer pick-your-own fruits and vegetables. Because the summer sun can be very hot, bring along hats and sunscreen and wear comfortable clothing. You will pay for your harvest by the pound. The kids will probably eat more than they pick, but this is a nice way to spend a breezy afternoon outdoors. **Ariel's Vegetable Farm** (194 Northern Pines Road, Wilton N.Y. [From Saratoga Springs take U.S. 9 north five miles to Wilton.] [518] 584–2189. Open April through September) has strawberries, asparagus, raspberries, beans, and peas for the picking. **Bullard's Farm** (New York 29, Schuylerville, N.Y. [Take Exit 14 from I-87.] [518] 695–3177. Open August through October) has pick-your-own pears and apples, but the farm stand is stocked with lots of local foods as well. **Knight Orchards** (Goode Street, Burnt Hills, N.Y. [Go west off New York 50 on Lake Hill Road, then north one mile to the orchards.] [518] 399–5174) has pears and apples on hand every day in September and October.

Rodeo at the Double M Arena. 678 New York 67, Ballston Spa, N.Y. (Take I-87 north from the Albany area Exit 12, and take New York 67 west one mile to the arena.) (518) 885–9543. Rodeos are held from mid-June through Labor Day, Friday, 7:30 pm. Admission.

A visit to a rodeo is exciting for adults and children alike, and this is the oldest professional weekly rodeo in the United States. Cowboys and cowgirls participate in bareback riding, barrel racing, Brahman bull riding, and calf roping, just like in the western shows. Rodeo clowns do their best to make you laugh and protect the cowboys by attracting the bulls' attention; trick riding and roping demonstrations are also given. The action takes place in a lighted, newly renovated outdoor arena, where the close-up view from the grandstand is excellent.

Facilities: Rest rooms; picnic area with tables; snack bar. Those in wheelchairs or pushing strollers can manage here.

Saratoga National Historical Park. New York 32, Stillwater, N.Y. 12170. (518) 664–9821. Open year-round, daily, 9 am to 5 pm. *Philip Schuyler House:* Open Memorial Day to Labor Day, daily; 9 am to 5 pm. Closed Thanksgiving, Christmas, and New Year's Day. Admission. Group tours and rates are available.

Any older child (age ten or older) who has ever studied the famous three-pronged plan of the British during the American Revolution or hissed at the memory of Benedict Arnold will enjoy a visit to this park. Your battlefield tour should begin at the Visitors Center, where elaborate displays of maps, miniature soldiers, battle arrangements, and slide shows guide the viewer through this all-important battle of the American Revolution. Next, take the two-hour drive-and-stop battlefield tour. Ten stations offer overlooks and descriptive markets about the days leading up to the battle. The most interesting stops include the only monument in America that is dedicated to a piece of a hero: in this case, Benedict Arnold's leg, which was injured during the battle (before he became a traitor). Another stop is the **Schuyler House,** which is in Schuylerville, eight miles from the park, and contains memorabilia of General Philip Schuyler and his wife, who were in residence during the battle. Younger children will enjoy the special events that are held throughout the summer in the park, including musketry displays, soldiers' encampments, and old-fashioned craft exhibitions. While the battlefield park is interesting, the tour is a long one and is not suitable for car-weary children or those who have no interest in revolutionary history.

Facilities: Rest rooms; gift shop; picnic area with tables.

Saratoga Performing Arts Center (SPAC). Spa State Park, Saratoga Springs, N.Y. 12866. (518) 587–3330. (Tickets for performances may also be purchased through major ticket services.) Open Mother's Day to early September; matinees and evening performances (hours vary). Ticket prices vary, but children twelve and under accompanied by a paying adult are given a free lawn ticket to the Philadelphia Orchestra, the New York City Ballet, and the New York City Opera if the tickets are picked up two hours before the performance at the SPAC box office. (Note that the New York City Ballet Thursday and Saturday matinees are not included in this discount program.)

One of the premier performance centers in America, SPAC offers an amazingly broad range of entertainment in a unique setting. Choose from among jazz, rock, folk, dance, opera, country, orchestral, and other music and dance performances throughout the season. While most performances are suitable only for adults, if your child enjoys a special type of entertainment, then by all means purchase lawn tickets the afternoon of the performance. There are covered seats available, but the lawn seating allows you to use blankets or chairs and to sit under the trees, off to the side, or anywhere you like with a stroller or baby carrier, and the views of the stage are not too bad. (If you like to see every movement of the performance, then bring a pair of binoculars.) Even if your child falls asleep, you can still enjoy the performance. One warning: there are some excellent food stands in the park that are open during the concerts, but food is not allowed in the covered seating area.

Facilities: Rest rooms; snack stands; restaurant. Preconcert dinners, picnics, and outdoor buffets are available by reservation; call (518) 587–8000 for information and reservations. Wheelchairs can manage on the walkways, but the lawn and the steps to the concert area may be a problem. SPAC is fine for strollers. There is lots of room, but be aware that if you attend a popular concert, you may have to walk quite a distance from the parking area to the lawn.

Adirondack Trout Fishing Preserve. U.S. 9, Lake George, N.Y. 12845. (At the intersection of U.S. 9 and I-87, Exit 21, go one-quarter mile north.) (518) 668–3064. Open July and August only, daily, 10 am to 5 pm. Free, but there is a rod rental charge. Groups are accommodated by reservation.

This lovely scenic preserve is stocked with brook, rainbow, and golden-rainbow trout. It's the perfect place to take young fishers for an afternoon's adventure when you are tired of other vacation activities. No fishing license is required, and you don't even have to bring your own equipment; rod rentals are available. Bring a picnic lunch and make this a relaxing afternoon stop.

Facilities: Rest rooms; picnic area; snack stand. Call ahead if wheelchair access is needed.

Adirondack Adventure. P.O. Box 31, Canada Street, Lake George, N.Y. 12845. (The site is on U.S. 9 in the village of Lake George.) (518) 668–9615 or 793–4051. Open May through October, daily, 10 am to 4 pm; the showings are continuous. Admission. Group and family rates are available.

This is a thirty-minute multimedia presentation about the history and lore of the Lake George and Adirondack area from the time of the American Indians to the present. The screen is thirty-six-feet wide and the theater is comfortable and air-conditioned (which is nice to remember on a sweltering afternoon when the kids are bored). This sight and sound show will keep even the youngest children interested, and there is enough history and adventure in the story to intrigue older kids and adults as well.

Facilities: Rest rooms.

Animal Land. P.O. Box 20, Lake George Road, Glens Falls, N.Y. 12801. (Take Exit 20 off I-87 and go one-half mile south.)

Open Memorial Day to Labor Day, daily, 9 am until dusk; and Labor Day to Columbus Day, weekends, 9 am until dusk. Admission (children under three are admitted free). Group rates are available.

This small game farm is perfect for younger children who enjoy being close to animals in a friendly setting. Deer, rabbits, and llamas all can be fed by young visitors. Three shows daily (at 10:30 am and 1:30 and 4:30 pm) feature bears, chimpanzees, and other trained animal entertainers that are sure to enthrall children and adults with their bike-riding, pole-climbing, and hoop-jumping tricks. We recommend this as a stop that will interest children who do not have pets or have not seen a larger zoo or other animal habitat. It's a nice way for kids to spend an active morning without doing a lot of walking.

Facilities: Rest rooms; gift shop; picnic area; snack bar. Wheelchair accessibility may be a problem, so it is recommended that you call ahead to make arrangements. Those with strollers can get around the site without too much difficulty.

Barton Garnet Mines. New York 28, North Creek, N.Y. 12853. (Take I-87 to Exit 23, U.S. 9, to New York 28. Go five miles north of North Creek, which is thirty-five minutes north of Lake George. Turn left at Shaw's General Store and proceed to the mines.) (518) 251–2706. Open late-June to Labor Day, Monday through Saturday, 9 am to 5 pm; and Sunday, 11 am to 5 pm. Admission. Group rates are available.

These mines, the oldest continuous garnet mining operation in the world, produce a major portion of the world's industrial garnets. The garnet, the New York State gem, is deep red in color and has long been popular in jewelry. A slide show introduces you to the story of the garnet. Then visitors are taken on a guided tour of the open-pit mines, where blasting and hand digging unearth the gems, which are later graded and polished according to the needs of the buyer. Since kids enjoy digging, a highlight of this site is the chance for visitors to spend time prospecting for their own garnets. You rent a hammer and a pail (or bring you own), stake out an area, and begin chipping away at the rock formations. Site guides will answer any questions you have about finding stones. Lucky prospectors will find a pocket in the rock where garnets are hidden; you can purchase the gems that you find. Unlucky souls may stop at the mineral shop, which has on display one of the largest collections of minerals in the country and offers an extensive selection of cut and polished gems. There are daily demonstrations of gem cutting and jewelry making, including cabachon cutting, a special way of cutting and polishing a garnet into a rounded shape. We recommend wearing sunglasses or safety glasses and supervising younger kids carefully because of the rock chips. Prospectors should bring hats and sunscreen and wear sturdy jeans and shoes for comfort. Also, bring a pillow to sit on if you are really serious about digging all afternoon.

Facilities: Rest rooms; gift shop; snack bar. This is not an accessible site for wheelchairs or strollers.

After digging in the mines, you may want to get above it all with the kids. At **Gore Mountain** (New York 28, North Creek, N.Y. 12853. [518] 251–2411. Open July to Labor Day, weekends only, 11 am to 4 pm. Admission), the gondola ride takes you up to the thirty-five-hundred-foot summit of Gore Mountain for a great view of the Adirondacks.

Baseball with the Glens Falls Tigers. East Field, P.O. Box 717, Glen Falls, N.Y. 12801. (Take I-87 to Exit 18 and follow the signs to field.) (518) 798–4600. Games are played from April through August at 7 pm, but schedules vary, so call in advance. Admission. For those baseball lovers in the family, watching this farm team of the Detroit Tigers is a unique opportunity to see tomorrow's major leaguers in action, close up. The ticket prices are very reasonable (less than what you might pay to see a movie) and the action is professional. Don't let the "farm-team" tag mislead you: you will see a full baseball game, with all of the excitement and thrills of a national competition. The stands are close to the action, and the hot dogs are just as good as the ones at Shea Stadium. This is a nice way to enjoy professional baseball—without the enormous crowds and parking problems of the larger stadiums.

Facilities: Rest rooms; gift concessions; snack stands. Wheelchairs and strollers can be maneuvered into some of the seating areas.

Beaches. Lake George has been famous for its water facilities for more than three centuries, and today, although many of the lake's beaches are now privately owned, there are still some excellent and convenient spots to go swimming with the kids. In general, the beaches are free, although there are some small parking fees. They are open from Memorial Day through Labor Day weekend, every day, from 9 am until 4:30 pm. Even though this is a resort area with lots of private beaches, remember that day-trippers fill up the parking areas and the best beach seats very early in the day, so plan accordingly. The famous **Million Dollar Beach** (Beach Road, Lake George), so-called because of the cost of construction and the ritzy clientele of the resort's early days, is at the head of Lake George. Park along the docks. This water playground is part of an extensive system of beaches that runs all along the southern end of the lake. These public beaches include: **Lake Avenue Beach** Lake Avenue, off Beach Road) and **Shepard Park** (off Canada Street, Lake George). Lake George Battlefield Park and Public Campground (Beach Road, Lake George), located directly in back of Million Dollar Beach, is a thirty-five-acre park that includes the remains of an old fort as well as monuments to the men who fought there during the French and Indian Wars and the Revolution. Rest rooms, picnic tables, barbecue pits, and water are available.

W. Keith DeLarm Bikeway. You can pick up the bikeway at Glenwood Avenue, U.S. 9, Exit 19 off I-87 (at the Glens Falls–Queensbury border), and cycle to the Lake George Beach State Park (I-87, Exit 21).

Warren County area offers a unique eight-and-one-half-mile trip along the W. Keith DeLarm Bikeway, through mostly flat terrain, complete with lovely mountain and valley views along the way, and ending at the southern tip of Lake George. The one-way trip takes approximately one to two hours and is along a paved, marked pathway, away from traffic. This is a side trip you may want to plan ahead for; a detailed map of the bikeway is available from the Warren County Department of Tourism, Municipal Center, Lake George, N.Y. 12845. (518) 761–6366. If you don't bring your own bikes with you and you plan on riding the full seventeen-mile round-trip, we recommend renting a bike at the Fort Mini Golf (Fort William Henry Museum, U.S. 9, Lake George, N.Y. 12845. [518] 668–5471), which rents out bikes daily from Memorial Day to Labor Day.

Candy Makers. Watching candy makers at work is always fascinating (and mouth watering), and Warren County has at least two candy factories open to the public. The **Boston Candy Kitchen** (21 Elm Street, Glens Falls, N.Y. 12801. [518] 792–1069. Open year-round, except major holidays, Monday through Friday, 7 am to 4 pm; and Saturday, 7 am to 3 pm. Candy making can be seen from early-November to April. Free) is a family-run confectionery and luncheonette that was founded in 1902 and still produces homemade ribbon candies and candy canes in flavors ranging from peppermint, wintergreen, lemon, and anise to cinnamon, molasses, cloves, and orange. You can watch the candy makers at work as they color, pull, knead, shape, and cut the candy into brightly colored ribbons and twists. The luncheonette has the original etched-glass soda fountain backing, a fine marble countertop, and old-fashioned stools that really spin. This is a nice, homey place to stop for a snack and give the kids a chance to see how candy-canes get their stripes. In the village of Lake George, you can stop at **Wagar's Soda Fountain and Candy Factory** (on Canada Street, across from the library. [518] 668–2693. Open July and August, daily, 10 am to 9 pm; and September to June, daily, 10 am to 5 pm.), a small, busy place redolent with the smells of rich chocolate and burnt sugar. Kids will love to watch as Adirondack bear claw candy is made, or to test the chocolate-covered strawberries or nut-crunchy turtle candies. For those on a special diet, note that this shop stocks a large variety of sugar- and salt-free candy.

Fort William Henry. Beach Road and U.S. 9, Lake George, N.Y. 12845. (518) 668–5471. Open May to June and September to mid-October, daily, 10 am to 5 pm; and July and August, 9 am to 10 pm. Guided tours take place every hour. Admission. Group tours are by reservation.

Fort William Henry was an important outpost during the tense years of the French and Indian Wars. In 1757 the fort was overrun by French troops, and the massacres that occurred became the basis for the James Fenimore Cooper novel *The Last of the Mohicans.* Today visitors to the fort will see a large restored site complete with innovative historical displays that bring the colonial period to life. Several stops will fascinate even the youngest in your group: the powder magazine (a log house underground) is reached by a long brick passageway and contains displays of how kegs of gunpowder were stored beneath the earth for safety. The cemetery was the resting place of more than twenty-five hundred soldiers, and some of the graves are on view (they are shown in an historical context, not a sensational manner). The dungeon, situated underneath the main museum, contains the remains of the original fireplace and cells and is dark and dismal—not so good for the original prisoners, but perfect for kids. At the Living History Wall, artifacts such as buttons and bullets that were found on the site are displayed. Their story is told in a multimedia presentation showing how the artifact fit into daily colonial life. The highlights of the Fort Henry tour are the musket and cannon firing demonstrations and the grenadier bomb toss. Kids receive a musket ball as a souvenir and will enjoy the noise and smoke of the show. There are many costumed guides at this site in eighteenth-century dress, and their uniforms are really spectacular. The fort itself looks down the length of Lake George, and the view is worth the stop all by itself.

Facilities: Rest rooms; gift shop; picn
There is some wheelchair access on the site,
generally good for strollers.

Gaslight Village. U.S. 9, Lake George, N.Y. 12845.
to Exit 21 and follow U.S. 9 north to the village
668–5459. Open mid-June to Labor Day, 10 am to 9 p
mission.

Gaslight Village is one of the oldest tourist attractions
Lake George, and it really hasn't changed much in the last
twenty-five years. There are lots of kiddie rides as well as a
collection of cars featuring automobiles owned by famous people, an ice show on a small rink, musical revues, and much
more. This is not a site for people who are seeking low-keyed
family entertainment: it's glitzy and noisy and the younger kids
will have a ball.

Facilities: Rest rooms; gift shop; picnic area with tables;
snack stand; restaurant. There is limited access for those in
wheelchairs, and parents with strollers will be able to manage.

Great Escape Fun Park. U.S. 9, Lake George, N.Y. 12845.
(518) 792–6568. Open Memorial Day weekend to Labor Day,
10 am to 6 pm. Admission. Group rates are available; call (518)
792–7056. They also will cater picnics for groups of more than
twenty-five; call ahead for information.

Once upon a time, this was a tiny park called Storytown.
Today it is the largest theme park in New York State, featuring
one hundred rides as well as daily shows including high divers,
circuses, magic puppeteers, and western gunfights. Storytown
is still there for the youngest visitors, complete with a ride in
Cinderella's pumpkin coach. Ghost Town hosts game arcades
and an old-fashioned saloon, Jungleland has animals galore, and
Raging River lets you bump over rapids in a family-sized rub-
ber tire–type boat. The bumper cars, ferris wheels, and other
rides are located in Fantasyland—although the large, more
scary rides, such as the Steamin' Demon roller coaster and the
Sky Lab, are reserved for older, braver children. Great Escape

do. You can easily spend the
going on rides, and eating at
's a nice way to let kids of all
bustling park.
; picnic area; snack stands;
stroller accessible.

159

ach Road, Lake George,
May to October, daily;
each boat has its own schedule, so
top by at their headquarters on the pier for up-
date tour information. Admission, with special children's
rates (children under three sail free). Special rates are also
available for groups of twenty or more, by reservation.

This cruise company offers a chance to see the Adirondack
scenery from a unique vantage point. It is the oldest boat excursion company in the country and has been offering passengers rides on Lake George since 1817. There are four cruise
ships that travel the length of Lake George on one- to four-and-
a-half-hour excursions. You can sail from the Lake George pier
to Ticonderoga or just take a short cruise and visit the lower
end of the lake. We suggest the one-hour cruise on the Minnie
Ha-Ha, an authentic paddle wheeler with steam-engine pistons
that are visible through a glass-paneled engine room. The ship
has a piercing steam whistle and is colorful and noisy as it
plows up and down the lake. A guided tour points out famous
homes and historical sites, although the kids may be more enthralled by the bright-red paddle wheel. Note that if you are
going to sit out on the deck, it is always windy, so you may
need to bring a sweater as well as a hat and sunscreen; however, there are enclosed observation areas.

Facilities: Rest rooms; snack bar concession; deck chairs.
Wheelchair and stroller accessible.

Magic Forest. U.S. 9, Lake George, N.Y. 12845. (518)
668–2448. Open Memorial Day to late-June, weekends only,

9:30 am to 6 pm; and late-June to Labor Day, daily, 9:30 am to 6 pm. Admission. Group rates are available by reservation.

This is a mellow, almost old-fashioned attraction that is actually set into a forest, so there is plenty of shade, even on the hottest days. Several entertainment theme areas offer displays and rides as diverse as a small Statue of Liberty to Santa's Workshop and Carousel. Younger children will delight in feeding Santa's reindeer, petting the baby animals, riding the Magic Forest railroad, and seeing the magic show. A colorful parrot show, with lovely bright-hued birds that are intelligent and fun to watch, is part of the attraction, as is a diving horse that jumps from a low diving platform into a pool. Everything here is geared toward children seven and under: the rides are not too fast or too scary, the colors are bright, and there are lots of places to stop and play make-believe.

Facilities: Rest rooms; gift shop; shaded picnic areas; snack stands.

Miniature Golf. Miniature golfing is a nice evening activity, especially after the heat of a summer's day. The village of Lake George offers several enjoyable miniature golf courses that will keep the kids busy for an hour or so. Then promenade through the village and buy an ice-cream cone, a perfect evening's ending. **Around the World in 18 Holes Mini-Golf** (Beach Road, Lake George, N.Y. 12845. [518] 668–2531. Open April 15 to September 30; hours vary. Admission) has two eighteen-hole miniature golf courses: Around the World and Around the United States, each complete with landmark buildings that will entertain the kids on their "trip." An ice-cream parlor is on the site, as are rest rooms. **Gift World, Gooney Mini-Golf, and the Haunted Castle** (located at the junction of U.S. 9 and New York 9N, Lake George, N.Y. 12845. [518] 668–2589. Open May through September; hours vary. Admission) combine to make a small but complete amusement park for younger children. We didn't get into the Haunted Castle, but the simple, colorful golf course is fun for all ages and is almost always packed on a summer's night. **Fort Mini-Golf** (Fort William

Henry Museum, U.S. 9, Lake George, N.Y. 12845. [518] 668–5471) is right in the center of town, which is convenient for those who want to spend a full afternoon at the fort.

Parks and Nature Trails. Warren County has thousands of acres of public campgrounds and parks, and it would take a lifetime to explore them all. Many of the Lake George–Warren County parks are in wilderness areas, and as such, they are not always suitable to the young day hiker or novice. So we have selected our favorites to include here, ones that will appeal to younger children as well as older kids and parents. In Glens Falls, **Crandall Park International** (Upper Glen Street, Glens Falls, N.Y. 12801. [518] 798–1761. Free. Open year-round, daily, 9 am to 6 pm) offers a large outdoor nature complex for exploration. There is a fishing pond on the site (bring your own poles), picnic areas, recreation areas, tennis and basketball courts, and a fitness trail, which has wooden exercise stations complete with directions for use for all levels of fitness. Hikers of all ages will appreciate the extensive trails, which lead through pine forests and cross over brooks and waterfalls. The trails are well marked for hikers and are not too challenging, so you can hike with the younger set and still have some energy left over for a cookout. **Pack Forest** (U.S. 9 [just past the junction of U.S. 9 and New York 28], Warrensburg, N.Y. 12885. [518] 623–9679. Open year-round, daily, 7:30 am to 4 pm. Free) boasts a very well marked one-mile nature trail, which offers a good way to spend some educational time outdoors with even the youngest naturalist. Ponds, forests, and a small river may be discovered on the site, and although there are no picnic tables, "picnic mountain" offers a mild climb, lovely views, and a nice place to stop for lunch.

The Sagamore Hotel. Bolton Landing, N.Y. 12814. (Take I-87 to Exit 24, turn right, and go six miles. Follow the signs in Bolton Landing to the Sagamore, which is located on Green Island.) (518) 644–9400. 1–800–358–3585 Open year-round.

Admission charged to day visitors. Family packages are available year-round.

Listed on the National Register of Historic Places, the Sagamore offers a combination of nineteenth-century charm and twentieth-century sophistication to family vacationers. The hotel opened in 1883 and catered for many years to a select, wealthy clientele that flocked to Lake George during the summer months. In 1981 the Sagamore underwent a $72-million restoration. This world-class resort now offers 350 rooms and suites in the Colonial Revival–style main building plus condominium accommodations designed especially for families. The condos include a fireplace, efficiency kitchen, studio couch, and terrace, and most have a fantastic view of the lake.

The site of the Sagamore is magnificent. Located on its own seventy-acre island, the hotel offers a wonderful getaway for families. We suggest visiting between June and August or during a school holiday (Presidents' Day week, Easter break, or Christmas recess). Although the family packages (with reduced winter rates) are offered by the hotel year-round, it is during school holidays that the children's program is in full swing. Extended hours (9 am to 4 pm and 6 to 9:30 pm daily) allow parents to enjoy a relaxing vacation because there are plenty of activities on tap for the kids. The program is directed by a children's entertainment coordinator and is well organized and well staffed. There is no surcharge for having your children participate in the program, which includes such fun-filled activities as face painting, kite flying, costume parties, musical chairs, "dinosaur" hunts, and poolside ice-cream socials, where the kids make their own sundaes. Older children—there are two age groups: 3 to 5 and 6 to 12—are taken on excursions to local attractions in the village of Lake George. From May to October there are trips on the *Morgan,* the hotel's own wooden yacht. Horse-drawn sleigh rides are enjoyed during the winter months, and there are ten miles of track-set trails for cross-country skiers. A free shuttle service runs to and from Gore Mountain (see page 164) for downhill skiers of all ages. If you want to go away with the kids, Sagamore is an ideal place for everyone to have a great time.

Facilities: This is a luxury resort with all of the amenities: gift shop; restaurants; indoor and outdoor pools; health club; championship golf course; indoor and outdoor tennis; table tennis racquetball; horseback riding; ice-skating; cross-country skiing; and jogging and nature trails. There are four restaurants, offering a range of dining options. Baby-sitting services can be arranged for guests of the hotel. Most areas in the main building are wheelchair accessible.

Skiing. Warren County ski areas are famous for their challenging slopes and ski conditions, but because of their location in the Adirondack Mountains you should consider a visit to the ski areas either as a vacation in itself or as part of a longer stay in the region. **Gore Mountain** (Box 470, North Creek, N.Y. 12853. [518] 251–2411. Open Thanksgiving to late March, daily, 9 am to 4:30 pm. Ski lift and gondola fees) is the largest state-run area in New York State, and it offers the only gondola lift in the state. The trails—there are forty-one of them—offer skiing at all skill levels, and complete snowmaking capabilities keep the fun coming all season. Cross-country skiers can take advantage of ten kilometers of set track, rentals, and a low trail-use fee. A nursery service is available, as are equipment rental and lessons, which cover all age groups, from toddlers on up. There are snack bars and restaurant and lodge at the ski area as well. **Hickory Ski Center** (New York 418, Warrensburg, N.Y. 12885 [located three miles west of Warrensburg]. [518] 623–2825. Open Saturday, Sunday, and holidays, 9 am to 4:30 pm. Lift fee) is a small, family-oriented area with a vertical drop of twelve hundred feet, fifteen slopes and trails, and four lifts. With no snowmaking capabilities, this site is at the mercy of the weather, but the people who work there are all very friendly and warm (we enjoyed their recorded messages). Lessons are available, as are snacks, but there is no nursery and, most important, there are no rentals—it's strictly bring your own. **West Mountain** (West Mountain Road, Glens Falls,

N.Y. 12801. [518] 793–6606. Open Thanksgiving to March, daily, 9 am to 4 pm, including holidays; also, night skiing is offered Monday through Friday, 6 to 9 pm. Lift fee) is near the capital district, so it is a busy slope. There are nineteen slopes and trails, six chairlifts, rentals, and lessons, but no nursery. Kids and adults who enjoy ski racing should check into this center's racing program, which runs all season.

Cross-country skiers can enjoy ski touring throughout the county. **Warren County Trails** (Hudson Street, Warrensburg, N.Y. 12885 [located one mile north of town]. [518] 623–4141. Open daily when weather permits. Free) is a twenty-five-kilometer park system of trails that weaves its way through forests and across meadows. The trails are easily accessible but there are no rentals or services, so go only with older children. If you want to know more about the trails before you set off, pick up a map at the Warren County Parks and Recreation Building, 261 Main Street, Warrensburg, on weekdays. We feel that the best cross-country ski area in the Warren County region that considers kids is the **Garnet Hill Ski Center** (Thirteenth Lake Road, North River, N.Y. 12856. [Take I-87 to Exit 23 and follow New York 28 west to Thirteenth Lake Road.] [518] 251–2444. Open, weather permitting, December to March, daily, 8:30 am to 5 pm. Trail-use fee; rental fee [children four and under ski free and are not charged for equipment use]). This center has fifty kilometers of trails, twenty-five with set track; a warming hut; instruction; rentals; and food. Guided tours and lessons available, as is night skiing (from 6 pm to 9 pm every evening). Snow-tubing and ice-skating are at this site, too; there is no additional charge for either. Free snow-tubes are provided, but there is a small fee for skate rental.

Warren County Fish Hatchery. U.S. 9, Hudson Street, Warrensburg, N.Y. 12885. (Take Exit 23 off I-87.) (518) 623–4141. Open, Memorial Day weekend to Labor Day, daily, 10 am to 5 pm. Free.

A stop at this site offers the kids a chance to view a slide show on the story of trout, their life cycles, and their environments, and then go outside to see trout feeding. Each year this hatchery produces thousands of fish, which are used to stock trout ponds and streams throughout the county. For a child who has never been fishing, this is an interesting stop either before or after a fishing expedition. We recommend this for kids who enjoy the outdoors; younger children will probably be bored during the slide show.

Facilities: Rest rooms; picnic area. Strollers can be used at this site, but call ahead if wheelchair accessibility is needed.

Water Slide World. U.S. 9 and New York 9L, Lake George, N.Y. 12845. (Take Exit 21 off I-87 and go one-half mile south of the village of Lake George. (518) 668–4407. Open June 20 to Labor Day, daily, 10 am to 6:30 pm, weather permitting. Admission (there are no refunds for inclement weather problems).

For kids who love water, plan a day at this wet and wild amusement park. Water Slide World offers dozens of water activities, including New York State's only wave pool, in which machine-made four-foot waves break over the swimmers in a sixteen-thousand-square-foot pool. An enormous series of water slides up to eleven hundred feet long allow older swimmers (no toddlers here) to plunge down watery ramps and splash into pools; one of the slides even has a 360-degree loop and a tunnel. For an extra charge there are bumper boats in their own lake and hot tubs for parents to relax in. Toddlers will really enjoy the Toddler Lagoon, with its tiny slides, watery rocking horses, and that all-time favorite: water guns. Throughout the park there are places to rent rafts or buy bathing suits and other sun paraphernalia, so even if you don't come prepared, you and the kids still can enjoy the park. Outdoor dry play areas offer volleyball and table tennis for a change of pace, and there is a game room, complete with video playthings. This is an excellent park for a hot day, but younger children must be supervised continuously, especially on a crowded day, when hundreds of people are splashing and sliding. A quieter time can be enjoyed by renting a raft and just floating along on the pools or sunbathing in the many chairs and rest areas that surround the pools.

Facilities: Rest rooms; lockers; showers; gift shop, with bathing suits and caps for sale; restaurant and snack bars with umbrella tables.

Bartholomew's Cobble. Weatogue Road, Ashley Falls, Mass. 01222. (Take U.S. 7 south from Great Barrington, then Massachusetts 7A to Ashley Falls. Follow Rannpo Road to cobble, which is eleven miles from Great Barrington.) (413) 229–8600. Open mid-April to mid-October, Wednesday through Sunday, 9 am to 5 pm. Admission.

This is a small (twenty-five acre), but extremely varied, natural site that is a delight to hike and explore. Even the youngest visitors will find rocks, five hundred species of wildflowers, forty species of ferns, numerous species of birds, and other natural objects that are lovely to look at and experience. A *cobble* is an old English name for an outcropping of rock. This particular cobble is more than several hundred million years old, is made of limestone, and overlooks the Housatonic Valley. You hike to the top and look out over valleys where cows graze and rivers run, or follow the resident naturalist on a walk and learn the names of all of the ferns and watch as a chickadee eats out of your hand. The Ledges Trail takes at least an hour to hike, but the views and the surrounding forests are worth the walk. At the Bailey Museum of Natural History (also open Wednesday through Sunday), changing displays offer views of local flora and fauna, and trail guides are available. This is also an excellent birdwatching site, so bring along the binoculars and let the kids enjoy nature close up at this designated national natural landmark. On Annual Cobble Day in late-June there are tours and special nature programs throughout the preserve.

Facilities: Rest rooms. Not suitable for wheelchairs or strollers.

Just adjoining the cobble is the **Colonel Ashley House** ([413] 229–8600. Open Memorial Day weekend to late June and post–Labor Day to Columbus Day weekend, Saturday,

Sunday, and holidays, 1 to 5 pm; and the last weekend in June to Labor Day, Wednesday through Sunday, 1 to 5 pm. Admission), the oldest house (1735) in Berkshire County and the site of the creation of the Sheffield Declaration, a declaration of personal freedom that predated the Declaration of Independence. Older children may enjoy the tour of the homestead, which includes a large tool collection of the last two hundred years, period furnishings, and decorative items. And if you head back to Great Barrington, there is a wonderful treat for the kids. **Rainbow's End Miniature Golf Course** (U.S. 7 [at Cove Lanes Bowling Center], Great Barrington, Mass. 01230. [413] 528–1220. Open year-round, daily, except major holidays. Admission) is an eighteen-hole golf course with scenes of local history, including a Shaker round barn and waterfalls. We've never heard of a kid who didn't enjoy this course.

Berkshire Garden Center. Route 102 and Massachusetts 183, Stockbridge, Mass. 01262. (413) 298–3926. Open mid-May to mid-October, daily, 10 am to 5 pm. Admission (children under six are admitted free).

If you have children with you who love gardens and flowers, then a stop here is a fine way to spend a summer's afternoon. The fifteen-acre botanic garden is planted with hundreds of rare and beautiful flowers, trees, and herbs. Several smaller gardens bloom with roses, hedges, and evergreens and there is a special raised-bed section for vegetables. Lily ponds and woodland walks let children explore the world of gardening firsthand: on a warm day they will enjoy smelling the scents of the herb garden. After you have finished your walk, stop by the greenhouses, where thousands of plants are raised each spring. While this is a garden center (adults should note that there are always experts on hand to answer your questions about weeds and such), it is also a lovely garden (complete with picnic areas but no tables) and is perfect for kids who love the earth. A special Harvest Festival in early October offers fire truck rides, food, and other entertainment for all ages; call ahead for the exact date.

Facilities: Rest rooms; gift shop; picnic area. Those in wheelchairs and parents with strollers will find limited access on the paths, but the terraced areas could be a problem.

Berkshire Museum. 39 South Street, Pittsfield, Mass. 01201. (413) 443–7171. Open year-round, Tuesday through Saturday, 10 am to 5 pm; and Sunday, 1 to 5 pm. Also open Monday, 10 am to 5 pm, in July and August. Free. Group tours are available by request.

Chock full of art, ancient history, and natural science collections, the Berkshire Museum is an educational stop for the kids. There are aquariums filled with both fresh and salt-water fish and displays of fossils, gems, minerals, and American Indian artifacts. Younger children will like the special bird room, including an owl exhibit. There are even some live animals on hand, such as a very popular armadillo. The biology room contains Uncle Beasley, the ten-foot-long dinosaur model that starred in the movie *The Enormous Egg*. Another room is filled with exhibits, dioramas, and photos depicting Berkshire animals, past and present, as well as other animals of the world depicted in miniature. And don't miss the Egyptian mummy, swathed in linen and still holding court, surrounded by other burial items. Older children who enjoy art will like the Hudson River paintings collection, which depicts many of the overlooks and mountains of the nearby Catskills. During Spring Break there are daily children's programs at the museum, including indoor gardening, a behind-the-scenes tour of the museum, and other special activities. Summer at the museum brings native American Day Camp (for children entering 3rd through 5th grades), a film series, and there is a concert series year-round (call ahead for scheduled performances).

Facilities: Rest rooms; gift shop. There is limited access for wheelchairs, but strollers should be manageable.

When you have finished your museum walk, stop by the **Children's Zoo** in Pittsfield (Springside Park, off North Street. Open June to mid-October, daily, 10 am to 6 pm), which features a small collection of farm animals, along with some raccoon, possum, an other local animals. On weekends there are talks and demonstrations by naturalists.

Berkshire Scenic Railway. P.O. Box 298, Lee, Mass. 01238. (Board at Lee, one mile north of I-90, Exit 2, on U.S. 20; make a left at the end of Canal Street.) (413) 243–2872. Open Memorial Day weekend through October, weekends, and holidays; call for daily schedules. Admission (children under five ride free). Group rates are available by advance reservation.

Take a two-and-one-half-hour round-trip train ride through the beautiful Berkshires and explore a small railroad museum as well. The train runs along the same tracks used by freight trains during the week to transport commercial goods throughout New England. Along the way, the kids will love seeing an old marble quarry (where the marble for the Washington Monument was mined) as well as waterfalls and maybe a deer running through the forest. The museum in Lee has railroad memorabilia as well as a working model railroad, which will delight even the youngest children. The depot is a nice place to stop for a snack before boarding the train for the return trip. There is often someone aboard who plays guitar and gets everyone singing, which makes for an enjoyable ride. The special Halloween ride is something to see: just about everyone is in costume, even the conductor!

Facilities: Rest rooms; gift shop; restaurant. If wheelchair accessibility is needed, call ahead. Strollers may not fit in the train ˙aisles.

Bousquet Ski Area. Tamarack Road, Pittsfield, Mass. 01201. (From U.S. 7 in Pittsfield, follow the signs.) (413) 442–8316. Open November through March, daily, 10 am to 4 pm, with night skiing from 5 to 10 pm, Monday through Saturday. Lift ticket fee. There are special rates for junior skiers.

This is the Berkshires' oldest ski center, dating back to 1932, and there is still an old-time, family-oriented atmosphere. Bousquet caters particularly to beginning, novice, and intermediate skiers, so you can expect to find easier skiing on many of the slopes. There is a nursery here for children who are at least age two, and graduated skiing classes accept toddlers and up.

Facilities: Rest rooms; lockers; ski shop; snack bar; restaurant; equipment rental; nursery.

If you still have some energy left in you after a day on the slopes at Bousquet, try an unusual New England tradition: ski tows. These rope tows (often run by old auto engines) haul you to the top of moderate-sized hills. Kids love the experience, both up and down. Most of the tows are owned by municipalities, so the skiing is family oriented and inexpensive. Try **Osceola Ski Tow** (Osceola Park, Pittsfield, Mass. 01201. [Take U.S. 20 West Housatonic Street.] [413] 499–9343. Open Monday through Friday, 6:30 to 9 pm; and weekends and holidays, 1 to 5 pm and 6:30 to 9 pm. Small fee), organized by the Pittsfield Recreation Department. You have to bring your own equipment.

Brodie Mountain. U.S. 7, New Ashford, Mass. 01237. (413) 443–4752. Open early-November to April, daily, 9 am to 11 pm. Lift ticket charge; there are discounts for children under age six.

This is a fine ski center for the younger set: the majority of trails here cater to the novice and there is a strong family atmosphere. Long hailed as part of the so-called Irish Alps, all of the mountains and trails bear names like Danny Boy's Trail and Gilhooley's Glade. Once in awhile—especially around March 17—the local leprechaun makes an appearance on the slopes, to the delight of the youngest skiers, who might even find that the snow is green! There are complete rentals and ski school classes for the children and a full-service nursery that accepts infants and older for the day. Early bird skiers will appreciate Brodie's snowmaking capabilities, which sometimes allows them to open as early as October. Brodie makes a day of skiing especially attractive to families and younger children just learning to schuss.

Facilities: Rest rooms; lockers; ski shop; snack bar; restaurant; equipment rentals; nursery.

Butternut Basin Ski Area. Massachusetts 23, Great Barrington, Mass. 01230. (413) 528–2000. Open early-November to April, daily, 9 am to 4 pm. Lift ticket fee; there is a special rate for children six and under.

With more than twenty-one trails, Butternut still manages to offer families a low-key place to ski and to learn. The ski area itself is lovely, and the two ski lodges offer excellent views of both Massachusetts and New York mountains. There is a separate beginner's slope, which is a perfect place for first-timers to take a tumble or two. A complete, friendly ski lesson program and rentals are offered. There is a full-service nursery on hand to care for kids age two and up who don't like the slopes; the nursery staff has a full-day program that is guaranteed to keep the kids happy and busy while Mom and Dad are out on the slopes.

Facilities: Rest rooms; lockers; ski shop; snack bar; restaurant; equipment rental; nursery.

Chesterwood. P.O. Box 827, Stockbridge, Mass. 01262. (413) 298–3579. (The site is located off Route 183, between Glendale and Stockbridge. This is not an easy place to find; you must follow the signs carefully from Route 183.). Open May 1 to October 31, daily, 10 am to 5 pm. Admission (children under six are admitted free).

This lovely site, part of the National Trust for Historic Preservation, was the summer home of Daniel Chester French, the sculptor who created the Lincoln Memorial and the Minute Man statues. Guided tours take you through the studio, residence, and gardens where French spent the summer months. The studio is filled with memorabilia as well as the tools and plaster casts used to make the Lincoln Memorial. Children will enjoy seeing how statues are made and are even able to handle some of the tools on display. Outside there are lovely gardens, walkways, and large sculptures, which kids have been known to climb over. A short woodland trail laid out by French still welcomes younger walkers who like nature.

Facilities: Rest rooms; gift shop. Wheelchair accessibility could be a problem in some areas of the studio, so call before you go if this is required. Those pushing strollers should be able to manage the several buildings on the site.

Sterling and Francine Clark Art Institute. 225 South Street, Williamstown, Mass. 01267. (The institute is located on the Williams College campus; watch for parking signs.) (413) 458–9545. Open year-round, Tuesday through Sunday, 10 am to 5 pm. Closed on major holidays. Free.

One of the best collections of fine art in the region is at this museum, which contains an incredible selection of French nineteenth-century paintings and sculpture. The colorful paintings by Renoir, Monet, and Degas are a wonderful introduction for older children to fine art. Many of the paintings are well known, and they all depict scenes and people who look like what they are: earthy peasant women, flowers, dancers, landscapes. Another exhibit hall displays a large collection of silver, from the seventeenth to the twentieth centuries; the candlesticks, ewers and plates are dazzling to all ages of viewers. This jewel of a museum is rarely crowded and permits children to get up close to rare, fine art.

Facilities: Rest rooms; gift shop. There are some wheelchair and stroller accessible areas.

While you are in Williamstown, stop at the **Williams College Museum of Art** (Route 2, Main Street. [413] 597–2429. Open year-round, Monday through Saturday, 10 am to 5 pm; and Sunday, 1 to 5 pm. Free), also on the Williams College campus. This museum has an excellent collection of nineteenth-and twentieth-century American art as well as ancient art of the Orient and South America. Combine this stop with the one above, and the kids will have seen two museums in a short period of painless museum hopping.

Cross-Country Skiing. The Berkshires is one of the finest areas in the country to pursue the sport of cross-country skiing. All ages enjoy gliding across meadows and trails on long, skinny skis, and it does not take a lot of lesson time to be able to maneuver on the snow. Kids as young as three can enjoy cross-country skiing, at least for limited periods of time. Most ski areas do rent equipment. Two downhill areas that also have several kilometers of groomed cross-country trails and rentals are **Brodie Mountain** and **Butternut Basin** (see separate entries for complete information). They also provide machine-made snow on their cross-country trails.

Ski-touring is also listed under the various state and local park entries. Many of the Berkshire cross-country areas are located in rugged regions with difficult trails and no facilities. The following cross-country areas were selected for their novice trails, easy access, and proximity to restaurants, public facilities, or towns. Please note that unless indicated, there are no rentals at the site, although skis may be rented at nearby sports shops. **Kennedy Park** (U.S. 7, Lenox, Mass. 01240. [The access point for the park is behind the Lenox House Restaurant, just north of Lenox on U.S. 7.] [413] 637–3010. Free) has more than forty miles of old carriage roads and bridle paths for skiing. The roads wind in and out of what was once the site of a grand old hotel. Each trail is well marked with colorful blazes of paint; the white novice trail is especially nice to try if the kids are new on skis. **Notchview Reservation** (Massachusetts 9, Windsor, Mass. 01270 [on Massachusetts 9, northeast of Pittsfield, in the town of Windsor]. [413] 684–0148. Open daily, 8 am to 4:30 pm, weather permitting. Small use fee) is a three-thousand-acre preserve that maintains twenty-five kilometers of marked trails. Its Visitors Center is open on weekends and holidays for use as a warming hut and waxing area. It also sells inexpensive maps of the trails. **Stone Hill Loop** (Clark Art Museum, Williams College, Williamstown, Mass. 01267. [Access

from the South Street parking lot of the Clark Art Museum.]
Open daily, weather permitting. Free) circles Stone Hill with
its lovely vistas of the nearby mountains. This is a neigh-
borhood-type ski trail that is perfect for a family outing. **Buck-
steep Manor** (Washington Mountain Road, Washington, Mass.
01223. [413] 623–6651 [ski center] or 623-5535 [lodging].) is a
complete cross-country ski center on six hundred acres. There
are twenty-five kilometers of groomed trails, including lots of
areas for beginners, and you can rent equipment and take
lessons on the site as well. The manor, an inn, also offers guests
sleigh rides.

Farms. Farms to visit are limited in number in the Berkshires,
and many of those that are open to the public have age limita-
tions on children. The following farms offer a chance to see
maple syrup making, poultry, and fruits and vegetables up
close. Some of them also offer tours. We do recommend that if
you are making a long drive to pick-your-own places, you
should call ahead and make certain that the harvest is ready.
The **Hopkins Farm Museum** (Hopkins Memorial Forest,
Northwest Hill Road, Williamstown, Mass. 01267. [413]
597–2346. Open May to October, weekends, 11 am to 4 pm) a
working farm museum, is on the grounds of a Williams College–owned two thousand-acre preserve. In addition to nature
trails, the farm has a collection of old tools on display, and
there are seasonal demonstrations of apple cider and maple
syrup making. **Sunset Farm Maple Products** (Tyringham Road,
Lee, Mass. 01238. [413] 243–3329. Open year-round, daily, 9
am until dusk. Free) is a working farm that produces maple
sugar, syrup, and cream. A stop here in maple season (March
to early April) will give visitors a look at the maple
syrup–making process, from sap to sweet. A tour of the sugar-
house includes a stop at the evaporators and the candy-making
area, where lucky visitors may even get to sample some hot,
fresh syrup! **Otis Poultry Farm** (Massachusetts 8, North Otis,
Mass. 01253. [413] 269–4438. Open daily, 8 am to 6 pm. Free)
is a large farm stand that offers a wide selection of fresh local

produce as well as honey, maple syrup, baked goods, and, of course, eggs. Kids will enjoy a short tour of the poultry farm. **Dennis March Farm** (U.S. 7, Great Barrington, Mass. 01230, [between Stockbridge and Great Barrington]. [413] 298–3217. Open September and October, daily, 9 am to 4 pm) has pick-your-own apples and raspberries (in August and September), but you have to make an appointment for the berries, and you have to pick at least five pints. Blueberries for picking are at none other than, **Blueberry Hill Farm** (East Road, Mount Washington, Mass. 01223. [413] 528–1479. Open July and August, daily, 9 am to 5 pm).

Hancock Shaker Village. P.O. Box 898, Pittsfield, Mass. 01202. (The village is on U.S. 20, five miles west of Pittsfield, at the junction of Massachusetts 41 and U.S. 20.) (413) 443–0188. Open April 1 to Memorial Day weekend and the month of November, 10 am to 3 pm; and Memorial Day weekend to October, daily, 9:30 am to 5 pm. Admission. Group rates and tours are available by advance reservation.

We recommend this unusual farming village for children ten and up who are especially interested in American history. At this one-thousand-acre site, which was the home of the Shakers, a religious sect of the eighteenth and nineteenth centuries, twenty of the original sixty buildings have been restored to their 1830s condition. The Shakers were a quiet, hardworking group who danced when they worshipped (their name came from "Shaking Quakers") and who believed that simplicity was an important tenet of life. Thus, the site is serene, neat, and quiet, and while it is filled with interesting stops, be warned that it does not bustle like other restorations. Some of the points of interest for the kids are the round barn, which held dairy cattle; the herb gardens, which stretch the length of the walkways and contain a variety of marked herbs; the village schoolhouse; and the machine shop and laundry, where some of the more popular Shaker inventions, such as the flat broom and the clothespin, are still used. Kids will be delighted to discover that lots of our everyday items had their start in Shaker communities: the round stove (for heating irons), the circular saw, mail order seeds and herbs, and rocking beds for the elderly. Beautiful Shaker woodwork and furniture are on display, too. Guides will explain the traditions of Shaker life, including the facts that men and women lived apart but had equal say in running the society, and that putting your "hands to work and your hearts to God" was considered the best way to use your talents. Changing exhibits of Shaker artwork and utensils are displayed in several different buildings, and the gift shop is stocked with lots of items that are made on the site. Throughout the season from late spring to late fall, you may find woodworkers, and weavers, and others at work, and there are often cows, sheep, and other farm animals available for petting. Special events, such as evening tours by candlelight, are offered, but you have to make reservations in advance for many of the events. A winter weekend is held each February, with Shaker craft demonstrations, baking, talks, walks, and sleigh rides as well as the World People's Dinners.

Facilities: Rest rooms; gift shop; picnic area; lunchroom, with homemade foods and reproductions of Shaker furniture. Wheelchairs and strollers will be difficult to maneuver at this site.

Jacob's Pillow Dance Festival. P.O. Box 287, Lee, Mass. 01238. (413) 243–0745. (The festival is on U.S. 20 in Becket, eight miles east of the Lee interchange on I-90; watch for signs.) Open late-June through late-August; schedules vary, so call for a brochure. Admission. Group rates are available by advance reservation.

This is one of the best dance festivals in the United States, and we recommend it for children who are interested in any kind of dance. A few of their offerings each summer will appeal to older children (and younger children who can sit through an entire performance). In the past, the colorful costumes and vibrant music of tap, ballet and exotic troupes have pleased all ages and have included the Magic of Creole troupe; Pilobolus, with its acrobatic and silly-shaped dances; and the Hubbard

Street Dance Company, complete with tap, jazz, and ballet's fancy footwork. Jacob's Pillow is an unusual way to introduce children to the world of dance, and the matinees make this a perfect place to stop on a Saturday afternoon. If you don't think the kids will sit through an entire show, watch a free performance of a work in progress. These are held an hour and a half before each scheduled main event at the Inside/Out Stage. Or watch the dancers at work in the studios, some of which are open to the public for viewing through special one-way mirrors.

Facilities: Rest rooms; gift shop; picnic area; cafe. Wheelchairs and strollers can be accommodated in some areas.

Jiminy Peak. Corey Road, Hancock, Mass. 01237. (From U.S. 7, take Massachusetts 43 to Brodie Mountain Road and follow the signs.) (413) 738–5500. Open late-November to late-March, weekends and Holidays, 8:30 am to 10:30 pm; and Monday through Friday, 9 am to 10:30 pm. Lift ticket fee. There are special rates for kids twelve and under.

This is a demanding mountain for skiers, so we recommend this ski center only for adults and children who are comfortable on the slopes. There are complete rentals and ski lessons, but this is a very busy (thirty-five-hundred-person-capacity) slope, and new skiers may feel a bit overwhelmed by all of the action. For parents who want to ski the advanced slopes, note that there is a fine supervised play area that is open daily and charges by the hour (children who attend this must be at least two years of age and toilet trained). Summer visitors will enjoy the Alpine Slide, a sort of coaster on wheels that wends its way down the slopes, and the miniature golf course.

Facilities: Rest rooms; lockers; ski shop; snack bar; restaurant; equipment rental; nursery. This ski center has a complete resort–condominium complex attached to it, and they offer special overnight rates for children.

Otis Ridge Ski Area. Massachusetts 23, Otis, Mass. 01253. (413) 269–4444. Open late-November to March, daily, 9 am to

4 pm. Lift ticket fee (kids five and under ski free on the beginner's slope). Special rates for junior skiers (over five are available.

A tiny hill in comparison to the other, behemoth Berkshire mountains, Otis Ridge has ten slopes and trails, one chairlift, and five tows. However, we can't think of a nicer place to take kids who want to learn to ski without pressure from large classes or advanced instructors. The whole setup considers careful ski instruction as the best way to manage younger skiers, and there is little of the competition found at larger slopes. Note that children must be at least four years old for group lessons. Only eight hundred lift tickets a day are sold, so the trails never become so crowded as to remove the real fun of skiing. Adults should note that there is a ski camp offered each year for kids from eight to sixteen, and that complete learn-to-ski packages are available for day or weekend use. No child care is available, but the lift ticket prices are so reasonable that we consider this the best place in the Berkshires for starting skiers.

Facilities: Rest rooms; lockers; snack bar; equipment rental; ski school.

Parks and State Forests. The Berkshires region extends over hundreds of square miles of villages, parks, and forests that offer a chance for young visitors to experience the outdoors firsthand. We have selected the following state forests as ones that offer the most facilities and activities for young children. The park season runs from Memorial Day weekend through Columbus Day, 9 am until dusk. There are daily-use fees; campsites are by advance reservation, and there is a separate campsite charge. Each park has picnic areas with tables, grills, and play areas, although they may be crowded on holidays and weekends. Unless otherwise noted, wheelchair accessibility is not offered; if accessibility is needed, we recommend calling the park before you plan your trip. **Beartown State Forest** (Blue Hill Road, Monterey, Mass. 01245. [Follow Route 17 from Monterey to the park entrance.] [413] 528–0904) is a huge, 10,500-acre reservation that has a full offering of outdoor activities, including camping, fishing, walking and hiking trails, and swimming in Benedict Pond. It is also open in the winter for cross-country skiing when the weather permits. **Mount Washington State Forest** (East Street, Mount Washington, Mass. 01223. [Take Massachusetts 23 to South Egremont and watch for the parking area.] [413] 528–0330) offers thirty-three hundred acres, including Bash Bish Falls, with its spectacular sixty-foot waterfall, which is said to be the home of a witch and her daughter. You can also swim, fish, and hike along the many well-marked trails (which are converted to cross-country ski trails in the winter). But the main attraction at this park is the falls. **October Mountain State Forest** (Woodland Road, Lee, Mass. 01238. [Take U.S. 20 from Lenox to the entrance of the park.] [413] 243–1778), once a private game preserve, is perfect for an overnight camping trip or even just a day-long picnic. There's swimming, fishing, and walking trails in the park, and picnic areas are numerous. Winter offers twenty-five miles of cross-country ski trails. **Pittsfield State Forest** (Cascade Street, Pittsfield, Mass. 00120. [From the junction of U.S. 20 and U.S. 7 in Pittsfield, drive west on West Street, go north on Churchill Street, then west again on Cascade Street to the park entrance.] [413] 442–8992) has ninety-six hundred acres filled with swimming, hiking, and camping facilities as well as an interpretive center. There is also a special paved wheelchair accessible trail. **Sandisfield State Forest** (West Street, Sandisfield, Mass. 01255. [413] 258–4774) is a popular site for swimming on York Lake. You can also picnic, hike, and camp at the park and cross-country ski in the winter.

Pleasant Valley Wildlife Sanctuary. 472 West Mountain Road (off U.S. 7), Lenox, Mass. 01240. (413) 637–0320. Open year-round, Tuesday through Sunday, dawn to dusk. Admission. Group tours are available by reservation.

This Audubon Society sanctuary covers 720 acres of land and contains a wealth of natural settings for animals and plants as well as seven miles of trails. The short and easy-to-walk trails lead through forests, ferneries and wildflower meadows and take you past wetlands and ponds. A beaver pond is always active with beaver, bullfrogs, and an occasional leaping fish. At the small trailside museum, local animals and plantlife are explained through a series of displays and live exhibits. Naturalists and guides are often on hand to answer any questions. If you are in the area during the summer, you may want to take advantage of the summer day camp, which runs for two-week sessions and includes lots of outdoor activities.

Facilities: Rest rooms; picnic area. We don't recommend this site for wheelchairs or for strollers.

Norman Rockwell Museum. Main Street, Stockbridge, Mass. 01261. (413) 298–3822. Open year-round, Wednesday through Monday, 10 am to 5 pm. Closed during the last two weeks in January. Admission (kids five and under are admitted free). Group educational tours are available by reservation.

Older children who visit this charming museum probably will recognize many of the paintings on display. Norman Rockwell was a creator of a special type of American art, one that celebrated everyday small-town life, with all of its joys and sorrows. The paintings on view offer the largest collection of Rockwell originals in the world, and the kids will enjoy seeing some familiar faces, such as those found in the *Four Freedoms* and many *Saturday Evening Post* covers. Rockwell's works are filled with humor that appeals to all ages. While the youngest children may not be enthralled by the large amount of art on view, we feel that children ten and up will appreciate seeing close up the same pictures they have seen in school, on calendars, and on television. Note that the museum is usually shown by tour only, but you may show yourself around on busy days; the tour lasts half an hour.

Facilities: Rest rooms; gift shop. Those in wheelchairs and parents with strollers may have a difficult time on the steps of the old house, but call ahead if this is a concern; the staff is friendly and helpful.

The Albert Schweitzer Center Hurlburt Rd., R.D. 1, Box 7, Great Barrington, Mass. 01230. (413) 528–3124. Open Tuesday through Saturday, 10 am to 4 pm; Sunday noon to 4 pm.

Dr. Schweitzer himself never visited the Berkshires, but the Nobel–Prize-winning humanitarian's reverence for life pervades this home of his archives. Films, concerts (Pablo Casals played here), and a summer children's program introduce families to the multifaceted legacy of this great doctor. The grounds include a wildlife sanctuary, Philosopher's Walk (with benches and quotations to ponder), and a children's garden.

Facilities: Rest rooms; picnic area; wheelchair accessible areas.

Skating. There are both roller- and ice-skating rinks in the Berkshires, and indoor skating is a good idea for kids on a rainy or blustery day. All of the rinks listed below offer skate rentals. Most of the rinks have sporadic open skating hours, so we suggest that you call ahead for the latest schedule. For roller skaters, there is **Roller Magic Roller Skating Rink** (Colonial Shopping Center, Massachusetts 2, Williamstown, Mass. 01267. [413] 458–3659), with its nine-thousand-square-foot skating surface. At certain times, the rink has its own disc jockey, light shows, video games, contests, and more for skating kids. Another indoor roller rink is **Broyle's Arena** (555 Dalton Avenue, Pittsfield, Mass. 01201. [413] 443–0611). For ice-skating there are a few indoor rinks for icy fun, and they all offer reasonably priced children's programs: **Boys Club of Pittsfield** (16 Melville Street, Pittsfield, Mass. 01201. [413] 448–8258); **Vietnam Veterans Skating Rink** (Church Street, North Adams, Mass. 01247. [413] 664–9474); and **Chapman Rink** (Williams College, Williamstown, Mass. 01267. [413] 597–2433).

Swimming. There are numerous places to swim in the Berkshires, from swimming holes to state forest preserves to private pools, but we think the following ponds and lakes offer

kid-sized water fun. Unless otherwise noted, each site charges
an admission fee and there are lifeguards on duty. Don't forget
to check the state parks listings (earlier in this chapter) for
other swimming spots. **Sand Springs Pool and Spa** (Sand
Springs Road, Williamstown, Mass. 01267 [just off U.S. 7].
[413] 458–5205. Open Memorial Day to Labor Day, daily, 10
am to 6 pm) is one of the oldest continuously running spas in
the country, and today it still soothes both adults and kids with
its heated mineral waters. Sand Springs has a full-sized pool fed
by natural mineral springs, a heated baby pool, beaches, and a
sauna. For river swimming at its best, **Green River** (one mile
west of Great Barrington, off Massachusetts 23; watch for other
cars parked along the roadside) offers a site to sunbathe and
swim for free (there are no lifeguards). **Onota Lake** (Onota
Boulevard, Pittsfield, Mass. Open Memorial Day to Labor
Day, daily, noon to 8 pm) is supervised until eight o'clock by
lifeguards, so you and the kids can take a summer's evening
swim in safety. **Windsor Lake** (Kemp Avenue via East Main
Street, North Adams, Mass. Open Memorial Day to Labor
Day, 10 am to 6 pm) is a large swimming area, so it may be
crowded on weekends, but the lake is lovely.

Theater. Theater in the Berkshire mountains is a summer
event that offers fine, professional entertainment for all ages,
but children will be particularly enchanted with many of the
productions. Everything from fairy tales to Shakespeare is on
tap, and it is a sure bet that if you are near a major town, you
will be able to find a theater group in residence during June,
July, and August. All of the following theaters have offered children's programming in the past, but each year their schedules
change and you have to call them for an up-to-date program.

The largest theater festival is The **Berkshire Theater Festival** (P.O. Box 797, Stockbridge, Mass. 01262 [located at Massachusetts 102, Stockbridge]. [413] 298–5536), which was
founded in the nineteenth century and has been going strong
ever since. Each summer, stars such as Katharine Hepburn,
James Cagney, and Montgomery Clift (he started here as a

twelve-year-old actor) have appeared in plays. A wide variety of programs is still offered, including a children's theater (offered on Saturday) and a series of plays written by children. It is well worth the stop. The **Berkshire Public Theater** (P.O. Box 860, Pittsfield, Mass. 01202 [located at 30 Union Street]. [413] 445–4634) uses local talent. Its shows take place year-round. A nice offering for children is the Robbins-Zust Family Marionettes, which do classic children's stories and fairy tales. Its annual presentation of *A Christmas Carol* is a popular tradition during the holiday season; other plays have included *Hansel and Gretel* and *Jack and the Beanstalk*. **Shakespeare and Company** (Plunkett Street, Lenox, Mass. 01240 [at the junction of U.S. 7 and Massachusetts 7A]. [413] 637–3353) specializes in the bard's works, and we can't think of a better way to spend a summer evening than to sit on the lawn (or bring chairs and a picnic) and watch the productions under the stars. The nice thing about this company is that the productions are light-hearted and fun. Older children are certain to enjoy this introduction to Shakespeare; also, younger kids can fall asleep on the lawn when they get tired.

There is a unique traveling theater group, **East-West Fusion Theatre**, (P.O. Box 141, Sharon, Conn. 06069. [203] 364–5220) which performs in libraries and schools. Their goal is to educate youngsters in the culture and history of Asia. It is America's first permanent professional company devoted to bringing together the Asian and Western performing arts. The performances are augmented by authentic costumes, masks, and puppets from Asia.

Tyringham Gingerbread House and Art Gallery. Tyringham Road, Tyringham, Mass. 01264. (413) 243-3260. Open June, July, and August, daily, 10 am to 5 pm; and Labor Day to Halloween, weekends only, 10 am to 5 pm. Admission.

This is a place to stop for both the kids and the adults on your trip. Inside there is a contemporary art gallery, but it is the outside that is captivating: once known as the Witch's House, this thatched roof cottage reminds one of Hansel and

Gretel. Built in 1916 by the sculptor Sir Henry Hudson Kitson, the rolling roof was supposed to imitate the rolling mountains of the area. There are some lovely walking paths through the surrounding gardens and woods, making this a fine stop for stretching your legs and letting the kids see an enchanting English cottage.

Part of the fun in visiting an area is attending the special events, which often reflect local traditions. These can range from grape-stomping festivals, country fairs, and Fourth-of-July fireworks to scarecrow contests, balloon festivals, strawberry socials, and even shad bakes and apple squeezes. The following calendar is organized by county and by month so that you can plan your trip around a specific celebration. You will need to call the sites to find out the specific dates (and to confirm their locations). Although the special events we've selected are ones that have been held consistently over the last several years, weather, scheduling difficulties, and other factors can change the date on which a festival is held. Every one of these events was kid-tested. We know that if you add just one of them to your vacation, it will make your trip all the more memorable!

WESTCHESTER COUNTY

February
Children's Mouse Hunt, Read Sanctuary
Rye, N.Y. (914) 967–8720
Tiny Tot Winter Walk, Marshlands Conservancy
Rye, N.Y. (914) 835–4466
Washington's Birthday, Washington's Headquarters Museum
North White Plains, N.Y. (914) 949–1236
Winter Fun Festival, Kenisco Dam Plaza
Mount Kisco, N.Y. (914) 763–3993
Winter Weekend at Sunnyside, Van Cortlandt Manor, and Phillipsburg Manor
Tarrytown, N.Y. (914) 631–8200

March
Maple Sugaring for Kids, Lenoir Preserve
Yonkers, N.Y. (914) 968–5851

Maple Sugaring for Kids, Trailside Nature Museum
   Cross River, N.Y.   (914) 763–3993
Maple Sugaring Party, Greenburgh Nature Center
   Scarsdale, N.Y.   (914) 723–3470
Old-Time Sugaring-Off Party, Trailside Museum
   Cross River, N.Y.   (914) 763–3993
Spring Egg Hunt, Greenburgh Nature Center
   Scarsdale, N.Y.   (914) 723–3470

April

Easter Egg Hunt, Westmoreland Sanctuary
   Mount Kisco, N.Y.   (914) 666–8448
Spring Egg Hunt, John Jay Homestead
   Katonah, N.Y.   (914) 232–5651

May

Crafts at Lyndhurst
   Tarrytown, N.Y.   (914) 631–0046
Pinkster Festival, Phillipsburg Manor
   Tarrytown, N.Y.   (914) 631–8200

June

Farm Day, John Jay Homestead
   Katonah, N.Y.   (914) 232–5651
Great Clearwater Revival
   Valhalla, N.Y.   (914) 454–7673
Ossining Village Fair
   Ossining, N.Y.   (914) 941–0009
Springfare, Greenburgh Nature Center
   Scarsdale, N.Y.   (914) 723–3470
Town Ball Game, Sunnyside
   Tarrytown, N.Y.   (914) 631–8200
Westchester County Fair, Yonkers Raceway
   Yonkers, N.Y.   (914) 968–4200

July

Fourth of July at Mount Vernon, Village Green
   Mount Vernon, N.Y.   (914) 667–4116
Independence Day, Sunnyside
   Tarrytown, N.Y.   (914) 631–8200
Summer Daze Scavenger Hunt, Greenburgh
Nature Center
   Scarsdale, N.Y.   (914) 723–3470

August

Annual Summer Festival at Emelin Theatre
   Mamaroneck, N.Y.   (914) 698–0098

Children's Craft Day, Ward Pound Ridge
Reservation
Cross River, N.Y.   (914) 763–3493
International Lantern Festival, Greenburgh Nature
Center
Scarsdale, N.Y.   (914) 723–3470

September
Culinary Arts Festival, Waterfront Park
Peekskill, N.Y.   (914) 739–8105
Grape-Picking Party, Greenburgh Nature Center
Scarsdale, N.Y.   (914) 723–3470
All About Apples, Muscoot Farm
Somers, N.Y.   (914) 232–7118
Crafts at Lyndhurst
Tarrytown, N.Y.   (914) 631–0046

October
Annual Archeology Day, Muscoot Farm
Somers, N.Y.   (914) 232–7118
Annual Fall Festival, Westmoreland Sanctuary
Mount Kisco, N.Y.   (914) 666–8448
Autumn Crafts and Tasks, Van Cortlandt Manor
Croton-on-Hudson, N.Y.   (914) 631–8200
Fall Festival, Greenburgh Nature Center
Scarsdale, N.Y.   (914) 723–3470
Halloween Night Hike and Party, Westmoreland
Sanctuary
Mount Kisco, N.Y.   (914) 666–8448
Harvest Festival, Muscoot Farm
Somers, N.Y.   (914) 232–7118
Legend of Sleepy Hollow Weekend, Sunnyside
Tarrytown, N.Y.   (914) 631–8200
Mushroom Day, Trailside Nature Museum
Cross River, N.Y.   (914) 763–3993

November
Marketplace, Van Cortlandt Manor
Croton-on-Hudson, N.Y.   (914) 631–8200
Royal Birthday of King George II, Phillipsburg
Manor
North Tarrytown, N.Y.   (914) 631–8200
Thanksgiving, Sunnyside
Tarrytown, N.Y.   (914) 631–8200

Turkey Scavenger Hunt, Greenburgh Nature
Center
    Scarsdale, N.Y.   (914) 723–3470

December
Candlelight Tours, Phillipsburg Manor
    North Tarrytown, N.Y.   (914) 631–8200
Candlelight Tours, Sunnyside
    Tarrytown, N.Y.   (914) 631–8200
Candlelight Tours, Van Cortlandt Manor
    Croton-on-Hudson, N.Y.   (914) 631–8200
Holiday Stories and Trim the Nature Tree,
Greenburgh Nature Center
    Scarsdale, N.Y.   (914) 723–3470

```
ROCKLAND COUNTY
```

January
Ice Harvesting Celebration, Rockland Lake
    Rockland Lake, N.Y.   (914) 268–3020
Ski Jumping Tournaments, Bear Mountain State
Park
    Bear Mountain, N.Y.   (914) 786–2701

February
Winter Carnival, Bear Mountain State Park
    Bear Mountain, N.Y.   (914) 786–2701

April
Easter Egg Hunt, Bear Mountain State Park
    Bear Mountain, N.Y.   (914) 786–2701

June
Military Encampment, Stony Point Battlefield
    Stony Point, N.Y.   (914) 786–2521

July
Battle of Stony Point Anniversary, Stony Point
Battlefield
    Stony Point, N.Y.   (914) 786–2521
Fireworks, Nyack Memorial Park
    Nyack, N.Y.   (914) 353–2221
Fourth of July, Bear Mountain State Park
    Bear Mountain, N.Y.   (914) 786–2701

Piermont Carnival
  Piermont, N.Y.   (914) 356–4650
Piermont Riverfront Festival
  Piermont, N.Y.   (914) 356–4650

August
Rockland County Fair, Rockland Community
College
  Suffern, N.Y.   (914) 359–1359

September
Septemberfest, Main Street
  Nyack, N.Y.   (914) 353–2221

October
Halloween Festival, Stony Point Battlefield
  Stony Point, N.Y.   (914) 786–2521
Paul Peabody Puppets, Nyack Library
  Nyack, N.Y.   (914) 358–3370

December
Candlelight Tours, Historical Society of Rockland
County
  New City, N.Y.   (914) 634–9629
Christmas Festival, Bear Mountain State Park
  Bear Mountain, N.Y.   (914) 786–2701
Holiday Festival
  Piermont, N.Y.   (914) 356–4650
St. Nicholas Festival, Historical Society of Rockland
County
  New City, N.Y.   (914) 634–9629
Winter Festival, Historical Society of Rockland
County
  New City, N.Y.   (914) 634–9629

PUTNAM COUNTY

June
Putnam Hospital Auxiliary Fair, Putnam Hospital
Center Grounds
  Carmel, N.Y.   (914) 279–5711

July
Cooperative Extension Youth Fair, Putnam County
Park
  Kent, N.Y.   (914) 628–0454

Ethnic Heritage Festival
  Cold Spring, N.Y.   (914) 265–2305
Victorian Fair, Grace Methodist Church
  Putnam Valley, N.Y.   (914) 528–0650

October
Family Environmental Discovery Weekend,
Fahnestock State Park
  Carmel, N.Y.   (914) 265–3773

December
Candlelight Holiday Tours, Boscobel
  Garrison-on-Hudson, N.Y.   (914) 265–3638

ORANGE COUNTY

February
Washington's Birthday, Washington's Headquarters
  Newburgh, N.Y.   (914) 562–1195

March
Family Winter Hike, Museum of the Hudson
Highlands
  Cornwall, N.Y.   (914) 534–7781

May
Spring Festival
  Greenwood Lake, N.Y.   (914) 477–8449

June
Kite Fly, Museum Village
  Monroe, N.Y.   (914) 782–8247
Martha Washington's Birthday, Washington's
Headquarters
  Newburgh, N.Y.   (914) 562–1195

July
Camp Day with the Third New York Regiment,
New Windsor Cantonment
  Vails Gate, N.Y.   (914) 561–1765
Great American Weekend
  Goshen, N.Y.   (914) 294–7741

Great American Weekend Fair, Historic Track
  Goshen, N.Y.   (914) 294–6330
Heritage Days, Farnum Building
  Port Jervis, N.Y.   (914) 856–3048
Major General Knox's Birthday Celebration, Knox's
Headquarters
  Vails Gate, N.Y.   (914) 561–5498
Orange County Fair, County Fairgrounds
  Middletown, N.Y.   (914) 343–3134

August
Kite Day, Washington's Headquarters
  Newburgh, N.Y.   (914) 562–1195
New York Renaissance Festival, Sterling Forest
  Tuxedo, N.Y.   (914) 351–5171
Onion Harvest Celebration
  Pine Island, N.Y.   (914) 386–5954

September
Civil War Weekend, Museum Village
  Monroe, N.Y.   (914) 782–8247
Grape-Stomping Festival, Brotherhood Winery
  Washingtonville, N.Y.   (914) 496–9101
Stewart Air Show, Stewart International Airport
  Newburgh, N.Y.   (914) 294–5151

October
Fall Festival, Museum Village
  Monroe, N.Y.   (914) 782–8247
Fall Festival, Sugar Loaf Village
  Sugar Loaf, N.Y.   (914) 469–4963
Halloween Celebration, Knox's Headquarters
  Vails Gate, N.Y.   (914) 561–5498
Halloween Party, Museum of the Hudson
Highlands
  Cornwall, N.Y.   (914) 534–7781
Halloween Party, Museum Village
  Monroe, N.Y.   (914) 782–8247
Revolutionary Encampment and Brigade, New
Windsor Cantonment
  Vails Gate, N.Y.   (914) 561–1765
Train Show, Howard Johnson's Restaurant and
Motel
  Middletown, N.Y.   (914) 344–2568

Warwick Fall Festival
Warwick, N.Y.   (914) 986–2720

December
Christmas at Washington's Headquarters
Newburgh, N.Y.   (914) 562–1195
Christmas Celebration, Sugar Loaf Village
Sugar Loaf, N.Y.   (914) 469–4963
Christmas in Museum Village
Monroe, N.Y.   (914) 782–8247

SULLIVAN COUNTY

January
Ice Carnival, Rotary Park
Livingston Manor, N.Y.   (914) 439–4820

February
Winter Carnival, Big Vanilla at Davos
Woodridge, N.Y.   (914) 343–1000
Winter Carnival, Holiday Mountain Ski Area
Monticello, N.Y.   (914) 796–3161

June
Frontier Living Days, Fort Delaware
Narrowsburg, N.Y.   (914) 252–6660

July
Colonial Military Encampment, Fort Delaware
Narrowsburg, N.Y.   (914) 252–6660
Fireworks, Monticello Raceway
Monticello, N.Y.   (914) 794–4100
Fourth of July Celebration
Narrowsburg, N.Y.   (914) 794–3000
Native American Pow-Wow
Barryville, N.Y.   (914) 794–3000
Ukrainian Youth Festival
Glen Spey, N.Y.   (914) 794–3000

August
Down on the Farm Day,
(location varies each year)   (914) 794–3000

Little World's Fair
  Grahamsville, N.Y.   (914) 794–3000
O&W Railway Festival, Railway Museum
  Roscoe, N.Y.   (607) 498–4753

September
Shandalee Fair, Lanza's Country Inn
  Livingston Manor, N.Y.   (914) 439–5070

October
Fall Festival Weekend, Canal Town Emporium
  Wurtsboro, N.Y.   (914) 888–2100
Giant Pumpkin Party, Fairgrounds
  Grahamsville, N.Y.   (914) 958–2998
Octoberfest, Lenape Farms Arena
  Narrowsburg, N.Y.   (914) 794–3000

ULSTER COUNTY

March
St. Patrick's Day Parade, Broadway
  Kingston, N.Y.   (914) 331–9300

April
Easter Egg Hunt, Benmarl Winery
  Marlboro, N.Y.   (914) 236–7271

May
Heritage Day
  Kingston, N.Y.   (914) 331–9300
Shad Festival, Hudson River Maritime Center
  Kingston, N.Y.   (914) 331–9300
Woodstock-New Paltz Art and Crafts Fair, County
Fairgrounds
  New Paltz, N.Y.   (914) 679–8087

July
Children's Day Parade
  Kingston, N.Y.   (914) 331–9300

Fourth of July Celebration
  Ellenville, N.Y.   (914) 331-9300
Fourth of July Celebration
  Kingston, N.Y.   (914) 331-9300
Fourth of July Celebration
  New Paltz, N.Y.   (914) 331-9300
Fourth of July Celebration
  Saugerties, N.Y.   (914) 331-9300
Old Stone House Day
  Hurley, N.Y.   (914) 331-9300
Woodstock Library Fair, Library Lane
  Woodstock, N.Y.   (914) 679-2213

August
Corn and Craft Festival, Reformed Church
  Hurley, N.Y.   (914) 331-9300
Stone House Day, Huguenot Street
  New Paltz, N.Y.   (914) 255-1660
Ulster County Fair, County Fairgrounds
  New Paltz, N.Y.   (914) 331-9300

September
Children's Day, Opus 40
  Saugerties, N.Y.   (914) 246-3400
Woodstock-New Paltz Art and Crafts Fair, County
Fairgrounds
  New Paltz, N.Y.   (914) 679-8087

October
Mum Festival, Seamon Park
  Saugerties, N.Y.   (914) 331-9300
Octoberfest, Belleayre Mountain
  Highmount, N.Y.   (914) 254-5600
Pumpkin Festival, Hudson River Maritime Center
  Kingston, N.Y.   (914) 338-0071

November
Kingston Model Railroad Club Open House, Susan
Street Clubhouse
  Kingston, N.Y.   (914) 338-7174

December
Holiday Traditions, Senate House
  Kingston, N.Y.   (914) 338-2786

DUTCHESS COUNTY

January

Family Farm Discovery Tour, Stony Kill
Environmental Center
Wappingers Falls, N.Y.   (914) 831–8780
Horse-drawn Sleigh Rally, Stony Kill
Environmental Center
Wappingers Falls, N.Y.   (914) 831–8780
Winter Carnival, James Baird State Park
Pleasant Valley, N.Y.   (914) 889–4100

February

Winter Weekend, Montgomery Place
Annandale-on-Hudson, N.Y.   (914) 758–5461

March

Easter Celebration, Montgomery Place
Annandale-on-Hudson, N.Y.   (914) 631–8200
Maple Syrup Demonstration, Stony Kill
Environmental Center
Wappingers Falls, N.Y.   (914) 831–8780

June

Strawberry Festival, Beacon Sloop Club
(Call for location)   (914) 831–1100
Strawberry Festival, Greig Farm
Red Hook, N.Y.   (914) 758–5762

July

Americana Festival, Webatuck Craft Village
Wingdale, N.Y.   (914) 832–6464
July Fourth Parade, U.S. 9
Hyde Park, N.Y.   (914) 229–8086
Town and Country Day Tour
Millbrook, N.Y.   (914) 677–5006

August

Corn Festival, Beacon Sloop Club
(Call for location)   (914) 831–1100
Crafts at Montgomery Place
Annandale-on-Hudson, N.Y.   (914) 758–5461

Day in the Park, Norrie State Park
   Staatsburg, N.Y.   (914) 889–4100
Dutchess County Fair, County Fairgrounds
   Rhinebeck, N.Y.   (914) 876–4001

September

Apple Harvest Fair, Montgomery Place
   Annandale-on-Hudson, N.Y.   (914) 631–8200
Apple-Raspberry Day, Greig Farm
   Red Hook, N.Y.   (914) 758–5762
Outdoor Food Fair, Culinary Institute
   Hyde Park, N.Y.   (914) 471–6608
Mid-Hudson Radio Control Society Old Rhinebeck
Jamboree, Old Rhinebeck Aerodrome
   Rhinebeck, N.Y.   (914) 758–8610

October

Annual Fall Harvest Festival, Stony Kill
Environmental Center
   Wappingers Falls, N.Y.   (914) 831–8780
Artscape
   (Call for locations)   (914) 454–3222
Beacon Sloop Club Pumpkin Festival
   (Call for location)   (914) 831–1100
Clearwater Pumpkin Sail, Sloop Clearwater
   (Call for locations)   (914) 454–7673
Fall Harvest Festival, Stony Kill Farm
Environmental Center
   Wappingers Falls, N.Y.   (914) 831–8780
Fall Harvest Festival, Webatuck Craft Village
   Wingdale, N.Y.   (914) 832–6464
Future Farmers of America Fall Festival
   Pine Plains, N.Y.   (518) 398–7181
Hudson Valley Railroad Show, Mid-Hudson Civic
Center
   Poughkeepsie, N.Y.   (914) 454–5800
Pumpkin Festival, Greig Farm
   Red Hook, N.Y.   (914) 758–5762

December

Christmas at the Roosevelt Home
   Hyde Park, N.Y.   (914) 229–9115

Gilded Age Christmas, Vanderbilt and Mills
Mansions
Hyde Park and Staatsburg, N.Y.   (914) 229–9115
Holiday Celebration, Montgomery Place
Annandale-on-Hudson, N.Y.   (914) 758–5461
The Nutcracker Ballet, Mid-Hudson Civic Center
Poughkeepsie, N.Y.   (914) 454–5800
Old Dutch Christmas
Rhinebeck, N.Y.   (914) 758–5519
Winter Holidays, Montgomery Place
Annandale-on-Hudson, N.Y.   (914) 631–8200

COLUMBIA COUNTY

June
Sheep-Shearing Festival, Clermont
Germantown, N.Y.   (518) 537–4240
Hudson Summer Festival, Warren Street
Hudson, N.Y.   (518) 828–4990

July
Independence Day Celebration, Clermont
Germantown, N.Y.   (518) 537–4240
Strawberry Shortcake and Flag Festival, Shaker
Museum
Old Chatham, N.Y.   (518) 794–9100

August
Ancram Summer Festival, Blass Memorial Field
Ancram, N.Y.   (518) 329–2234
A Day on the Van Alen Farm
Kinderhook, N.Y.   (518) 758–9265
Fire Fighter's Competition, Firemen's Home
Hudson, N.Y.   (518) 828–7695
Hayrides and Barn Dance, Olana
Hudson, N.Y.   (518) 828–0135
Hudson River Steamboat Days, Clermont
Germantown, N.Y.   (518) 537–4240
Victorian Picnic, Olana
Hudson, N.Y.   (518) 828–0135

September
Columbia County Fair, Fairgrounds
Chatham, N.Y.   (518) 392–3951

Family Day, Shaker Museum
Old Chatham, N.Y.   (518) 794–9100
Harvest Festival, Shaker Museum
Old Chatham, N.Y.   (518) 794–9100
Harvest Time, Clermont
Germantown, N.Y.   (518) 537–4240
Octoberfest, Palatine Park
Germantown, N.Y.   (518) 537–6686

October
Pumpkin-Painting Festival, Clermont
Germantown, N.Y.   (518) 537–4240

December
Christmas at Clermont
Germantown, N.Y.   (518) 537–4240
Christmas at Olana
Hudson, N.Y.   (518) 828–0135

GREENE COUNTY

February
Ski Fest, Ski Windham
Windham, N.Y.   (518) 734–4300

May
Catskills Irish Festival
East Durham, N.Y.   (518) 634–7100

June
Festival of Circus Acts, Bond Street Theater
Palenville, N.Y.   (518) 678–3332

July
Cairo Country Fair
Cairo, N.Y.   (518) 622–8654
Great American Paper Hat Parade, Main Street
Athens, N.Y.   (518) 945–2548
Greene County Youth Fair
Durham, N.Y.   (518) 622–9820
Medieval Fair, O'Brien's Field
Leeds, N.Y.   (518) 945–1207

Old Catskill Days, Main Street
Catskill, N.Y.   (518) 943–3600

August
Athens Street Festival
Athens, N.Y.   (518) 945–1617
Coxsackie Riverside Festival, Riverside Park
Coxsackie, N.Y.   (518) 731–6905
Crazy Wacky Raft Race, Hudson River
Coxsackie, N.Y.   (518) 945–1858
Irish Feis, Irish Cultural Center
East Durham, N.Y.   (518) 634–2582

September
Boomerang Tournament, Bond Street Theater
Palenville, N.Y.   (518) 678–3332
Country Fair, Ski Windham
Windham, N.Y.   (518) 734–4300

October
Pumpkin Sail, Sloop Clearwater
Coxsackie, N.Y.   (518) 943–3223

DELAWARE COUNTY

June
Arkville Fair,
Arkville, N.Y.   (607) 746–2281
Home and Hearth Day, Delaware County
Historical Association
Delhi, N.Y.   (607) 746–3849

July
Delaware and Ulster Rail Ride Train Robbery,
Arkville Depot
Arkville, N.Y.   (914) 586–3877
Farm Festival, Delaware County Historical
Association
Delhi, N.Y.   (607) 746–3849
Firemen's Field Days
Margaretville, N.Y.   (607) 746–2281

Independence Day, Hanford Mills Museum
East Meredith, N.Y.   (607) 278–5744
Lumberjack Festival, Riverside Park
Deposit, N.Y.   (607) 467–2673
Peaceful Valley Bluegrass Festival, Peaceful Valley
Campsites
Downsville, N.Y.   (607) 363–2211
Strawberry Festival, Presbyterian Church
Andes, N.Y.   (607) 746–2281
Teddy Bear Picnic, Delaware and Ulster Rail Ride
Arkville, N.Y.   (914) 586–3877

August
Children's Fair, Hanford Mills Museum
East Meredith, N.Y.   (607) 637–5205
Delaware County Fair, Delaware County
Fairgrounds
Walton, N.Y.   (607) 829–5011
Margaretville Street Fair, Main Street
Margaretville, N.Y.   (914) 586–3770
Old Franklin Day, Main Street
Franklin, N.Y.   (607) 829–8725

September
Antique Engine Jamboree, Hanford Mills Museum
East Meredith, N.Y.   (607) 278–5744
Lumber Jack Round-Up, Bobcat Ski Center
Andes, N.Y.   (914) 676–3143
Roxbury Country and Children's Fair, Main Street
Roxbury, N.Y.   (607) 326–7908
Tavern Day, Delaware County Historical
Association
Delhi, N.Y.   (607) 746–3849

October
Ghost Train, Delaware and Ulster Rail Ride
Arkville, N.Y.   (914) 586–3877
Historic Halloween, Delaware County Historical
Association
Delhi, N.Y.   (607) 746–3849
Lumberjack Festival, Hanford Mills Museum
East Meredith, N.Y.   (607) 278–5744

OTSEGO COUNTY

January

Richfield Springs Winter Carnival
Richfield Springs, N.Y.   (315) 858–2702

February

Cooperstown Winter Carnival
Cooperstown, N.Y.   (607) 547–9983

May

Memorial Day Parade, Main Street
Richfield Springs, N.Y.   (315) 858–0492

June

Doll Show, State University College
Oneonta, N.Y.   (607) 432–3812

July

Firemen's Field Days and Parade, Main Street
Richfield Springs, N.Y.   (315) 858–0863
Fourth of July, Farmers Museum
Cooperstown, N.Y.   (607) 547–2533
Great American Balloon Fest and Family Fun Day,
Fairgrounds and High School
Norwich, N.Y.   (607) 334–5454
National Baseball Hall of Fame Induction
Ceremony and Game
Cooperstown, N.Y.   (607) 547–9988

August

Otsego County Fair, Otsego County Fairgrounds
Morris, N.Y.   (607) 432–6610

September

Autumn Harvest Festival, Farmers Museum
Cooperstown, N.Y.   (607) 547–2533

October

Fly Creek Applefest, Fly Creek Cider Mill
Fly Creek, N.Y.   (607) 547–9602

Scarecrow Contest, Butternut Barn
  Richfield Springs, N.Y.   (315) 858-0964

December
Winter Carnival, Canandarago Lake
  Richfield Springs, N.Y.   (315) 858-2705

```
┌────────────────────────────────────────────────────────────┐
│                    SCHOHARIE COUNTY                          │
└────────────────────────────────────────────────────────────┘
```

May
Johnnycake Festival, Bramanville Gristmill
Museum
  Bramanville, N.Y.   (518) 827-5247
Maple Festival, Village Green
  Jefferson, N.Y.   (607) 652-7473
Spring Festival, New York Power Authority Visitors
Center
  North Blenheim, N.Y.   (607) 588-6061

June
Children's Day Celebration, New York Power
Authority Visitors Center
  North Blenheim, N.Y.   (607) 588-6061
Colonial Craft Weekend, Esperance Historical
Museum
  Esperance, N.Y.   (518) 875-6417
Founders Day Celebration
  Sharon Springs, N.Y.   (518) 284-2438
Strawberry Festival, Bohringers Fruit Farm
  Middleburgh, N.Y.   (518) 827-5783

July
Mettawee River Theater Company
  (Various sites throughout the county)   (518) 234-3940

August
Sunshine Fair, Cobleskill Fairgrounds
  Cobleskill, N.Y.   -   (518) 234-2125

September
Colonial Days, Lutheran Parsonage
  Schoharie, N.Y.   (518) 295-8617
Iroquois Indian Festival, SUNY
  Cobleskill, N.Y.   (518) 295-8553

Schoharie County Country Music Festival,
Cobleskill Fairgrounds
Cobleskill, N.Y.   (518) 234–7380
Wildlife Festival, New York Power Authority
Visitors Center
North Blenheim, N.Y.   (607) 588–6061

October
Stone Fort Days, Old Stone Fort
Schoharie, N.Y.   (518) 295–7192

ALBANY, SCHENECTADY, AND RENSSELAER COUNTIES: THE CAPITAL REGION

January
Twelfth Night, Crailo
Rensselaer, N.Y.   (518) 463–8738
Winter Carnival, Washington Park
Albany, N.Y.   (518) 434–1217
Winter Festival, Grafton Lakes State Park
Grafton, N.Y.   (518) 279–1155

February
Colonial Festival
Schenectady, N.Y.   (518) 372–5656
Winter Festival, John Boyd Thacher Park
Albany, N.Y.   (518) 827–1237

March
Northeastern Wildlife Expo, Empire State Plaza
Albany, N.Y.   (518) 783–1333

May
Farm Day in the City Springfest, Schuyler Mansion
Albany, N.Y.   (518) 434–0559
Festival of Nations, Schenectady Museum
Schenectady, N.Y.   (518) 372–7890
Imagination Celebration, New York State Museum
Albany, N.Y.   (518) 473–0823
Shaker World's People Day, Watervliet Shaker
Community
Albany, N.Y.   (518) 456–7890

Tulip Festival, Washington Park
Albany, N.Y.   (518) 434–2023
Waterford Canalfest, Button Park and Broad Street
Waterford, N.Y.   (518) 237–7999

June

Arts and Crafts Festival, Riverfront Park
Troy, N.Y.   (518) 273–0552
Cohoes Heritage Festival, Remsen Street
Cohoes, N.Y.   (518) 237–7999
Empire State Regatta, Corning Preserve
Albany, N.Y.   (518) 434–5073
Flagfest Weekend, Riverfront Park
Troy, N.Y.   (518) 274–7020
Food Festival Country Style, Urban Cultural Park
Schenectady, N.Y.   (518) 372–5656
Great Northeast River Festival, Freedom Park
Scotia, N.Y.   (518) 372–5656
Northville Independence Celebration, Village
Center
Northville, N.Y.   (518) 863–8775
Old Songs Festival, Altamont Fairgrounds
Altamont, N.Y.   (518) 765–2815

July

Black Arts and Cultural Festival, Empire State
Plaza
Albany, N.Y.   (518) 474–4712
Independence Day Celebration, Empire State
Plaza
Albany, N.Y.   (518) 473–0559
Meet-Your-Past Day for Kids, Schuyler Mansion
Albany, N.Y.   (518) 434–0834
Northeast Air Show, Schenectady County Airport
Scotia, N.Y.   (518) 382–0041

August

Altamont Fair, Altamont Fairgrounds
Altamont, N.Y.   (518) 861–6671
Children's Day, Empire State Plaza
Albany, N.Y.   (518) 474–5986

September

Capital District Scottish Games, Altamont
Fairgrounds
Altamont, N.Y.   (518) 372–2835

International Bazaar, Empire State Plaza Patio
Albany, N.Y.   (518) 474–5986
Larkfest, Lark Street
Albany, N.Y.   (518) 449–5011
Melting Pot Food Festival, State Street
Schenectady, N.Y.   (518) 372–5656
Stockade Walk-About, Stockade District
Schenectady, N.Y.   (518) 374–0263
Uncle Sam Parade and Celebration, Riverfront Park
Troy, N.Y.   (518) 274–7020

October
Octoberfest, State Street
Schenectady, N.Y.   (518) 372–5656
Stuyvesant Apple Festival, Stuyvesant Plaza
Albany, N.Y.   (518) 482–8986

November
Christmas Parade, State Street Terrace
Schenectady, N.Y.   (518) 372–5656
Festival of Trees, Albany Institute of History and
Art
Albany, N.Y.   (518) 463–4478

December
Children's Christmas, Pruyn House
Albany, N.Y.   (518) 783–1435
Christmas Open House, Schuyler Mansion
Albany, N.Y.   (518) 434–0834
Family Christmas, Cherry Hill
Albany, N.Y.   (518) 434–4791
First Night Celebration, Empire State Plaza
Albany, N.Y.   (518) 434–1217
Holiday House Tour, Albany Homes
Albany, N.Y.   (518) 463–0622
Toy Train Exhibit, New York State Museum
Albany, N.Y.   (518) 474–5877

SARATOGA COUNTY

July
Duck Derby
Saratoga Springs, N.Y.   (518) 587–4709

Family Day, National Museum of Racing
Saratoga Springs, N.Y.   (518) 584–0400
A Revolutionary Fourth of July, Saratoga National
Historical Park
Stillwater, N.Y.   (518) 664–9821
Saratoga County Fair, Saratoga County Fairgrounds
Ballston Spa, N.Y.   (518) 885–9701

August
Eighteenth-Century Day, Philip Schuyler House,
National Historic Park
Schuylerville, N.Y.   (518) 664–9821

September
Eighteenth-Century Military Encampment,
Saratoga National Historical Park
Stillwater, N.Y.   (518) 664–9821

December
Historical Society Museum Christmas Display,
Congress Park Casino
Saratoga Springs, N.Y.   (518) 584–6920
Victorian Christmas, National Museum of Dance
Saratoga Springs, N.Y.   (518) 584–9330
Victorian Street Walk, Broadway
Saratoga Springs, N.Y.   (518) 584–3255

WARREN COUNTY: THE LAKE GEORGE REGION

February
Mardi Gras Parade, Main Street
Lake George, N.Y.   (518) 668–4644

May
Memorial Day Parade, U.S. 9
Lake George, N.Y.   (518) 668–5755

June
Sights and Sounds Festival
Lake George, N.Y.   (518) 668–5755

July
Fourth of July Fireworks
Lake George, N.Y.   (518) 668–5755

Smoke-eaters Jamboree
  Warrensburg, N.Y.   (518) 623–9598

August
Family Festival Week
  Lake George, N.Y.   (518) 668–5755
Mountain Days
  Stony Creek, N.Y.   (518) 696–2035
Warren County Country Fair, Warren County
Fairgrounds
  Warrensburg, N.Y.   (518) 623–3291

September
Adirondack Balloon Festival
  Queensbury, N.Y.   (518) 761–6366
Oktoberfest
  North Creek, N.Y.   (518) 251–2612

THE BERKSHIRES

February
Winter at Hancock Shaker Village
  Pittsfield, Mass.   (413) 443–0188

May
Berkshire Highland Games
  Pittsfield, Mass.   (413) 442–2759

June
Cobble Day, Bartholomew's Cobble
  Ashley Falls, Mass.   (413) 229–8600

July
Americana Day, Berkshire Scenic Railway
  Lee, Mass.   (413) 243–2872
Artabout Summer Arts Festival
  Pittsfield, Mass.   (413) 663–3735
Big Apple Circus, Arrowhead
  Pittsfield, Mass.   (413) 442–1793

Fourth of July Fireworks, Stockbridge Bowl
Stockbridge, Mass.   (413) 528–1510

August
Cummington Balloon Festival
Cummington, Mass.   (413) 634–2111
Berkshire County 4-H Fair, Holmes Rd.
Pittsfield, Mass.   (413) 443–9186
Pittsfield Grange Fair, 1123 West St.
Pittsfield, Mass.   (413) 443–9186
Stockbridge Grange Fair, Church St.
Stockbridge, Mass.   (413) 443–9186

September
Apple Squeeze Festival
Lenox, Mass.   (413) 637–3646

October
Halloween Special, Berkshire Scenic Railway
Lee, Mass.   (413) 243–2872
Harvest Festival, Berkshire Garden Center
Stockbridge, Mass.   (413) 298–3926

December
Hancock Shaker Christmas, Hancock Shaker Village
Pittsfield, Mass.   (413) 443–0188
The Nutcracker Ballet, Berkshire Ballet
Pittsfield, Mass.   (413) 442–1307

Index